Bright Seas, Pioneer Spirits

Bright Seas, Pioneer Spirits

A HISTORY *of the* SUNSHINE COAST

BETTY KELLER *and* ROSELLA LESLIE

TouchWood
Editions

First published in 1996 by Horsdal and Schubart
Revised and expanded TouchWood Edition 2009

TouchWood Editions
www.touchwoodeditions.com

Library and Archives Canada Cataloguing in Publication
Keller, Betty
Bright seas, pioneer spirits: a history of the Sunshine Coast / Betty Keller and Rosella Leslie.

Includes bibliographical references and index. ISBN 978-1-894898-87-4

Sunshine Coast (B.C.)—History. 2. Sunshine Coast (B.C.)—Description and travel. I. Leslie, Rosella M., 1948– II. Title.

FC3845.S95K45 2009   971.1'31   C2009-900992-7

Library of Congress Control Number: 2009920170

Edited by Marlyn Horsdal
Front cover photos: Large colour photo by Rosella Leslie. Archival photo on the left is the Sechelt Indian band celebrates the opening of the first St. Augustine's School on June 29, 1904. On the left Our Lady of the Rosary Church which was destroyed by fire on January 14, 1906. The flags of the four hereditary Sechelt chiefs fly atop the arch of greenery. Photo 0099, Courtesty of the Sunshine Coast Museum and Archives. The Archival photo on the right is the Union Steamship *Lady Evelyn* at Granthams Landing. Purchased in 1923 from the Howe Sound Navigation Company. Photo 0380, courtesy of the Sunshine Coast Museum and Archives.
Back cover photo by Rosella Leslie
Front cover design by Caroline Goodrich
Interior layout by Duncan Turner

TouchWood Editions acknowledges the financial support for its publishing program from the Government of Canada through the Book Publishing Industry Development Program (BPIDP), Canada Council for the Arts, and the province of British Columbia through the British Columbia Arts Council and the Book Publishing Tax Credit.

Mixed Sources
Cert no. SW-COC-001271
© 1996 FSC
FSC

The interior pages of this book have been printed on 100% post-consumer recycled paper, processed chlorine free, and printed with vegetable-based inks.

1 2 3 4 5 12 11 10 09

This book is dedicated to all of those people
who generously provided us with the memories,
family records, archives and photos that enabled
us to tell the story of the Sunshine Coast.

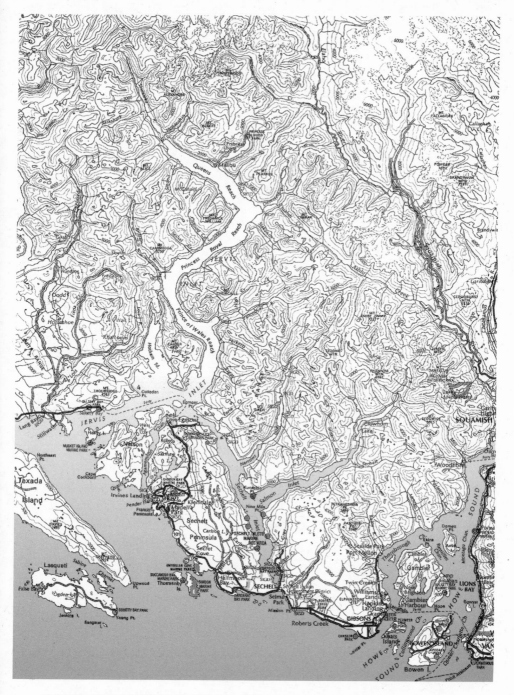

PORTION OF BC GOVERNMENT MAP SGS1. (REPRODUCED WITH PERMISSION OF MINISTRY
OF ENVIRONMENT, LAND AND PARKS, GEOGRAPHIC DATA BC).

CONTENTS

A DREARY AND INHOSPITABLE COUNTRY

When Captain George Vancouver surveyed and charted the coastline of British Columbia in the summers of 1792 to 1795, he found the lands lying in between each of its long narrow inlets depressingly similar to one another. "Mostly a repetition of dreary and inhospitable countries,"[1] he called them. Superficially, they are very similar—steep-sided mountains laced with icy cataracts that disappear into deep water, with the same coniferous trees clinging to bedrock slopes and the same fish swimming beneath the waves.

When these "countries" were eventually settled and their resources developed, the ruggedness of the landscape ensured that they would remain isolated from one another. Travel by land over the mountain divides that separated them was virtually impossible and travel by water in small, underpowered boats was laborious and dangerous. As well, since they all had the same resources, there was little excuse for commerce to develop between them. Instead of becoming interdependent, these pioneer inlet settlements came to depend on the steamers from coastal cities like Vancouver and Victoria for their supplies and their markets. As a result, it was possible for each inlet to nurture an almost separate culture and lifestyle to which people were bound by economic realities.

The Sunshine Coast is one of these unique coastal units—or rather, it is two units welded together because of a narrow strip of lowland at Sechelt that provides a connecting link between the inlet systems that form its boundaries: Jervis Inlet and Howe Sound, the two most southerly of British Columbia's fiords. It includes a 1,500-square-mile area and coincides closely with the Sechelt Forest District as it was defined by the BC Forest Service shortly before World War I and as it remained until it was combined with the Powell Forest in 1989. Roughly speaking, this area is bounded on the north by the Toba River divide, on the east by the Elahoe and Squamish River divides, Howe Sound and Thornbrough Channel, on the south by the Strait of Georgia, on the southwest by Malaspina Strait and on the west by the Powell Forest.

Credit for inventing the name "Sunshine Coast" was claimed by Harry Roberts (1884–1978), the most famous member of the clan that founded Roberts Creek. In an anecdote reprinted in *Remembering Roberts Creek 1889–1955*, Roberts explained that he had painted the words "Sunshine Belt" in large white letters on the side of the red freight shed on the first wharf built in Roberts Creek in 1914. The name had apparently originated with his grandmother, Charlotte Roberts, who had homesteaded there with her husband Thomas from 1890 to 1897. She cherished a dream that in time there would be a long dock built there and that steamers would arrive every day with tourists who wanted to enjoy the sunshine, "for there is more of it along this part of the coast than at any other place."[2] She had foreseen a summer resort with hundreds of cottages among the trees where only three houses then stood, and she decreed that this community of happy holidayers would be called "The Sunshine Belt."

According to Harry Roberts, the word "Coast" was substituted for "Belt" by "the young fellow who started the real estate office at Gibsons . . . so the belt had stretched as I watched Grannie's old dream stretch each year."[3] The identity of the "young fellow" is unknown, but if he really was the originator of the second half of the name, he must have invented it before 1951 because that was the year Black Ball Ferries established the first car ferry service between Horseshoe Bay and Gibsons and began advertising the whole coastline from Port Mellon to Pender Harbour as "The Sunshine Coast."

The name became so generally used that on July 18, 1957, Highways Minister P.A. Gaglardi christened the highway from Gibsons to Powell River the Sunshine Coast Highway. Thus, in 1965, when the provincial government divided the unincorporated areas of the province into regional districts, it was no surprise that this area was officially named the Sunshine Coast Regional District. When the new district's boundaries were established, they included Gambier, Anvil and Keats islands in Howe Sound, the Trail Islands, North and South Thormanby and Merry Island in Malaspina Strait, and Nelson, Hardy, Kelly and Captain islands in Jervis Inlet, as well as all the rocky little islets that surround them.

PART ONE
FORMING THE LAND

When the earth was young, the portion of its crust that is now called the Sunshine Coast bore no resemblance to the land forms that exist here today. Over billions of years the ancient igneous rocks that formed the original building blocks of this area were twice raised into mountain ranges and twice eroded away by glaciation. Then, 250 million years ago, the eroded remnants gradually subsided until they were either below or at our present-day sea level. The depressed land remained under water for more than 100 million years while dinosaurs evolved, went into decline and abruptly vanished from the earth. During these years, layer after layer of marine sediment settled over the basic igneous rock.

The creation of the Sunshine Coast's present profile began in the Cretaceous Period, approximately 130 million years ago, when earthquakes and volcanic action began to fault and fold the land lying under the sea, thrusting it upward until it eventually formed the tops of the Coast Range mountains. At the same time, the area that we know as the Strait of Georgia subsided still further, leaving above sea level only a flattish platform of land at the base of the new mountains. This Georgia Lowland exists today in two fragments: the low-lying Gulf Islands on the strait's western edge and a narrow fringe of land at the foot of the coastal mountains on its eastern side. The settlements of Pender Harbour, Sechelt and Gibsons all lie on this eastern fringe.

The top layer of the new Sunshine Coast mountains was composed of the marine sediments deposited during the previous 100 million years, and beneath them lay the original igneous rocks. However, the largest component of the new mountains was granite that had travelled upward in molten form from so deep within the earth that it cooled and crystallized before it could push its way through the igneous and sedimentary layers to reach the surface. In the millions of years after this granite cooled and became solid rock, it was repeatedly folded, faulted and fractured by earthquake action and alternate freezing and thawing. The cracks that developed in it were filled by fresh molten rock from renewed volcanic action, either pushed up from below or spilled down the sides of new volcanoes. These cracks or sutures sometimes opened enough to allow as much as a half-mile-wide strip of molten rock to enter. Later, with renewed faulting, many of the cracks shifted and closed again, and because the trapped rock was generally softer than the granite around it, it was compacted and structurally changed.

Throughout this long-ago mountain-building period the climate of the

Sunshine Coast was much warmer and wetter than it is now. Subtropical plants grew here, and as they died, the warmth and humidity turned their remains into peat and coal. The extensive Nanaimo coal deposits just across the Strait of Georgia on Vancouver Island are the most obvious proof of this climatic difference, but there are also small isolated pockets of low-quality coal and peat on the Sunshine Coast.

Hundreds of new rivers and streams developed to carry the heavy rainfall to the sea, and while it took a mere millenium or two for them to cut through the relatively soft sedimentary and igneous crustal rocks, it was much more difficult for them to wear a channel into the granite bedrock that lay below. As a result, they were diverted into the belts of newer and softer rock that lay in the cracks of the granite. In this way the "Jervis River," that flowed where Jervis Inlet lies today, cut its distinctive channel, abruptly changing direction where it was diverted into zigzagging belts of softer rock. The deep valley that extends from McMurray Bay on the west side of Prince of Wales Reach southwestward to the head of Hotham Sound shows that in some early stage of its development, this prehistoric Jervis River must have followed this shortcut to the sea, abandoning it when erosion provided a deeper channel down Prince of Wales Reach. The Jervis River's tributary streams, the "Sechelt River," "Salmon River," and "Narrows River," developed comparatively straight channels because they followed uninterrupted faults in the granite bedrock.

THE LAST ICE AGE

The geological period that saw the final shaping of the Sunshine Coast landscape was the Pleistocene Ice Age, which began approximately one million years ago with relentless snow over all of the northern half of this continent. In time, the bottom layers of this snow turned to ice, and centuries of pressures from above started it moving downhill. The ice that moved over the Sunshine Coast originated in the Rocky Mountains, but it travelled so quickly that by the time it arrived here, it had become a series of glaciers rather than a single sheet. Scientists know from studying the striae and grooves etched into the bedrock that one glacier moved southward down Howe Sound toward Gibsons and a second travelled more or less southeasterly down the Sechelt Peninsula, approaching Gibsons from the other side. The most accessible examples of these glacial grooves and striae can be found on the exposed bedrock along the shoreline at Wilson Creek and Roberts Creek.

Everything in the path of the glaciers—from particles of rock to house-sized boulders—became frozen onto their undersides so that they acted like giant rasps. Where these rasps went over small hills, the crust of sedimentary and original igneous rocks was scoured completely away, exposing the hard granite mass underneath it. They chewed at the sides of high mountains, leaving only sharp peaks. Where the rasps followed riverbeds, making contact with the softer rock infusions, they scooped out long, U-shaped channels, and this is how Jervis River became Jervis Inlet, and its tributary streams became Sechelt Inlet, Salmon Inlet and Narrows Inlet.

One of the gaps in the ice sheet occurred over the main valley of Bennett Creek, northeast of the Clowhom Lakes. Although it is some distance from the coast where the glaciers actually ended, this entire valley is plugged with talus slopes and crisscrossed with moraines of rock and gravel that are typical of the kind of deposits found at glacier edges.

The layer of ice over most of the coastal area and the Strait of Georgia was at least 3,000 feet thick, but where it scoured out the deepest part of Jervis Inlet, it may have been as much as 6,000 feet thick. All that would have been visible above the ice surface were the tops of the tallest peaks—Mounts Frederick William, Alfred, Diadem, Churchill and Spencer on Jervis Inlet, Mount Pearkes south of Princess Louisa Inlet, Mount Hallowell on the Sechelt Peninsula, and Tetrahedron Peak on the southern mainland. The rounded granite tops of most other Sunshine Coast mountains show that the glaciers went right over them.

Changes were also happening in the sea, mostly because the moisture forming the continual snow was coming out of the oceans, gradually lowering their levels worldwide. However, at the same time, the enormous weight of the ice sheets was causing the northern half of North America to subside. The net result was that sea levels in this part of the world actually rose by about 500 feet.

AFTER THE ICE AGE

When North America's climate began warming up again, the seaward edges of the glaciers began to recede, water from melting ice rushed down from the higher glacial masses to fill the seas again, and the land that was relieved of its ice burden began rebounding. But since it took much longer for the land to rebound than it took the seas to refill—possibly as much as two or three thousand years—there was a period when the seas still covered the slopes of the Coast Mountains. This meant that in immediate postglacial times the sea level along the Sunshine Coast continued to climb until it was roughly 600 feet higher than it is today. During this period the Sechelt Peninsula was an island and all the presently inhabited lowlands along the coast lay under water. And this is why the fossils of marine creatures from the Pleistocene Age have been found as high as 500 and 600 feet above sea level in the Roberts Creek area, along Gray and Angus creeks and along the coast northeast of Gibsons on Thornbrough Channel.

While the ice was melting, fine glacial debris was deposited on the lowlands lying under the sea, most of it along the south coast where the glaciers had ended. This debris or "till" was overlain with marine sediment, the result of the sea's continual attack on the lower slopes of the mountains and on the boulders left behind in the surf zone. Bits of rock, constantly flung against these boulders and cliffs, continued the erosion that the ice sheet had begun. Over this marine sediment was deposited the silt, sand and fine gravel that had been loosened by the ice sheet and washed toward the sea by streams and rivers. The uppermost layer of debris consisted of cobbles, rocks and even huge boulders that had been imbedded in the ice and only released when it melted. Some of these rocks, known as "erratics," had been broken from distant mountains and carried hundreds of miles. Spectacular examples can be found at Granville Bay in Hotham Sound where black boulders the size of boxcars sit incongruously on top of solid granite shoreline rocks, and in Square Bay where one solitary boulder lying among the granite rocks below the cliffs is composed of green porphyry.

The land's rebounding process was complete about 10,000 to 12,000 years ago, stabilizing the shoreline at more or less its present level. However, above that shoreline was a very different landscape than the one that had existed before the ice came, because as the land rose again, the Georgia Lowland re-emerged from the sea covered with its fresh deposits of glacial till alternating with layers of marine and river sediments and capped with cobbles and boulders. Six deep inlets now bordered or bisected the region. In fact, Jervis Inlet, which forms the northwestern boundary of this area, has the distinction of registering the greatest maximum depth of any of BC's 37 inlets: 2,400 feet or almost half a mile. Its average mid-inlet depth is nearly one-third of a mile: 1,620 feet. At 48 nautical miles from head to mouth, it is also one of the longest of the 37, yet its width rarely exceeds one and a half miles.

The other inlets are neither as deep nor as long. Howe Sound, which borders the southern side of the Sunshine Coast, is only 23 miles long, its average mid-inlet depth less than half that of Jervis— only 740 feet—although one area has been charted at 1,060 feet. The deepest part of the fiords of the inland sea— Sechelt, Salmon and Narrows inlets—registers only 980 feet, but they are long and narrow. All of them are prone to sudden, violent storms.

Dominating the landscape were jagged peaks and bald, rounded mountains, composed primarily of granite bedrock, although pockets of debris had been left behind in depressions that had been worn into the bedrock by the ice and in the cracks where some of the lava and sedimentary deposits had been scoured out. In time, these deposits, although not much more than gravel, allowed mineral-loving plants to gain a foothold, and as they developed and decomposed, a thin veneer of humus was built up over the glacial debris.

Wherever pockets of this enriched soil accumulated—especially in the limited areas of protected coastal plain and at river mouths—seeds deposited by the wind and by birds and animals took root. Skunk cabbages *(Lysichitum americanum)* found their place in boggy ground, their bright yellow flower wrappers attracting the attention of the insects that would propagate them. Alongside them "Hudson's Bay Tea," and a wide variety of marsh lilies, rushes, reeds and grasses developed. On the moist slopes nearby grew mosses and ferns such as the majestic sword ferns *(Polystichum munitum)* with their five-foot fronds, deer ferns *(Blechnum spicant)* with dark-stemmed spore-bearing central fronds towering over their basal leaves, and the delicate maidenhair fern *(Adiantum pedatum)* with its wedge-shaped leaflets. A dozen species of wild onions established themselves on the new land, along with wild strawberries *(Fragaria, vesca)*, thimbleberries *(Rubus parviflorus)*, salmonberries *(Rubus spectabilis)*, red huckleberries *(Vaccinium parvifolium)*, Oregon grape *(Berberis nervosa)*, and several species of snowberries *(Symphoricarpos)*. Kinnikinnick *(Arctostaphylos uva-ursi)* and twin-flower *(Linnaea borealis)* crept over the ground. In places where lightning fires cleared the land again, fireweed *(Epilobium angustifolium)* flourished.

Taller shrubs took root here as time went by. Pussy willow *(Salix scouleriana)* and salal *(Gaultheria shallon)*—sometimes growing to a height of 10 feet—and two or three species of highbush cranberries and red flowering currants *(Ribes sanguineum)* all became part of the natural landscape. Spiny devil's club *(Oplopanax horridum)* took over moist valleys, and heathers *(Cassiope mertensiana* and *Phyllodoce)* ranged over the upland meadows. Red alder *(Alnus rubra)* was probably the first tree to put down roots here because, in the natural course of events, it is the one that reseeds areas devastated by fire, ice or windstorms, major insect infestations or disease. Alders also have a unique symbiotic relationship with frankia, a bacteria-like soil organism that fixes nitrogen so that when alder leaves fall they add a nitrogen layer to the soil. And since they have a maximum lifespan of 80 years, it is not long before they add even more nitrogen to the soil as the trees themselves fall and quickly decay.

This steady accumulation of soil encouraged the establishment of more long-lived forests. While the trees along the exposed shorelines and in fissures of the bedrock were generally dwarfed by lack of soil and misshapen by the wind, stands of tall, straight timber developed farther back from the water's edge. In most cases they grew in the protected valley bottoms that ran back from tidewater, where humus had accumulated to greater depths. Each of these valleys provided a separate forest unit isolated from other units by mountain crests that were either barren or, at most, lightly covered with scrub forest. The forests of the Sunshine Coast developed and matured, and when these first trees fell and decayed, they nurtured the seedling trees that took their places.

In time, the forests came to be dominated by coniferous, resinous-sapped evergreens: Douglas fir *(Pseudotsuga taxifolia)*, western hemlock *(Tsuga heterophylla)*, both western red cedar *(Thuja plicata)* and yellow cedar *(Chamacyparis nootkatensis)*, silver and balsam fir *(Abies amabilis* and *Abies grandis)*, white pine *(Pinus monticola)* and sitka spruce *(Picea sitchensis)*. While these eight species constitute what would eventually become the most commercially valuable trees on the Sunshine Coast, many others are important for their ornamentation. The spring display of the Pacific flowering dogwood *(Cornus nuttallii)*, scattered throughout lowland evergreen forests, is spectacular. The arbutus *(Arbutus menziesii)* is common on headlands and slopes exposed to the ocean. An elegant tree that the wind often bends into an artful shape, it can reach a height of 75 feet.

No tree in the Sunshine Coast forest has as distinctive a form as the broadleaf maple *(Acer macrophyllum)* with its massive and squat main trunk dividing into several huge vertical limbs that may soar up to 100 feet high with a breadth of 50 feet or more. Western yew *(Taxus brevifolia)*, a shrubby evergreen that can be found in the Sunshine Coast's mixed evergreen stands, is somewhat scraggly as the result of competing for light. It is valuable for its extremely hard wood and the medicinal properties of its bark. Cascara *(Rhamnus purshiana)* is also valuable for its medicinal properties and hazel *(Corylus cornuta)* for its hazelnuts. Literally hundreds more varieties of trees and shrubs and thousands of herbaceous perennials and annuals colonized the Sunshine Coast after the last ice age, and each plant that was successful made it possible for certain insects or animals to survive here.

As the centuries passed, the waters became populated with five species of salmon and many species of bottom fish, shellfish, Pacific white-sided dolphins *(Lagenorhynchus obliquidens)*, orcas *(Orcinus orca)* and other whales, sea lions—both California *(Zalophus californianus)* and Steller or northern *(Eumetopias jubatus)*—and seals *(Phoca vitulina)*. The animals that roamed the land ranged from Roosevelt elk *(Cervus elaphus roosevelti)*, grizzly bears (*Ursus arctos*) and black bears (*Ursus americanus*), to black-tailed deer (*Odocoileus hemionus columbianus*), cougars *(Felis concolor)*, bobcats *(Felis rufus)*, wolves *(Canus lupus)* and mountain goats *(Oreamnos americanus)*, to river otters *(Lutra canadensis)*, beavers *(Castor canadensis)* and raccoons (*Procyon lotor*). Birds became plentiful: bald eagles *(Haliaetus leucocephalus)*, ospreys *(Pandion haliaetus)*, turkey vultures *(Cathartes aura)*, Canada geese *(Branta canadensis)*, blue herons *(Ardea herodias)*, many species of ducks, gulls and cormorants, hawks, owls, shorebirds, forest birds and songbirds.

It was into this land of deep inlets, granite bedrock, dense evergreen forests and abundant wildlife that the first Native people ventured about 10,000 years ago. When European explorers and traders arrived in the 18th century, little had changed, but the 20th century saw the disruption of many wildlife cycles. Roosevelt elk were hunted into extinction, but between 1987 and 1989 a small group of animals was reintroduced into the Pender Harbour area. As this herd increased, some were transferred to the Tzoonie and Skwakwa watersheds to repopulate those areas. Grizzly bears became so scarce that they were "blue-listed" (designated a species of special concern), although by the beginning of the 21st century they were returning to the watersheds of the Skwakwa, Hunechin and Deserted rivers, now established as wildlife habitat areas for recovery of the species. Although the current total for bird species recorded on the Sunshine Coast is 301, some birds have not fared well here. As the original forests of the Sunshine Coast were logged off, the marbled murrelet *(Brachyramphus mamoratus)*, which nests in old-growth forest, came close to extinction, was "red-listed" (designated a threatened or endangered species) and is now found only in small pockets of untouched forest along Jervis Inlet. The spotted owl *(Strix occidentalis)* is also red-listed. Among amphibians, the red-legged frog *(Rana aurora)*, the coastal tailed frog *(Ascaphus truei)* and the painted turtle *(Chrysemys picta)* are all considered at risk. On the other hand, some new species have appeared. For example, coyotes *(Canis latrans)*, which were formerly confined to the drier Interior, made their appearance on the Sunshine Coast in the late years of the 20th century as their natural enemies— grizzlies and cougars—diminished in number.

PART TWO

PUTTING THE SUNSHINE COAST ON THE MAP

GEORGE VANCOUVER

When Captain George Vancouver of His Majesty's Ship HMS *Discovery* surveyed the Sunshine Coast in the summer of 1792, he was not favourably impressed. "These shores," he wrote in his three-volume survey report, "are composed principally of rocks rising perpendicularly from an unfathomable sea; they are tolerably well covered with trees, chiefly of the pine tribe, though few are of a luxuriant growth. . . . It is," he concluded, "a dreary and comfortless region."[1] In spite of his poor opinion of the landscape, however, he devoted 14 pages of his report to its description, and it is these pages that launch the written history of the area.

Vancouver had been carrying out a survey of the whole Pacific coast of North America when at the beginning of June 1792, he ordered his ships, the *Discovery* and the *Chatham,* to anchor off Point Roberts in Birch Bay. This was to be the base for his fourth boat expedition, which would go northward to survey the uncharted coast of the mainland. The ship's observatory was set up on the nearby point of land to establish the latitude and longitude and provide corrections for the observations that would be made from the boats.

Meanwhile, the *Discovery's* launch and the 25-foot pinnace, the *Elizabeth Bonaventure,* were lowered over the side of the ship. The pinnace, which on this expedition would be commanded by Vancouver, rowed eight double-banked oars and sailed with a three-masted lugsail rig. The launch was in the charge of Lieutenant Peter Puget; it had a single sail but was usually rowed. A total of 30 men were embarked, eight of them marines. Both boats were heavily armed, and each was stocked with a seven-day food supply.

EXPLORING HOWE SOUND

June 12, the first day of the expedition, the boat crews spent charting the area off the mouth of the Fraser River; the following day they mapped Burrard Inlet. Then at four on the morning of Thursday, June 14, they rowed the pinnace and the launch north past Point Atkinson into the inlet that Vancouver would christen Howe's Sound, in honour of one of his heroes, Admiral Richard Scrope Howe, Earl and Baron, First Lord of the Admiralty from 1783 to 1788. Just after daylight, when a fine southerly gale blew up, the crews raised the sails on both boats.

Vancouver's disappointment in the landscape was immediate. "The low fertile shores we had been accustomed to see," he wrote, "no longer existed;

their place was now occupied by the base of a stupendous snowy barrier, thinly wooded, and rising from the sea abruptly into the clouds; from whose frigid summit, the dissolving snow in foaming torrents rushed down the sides and chasms of its rugged surface . . . Not a bird, nor living creature was to be seen."[2]

For the survey, Vancouver took the compass bearings on the main bays and headlands and checked the angles between them with the sextant. One crewman kept track of the direction and speed of the boat's run, a second was in charge of the depth-sounding equipment, and a third compiled the survey data and sketched the more prominent landforms to help in later identification. The accuracy of the maps they produced, however, depended on the astronomical observations that were taken routinely from the boats to be checked later with the ship's observatory. On the Sunshine Coast, Vancouver was able to vary the system by landing the launch crew on each promontory to take compass bearings on all the other prominent features within sight while the pinnace's crew took a second set of bearings from the sea. As a result, the landing party brought back numerous plant samples for identification by the ship's botanist.

With a strong wind to carry them northward, the survey made good time, but toward noon, black clouds blotted out the sun and the day grew cold. When the sky cleared briefly, the crews hurriedly measured the altitude of the sun to determine the latitude and longitude of the island that lay ahead. Because of its shape, Vancouver named it Anvil; it was the only island to which he gave a name during his Sunshine Coast survey although his charts show the existence of the islands that would later be called Gambier, Bowen, Bowyer and Keats. Puget's launch arrived at Anvil Island first, and while waiting for the pinnace to catch up, the men shot long-billed curlews to add to their dinner rations.

With rain threatening, they continued up the inlet, "which was now only a mile and a quarter broad, each side formed by high stupendous mountains rising nearly perpendicular from the sea."[3] Near the head of the inlet, the water became less salty and somewhat whitish in colour. Convinced that these were signs of shallow water, the crew tried to take soundings but were surprised to find that they could not touch bottom even using 85 fathoms of line. In spite of the inlet's great depth, they came to its head only 10 miles beyond Anvil Island.

Vancouver's log reads: "my expectations vanished in finding it to terminate in a round basin, encompassed on every side by the dreary country already described."[4] He had hoped that it would turn out to be the fabled Northwest Passage that the adventurer Juan de Fuca had reported discovering at 50° north latitude, a location that should have placed it somewhere on the Sunshine Coast. Puget, however, found the country to have "a pleasant though romantic appearance" and noted that the land on the nearby islands of Bowen, Gambier and Keats was "low and well wooded, but its shores are in general rocky."[5]

After a brief exploration at the head of Howe Sound, the expedition returned along the shoreline for about three miles to a little cove where they made camp for the night. They were scarcely settled when the wind "became excessively boisterous from the southward, attended with heavy squalls and torrents of rain." Fog rolled in, completely obscuring the land.

"But for this circumstance," Vancouver wrote in his history of the expedition, "we might too hastily have concluded that this part of the gulf was uninhabited. In the morning we were visited by near forty of the Natives on whose approach, from the very material alteration that had now taken place in the face of the country, we expected to find some difference in their general character. This conjecture was however premature, as they varied in no respect whatever, but in possessing a more ardent desire for commercial transactions; into the spirit of which they entered with infinitely more avidity than any of our former acquaintances, not only in bartering amongst themselves the different valuables they had obtained from us, but when that trade became slack, in exchanging those articles again with our people; in which traffic they always took care to gain some advantage, and would frequently exult on the occasion. Some fish, their garments, spears, bows and arrows, to which these people wisely added their copper ornaments, comprised their general stock in trade. Iron, in all its forms, they judiciously preferred to any other article we had to offer."[6]

The eagerness of the Native traders of Howe Sound convinced Vancouver that they had previously traded with Europeans or Americans. In the seven years before his arrival on this coast, over a hundred trading vessels were known to have visited the Pacific Northwest coast in search of furs, or rather, for Natives who could supply them with furs. Many of these traders were British ships licensed by the East India Company, which held the exclusive trading rights for the area, but others belonged to American entrepreneurs who were conducting a triangular trade between Boston, the Northwest Pacific and Canton. Since none of these traders kept logs of their coastal journeys—or at least never made them public—Vancouver did not know how far their ships had penetrated or which tribes they had offended.

The people of Howe Sound, however, did not appear to recognize any words in either Spanish or English, and when Vancouver, who knew a little of the Nootka language, tried that on them, they still showed no understanding. When all these attempts failed, he and his crew resorted to sign language to explain themselves.

Both Vancouver and Puget speculated on the source of the Natives' copper ornaments and why they preferred iron trinkets over copper ones. Neither of them believed that the copper had come from European visitors. Instead, Puget suggested that it might have come from "other tribes on commercial pursuits who have in exchange for furs, collected these articles and bartered them away to the more inland nations."[7] It was even possible, he wrote in his log, that these inland people were trading with people living still farther inland who had actually mined the copper. It is ironic that the little cove in which Puget wrote these words on June 14, 1792, was close to the spot on which one of the most productive copper mines in Canada's history would operate from 1905 to 1975—Britannia Beach.

Continuing high seas and heavy rain on June 15 prevented the expedition from setting out again until the afternoon. Then they were forced to row against the wind, working their way along the western shoreline of Howe Sound into the channel between Gambier Island and the mainland (later named Thornbrough Channel), right past the site of the present-day Howe Sound Pulp and Paper Mill at Port Mellon. Once into this channel there was little wind, and in the calmer waters, Vancouver noted that the water had become saltier again, and at a distance of a hundred yards from the shore, they could not touch bottom with 60 fathoms of line.

At nine o'clock on the evening of Friday, June 15, the boats' crews came ashore for the night on a point of land that Vancouver calculated to be the west point of entrance into Howe Sound. Modern survey instruments place it at latitude 49° 23' N, longitude 123° 32' W, which is just 22' west of where Vancouver placed it on his charts. He named it Point Gower after Admiral Sir Erasmus Gower. It is now part of the town of Gibsons.

During the night, although the skies remained cloudy, the rain held off. Vancouver slept well, but he might not have rested so comfortably if he had known that a Spanish naval ship had been there only a year earlier in an attempt to establish Spain's ownership of the land. Although the *Santa Saturnina*, commanded by Jose Maria Narvaez, had not entered Vancouver's Howe Sound, it had sailed across the mouth of the sound and Narvaez named it *Boca del Carmelo* or Camel's Mouth. He left no written description of the lands that he saw, but the map that he drew shows some recognizable landmarks, among them Point Gower.

Travelling westward, Narvaez had anchored the *Santa Saturnina* just east of the mouth of Wilson Creek while his crew rowed ashore to replenish their fresh water supplies. At that time, an eastern arm of Chapman Creek also emptied into the small bay at the mouth of Wilson Creek, and Narvaez, thinking that he was looking at two mouths of the same river, named them *Rio de la Aguada,* or River of Swift Water. After leaving Wilson Creek, he had sailed northwest up Malaspina Strait, then west to Cape Lazo on Vancouver

Island, before turning south again to rejoin his commander, Francisco de Eliza, at the entrance to Puget Sound.

SURVEYING WELCOME PASSAGE AND MALASPINA STRAIT

At four on the morning of Saturday, June 16, Vancouver's crews re-embarked, setting their course northwestward along the continental shore of the Strait of Georgia. The landscape had "a more pleasing appearance than the shores of Howe's Sound. This part of the coast is of moderate height for some distance inland, and it frequently jets out into low sandy projecting points." These points would have included the Wilson Creek mud flats and Mission Point just west of Chapman Creek's main mouth. The trees that covered the site of present-day Sechelt grew "in great abundance of some variety and magnitude; the pine [coniferous evergreen] is the most common, and the woods are little encumbered with bushes or trees of inferior growth."[8] During the early afternoon they passed the Trail Islands without mapping them in detail, and then about 15 miles from their previous night's stopping place, they surveyed three more islands, which are now known as the Thormanbys.

While still aboard the *Discovery* at Birch Bay, Vancouver had sighted a "small though very high round island" far to the north. Now, after entering the passage that runs between the mainland and the Thormanbys, he could see that it was actually a very long island lying parallel to the mainland. Strictly following his orders to map only the continental shore, Vancouver did not even bother to give the island a name; Narvaez, however, had already named it *Isla de San-Felix*. In 1792 another Spanish survey crew renamed it Texada Island and christened the passage between the island and the mainland Malaspina Strait.

Sailing northward close to the rocky shore of the mainland, Vancouver's crews sighted "two smokes" on the long island but saw no other signs of life. Late that evening they navigated past shoals and rocky islets into Bargain Harbour, only to find the passageway into Pender Harbour too narrow for the boats to negotiate. It was after dark when they landed for the night in "a very dreary uncomfortable cove near the south point of an island about a mile long and about two miles to the S.S.E. of a narrow opening leading to the northward."[9] This island was later named Beaver Island, although since a bridge was built to connect it to the mainland, it has been generally known as Francis Peninsula. The cove where the expedition spent the night was probably Francis Bay on the west side of the island, just south of the entrance to Pender Harbour.

The "narrow opening leading to the northward" was not the entrance to Pender Harbour—which Vancouver's crews ignored, having seen that harbour already from Bargain Harbour—but a passageway just north of it that a year earlier Narvaez had labelled *Boca de Monino,* although he had not investigated beyond its entrance. It is the southern entrance to Jervis Inlet and it is now known as Agamemnon Channel.

SURVEYING JERVIS INLET

Although it was pouring when dawn came on June 17, the wind died around eight o'clock, and Vancouver ordered his men into the boats again to begin rowing. The entrance to the channel was studded with rocky islets at its mouth, but once past them, they found the passage was very deep, and Vancouver, once again encouraged to believe that he may have found the fabled Northwest Passage, returned to the survey with new enthusiasm.

Lieutenant Puget was impressed with the landscape. "The shore we now passed," he wrote, "was indented with bays whose beaches were in general composed of loose gravel. The country was low and thickly covered with pines, every place abounding with streams of fresh water, but whether these are occasioned by the late rains or are perpetual streams we could not determine."[10]

The boats emerged from Agamemnon's narrow channel into the junction of two broad waterways. Vancouver chose the one to the northeast as soundings showed that it was more than 100 fathoms deep. By this time, however, a gale had sprung up from the northeast, and the crew was forced to row into it, passing the mouth of Sechelt Inlet with neither Vancouver nor Puget commenting on it in their logs. Vancouver's map shows only a deep bay at this point. About 18 miles from their previous night's stopping place, they went ashore to make their noon meal in a narrow cove (probably Clam Cove just east of Egmont Point). As they had arrived at low tide, they were able to collect clams for their lunch. In this way "the provisions were made to last far beyond their proportioned time."[11]

During the afternoon, the expedition was approached by two canoes carrying 17 Indians, and from them Vancouver's men acquired some fish and several bows and arrows. Two things about these people particularly interested him: first, they were "much more painted than any we had hitherto met with," and second, some of their arrows were pointed with slate, the first that he had seen since visiting Nootka in 1778 with Captain Cook. "These" he wrote, "they appeared to esteem very highly, and like the inhabitants of Nootka, took much pains to guard them from injury."[12] What he had seen were the arrowheads specially designed by the Native people of Pender Harbour for hunting sea lions. The sources of the slate were deposits on Texada Island and at Deserted Bay farther up Jervis Inlet.

All afternoon the wind increased and the rain fell in torrents, but they rowed on, partly because Vancouver had made up his mind not to go back before he had examined the full extent of the waterway ahead of them but also because they could not find any place to land. At 11 o'clock that night, after what Puget described as "a most disagreeable and laborious row," they finally found a bay where they could drop anchor out of the wind. All of the boat's equipment and the men's clothing were thoroughly drenched, but "as it was equally uncomfortable either remaining in the water afloat or on shore, most preferred the ground and fire for the remainder of the night."[13] Nearly a century later this bay was identified from Vancouver's charts and given his name. Much later, the 13-mile-long river that flows into it was given the name Vancouver River.

The rain had stopped by the time the crews began rowing again at four the following morning, Monday, June 18, and within a few hours the sky had been swept clear. Puget, going ashore to survey near one of the inlet's numerous waterfalls, "ascended a small hill not far from the fall, and here a very light surface of earth covered an immense mass of rock which appeared to compose the foundation of the hill; yet with so bad a soil, it did not prevent a thick growth of pines, which here were large, but not so tall or straight as in the lower country, the ground not being of sufficient nourishment to bear such fine sticks."[14]

They stopped for the noon meal on a point of land which Vancouver established to be at latitude 50° 1' N and longitude 123° 46' W; it is now known as Patrick Point. Beyond this point the waterway swung abruptly to the northwest, and Vancouver's hopes rose. "By the progress we had this morning made, which comprehended about six leagues [18 miles], we seemed to have penetrated considerably into this formidable obstacle; and as the more lofty mountains were now behind us . . . I was induced to hope we should yet find this inlet winding beyond the mountains."[15]

While Vancouver fervently hoped that this waterway would not turn out to be just another inlet, he knew that if he did not find the end of it soon, he would run out of food and have to come back a second time. But at five o'clock that evening, the expedition reached the head of the inlet. They had travelled nearly 60 miles from their stopping place at Beaver Island, rowing most of the way, only to find a patch of "swampy low land producing a few maples and pines." At the high tide level they found a small encampment consisting of two huts and five or six aged men and women. "Their sole employment," Puget wrote, "appeared catching salmon and curing them with any other fish that fell their way."[16]

Vancouver named this inlet Jervis's Canal, in honour of Admiral Sir John Jervis. In time the name evolved to Jervis's Channel and then Jervis Inlet. The valley at the inlet's head interested him as a possible overland route to the eastern part of the continent because it "took nearly a northerly uninterrupted direction as far as we could perceive, and was by far the deepest chasm we had beheld in the descending ridge of the snowy barrier, without the appearance of any elevated land rising behind it."[17] But since the expedition's boats could not navigate the streams that flowed into the inlet from this valley, and the crew could not afford the time to explore on foot, Vancouver traded some iron trinkets for salmon from the Natives and started on his return journey.

THE JOURNEY BACK TO THE *DISCOVERY*

By Vancouver's reckoning, he and his crews were 114 nautical miles via the most direct route from the *Discovery* and the *Chatham,* a trip that would take at least three days of steady rowing. On their way up "Jervis's Canal," he had spotted "a small creek with some rocky islets before it" about five miles from the end of the inlet, and they began rowing for it now, believing it to be a suitable place to spend the night. They found it to be "a fall of salt water, just deep enough to admit our boats against a very rapid stream." The crew of Puget's launch "with great difficulty pulled a little way up" it, but quickly returned, afraid that when the tide fell, their boats would ground on the "sharp sunken rocks whose heads by the rapidity of the stream were frequently visible above the surface of the water."[18] As a result, Vancouver's expedition missed seeing the spectacular little inlet that was later christened Princess Louisa, a waterway that 20th century boaters would come thousands of miles to see.

The crews rowed until 10 that night then slept in the open on a bare rocky point on the west side of the inlet. The next morning, Tuesday, June 19, Puget joined Vancouver in the pinnace so that they could consolidate their survey notes; Lieutenant Thomas Manby was put in charge of the launch. All that day the men pulled on the oars against a strong southerly breeze, and at nine that night the pinnace took shelter in a small cove across from Vancouver Bay; the launch failed to rendezvous with them. When morning came, there was still no sign of the boat, but Vancouver went ahead with a survey of the inlet's northerly arm, though this was difficult with only one boat.

Just before noon the pinnace reached the north point of the inlet, "which producing the first Scotch firs we had yet seen, obtained the name of Scotch-Fir Point." From here, the surveyors could see that the largest of the islands separating the two mouths of Jervis Inlet was "three leagues [nine miles] in length with several small islets about it. This island and its adjacent shores, like those in the other channel, are of a moderate height and wear a similar appearance."[19] The island is now known as Nelson Island.

The crew of the pinnace spent that night on the eastern shore of Texada Island, directly opposite the entrance to Agamemnon Channel, but when morning came and the launch had still not reappeared, Vancouver's crew began pulling for the ships, still 84 miles away to the south. On his way, Vancouver encountered two Spanish ships, the brig *Sutil* commanded by Dionisio Alcala Galiano and the schooner *Mexicana* commanded by Cayetano Valdes. Since they had been ordered by their governments to co-operate with each other, Vancouver and the Spanish surveyors traded information on their discoveries. As a result, their maps of the area are very similar. When Vancouver's pinnace arrived in Birch Bay two days later, Manby and the launch crew were there to greet them.

WILLIAM DOWNIE

For close to 70 years after Vancouver's survey was completed, no government agency took an interest in more detailed mapping of the Sunshine Coast. Then in the 1850s both the colonial government and the British Admiralty sent surveyors to gather more information on this coast and on the land lying behind the shoreline.

In 1859 a California surveyor named William Downie was commissioned by the government of British Columbia to investigate the deep valley at the head of Jervis Inlet as a possible alternate route to the goldfields of the Cariboo. But it was late November before Downie's party arrived in the inlet, and in the report that he filed with the Department of Lands on December 12 of that year, he wrote, "The snow and rain set in so as to make it impossible to start over the mountains from the head of Jarvis [sic] Inlet to the Upper Fraser River for some time."[20] He went instead to investigate Desolation Sound and never returned to Jervis Inlet. The colonial government's interest in the area was never rekindled.

BRITISH ADMIRALTY SURVEYS 1856 TO 1862

By 1856 the discrepancies in longitudes between the survey maps of Captains Cook and Vancouver had made navigation of BC's coastal waters so hazardous that the British Admiralty commissioned a new survey of the coastline to reconcile and correct the earlier maps. The ship provided for the survey was HM Surveying Vessel *Plumper*, a 19-year-old, bark-rigged sloop of 484 tons with 60-horsepower auxiliary steam engines. Under steam, she could make six knots an hour.

The *Plumper's* captain was George Henry Richards, who had spent nearly 20 years as a marine surveyor. He was already famous for his participation in the second attempt to locate the ill-fated Franklin Expedition in Canada's Arctic. When the would-be rescue ships had to be abandoned in the ice, Richards made one of the most extraordinary sledging journeys on record to find help. According to his naval record, his subsequent surveys were carried out "with extraordinary energy and almost severe zeal."[21]

Chief Assistant Surveyor and Second Master aboard the *Plumper* was

Daniel Pender. He was promoted to the rank of master in 1859 when the *Plumper*, having proved too small and unsuitable for these waters, was replaced by the *Hecate*—"a fine, roomy paddle sloop, carrying an abundance of coal"[22]— which proved better suited to survey work of this kind. After Captain Richards and the *Hecate* were ordered back to England in December 1862, Pender, now a captain, was left to complete the survey of the coast adjacent to Vancouver Island. The ship he used was the famous paddle steamer *Beaver*, hired from the Hudson's Bay Company.

In the course of the *Plumper/Hecate/Beaver* survey expedition most of the mountain peaks, channels, points, bays and islands that had been vague entities on existing maps were charted and named. In Howe Sound, Richards added more place names to honour that admiral's most famous battle—that of the First of June, 1794, when his small fleet captured seven line-of-battle French ships and sank a dozen more. Gambier Island is named for the captain of one of the ships participating in the battle—HMS *Defence;* the ship itself gives its name to a group of small islands in the sound. Ramillies is the name that Richards gave to the channel between Anvil and Gambier islands to commemorate the service of the ship of that name. The channel between Anvil and the mainland is named after HMS *Montagu* and her captain, James Montagu, who died during the battle. Irby Point at the south end of Anvil and Domett Point at the north end are named after officers who served on board that ship. On the mainland above present-day Gibsons, 4,000-foot-high Mount Elphinstone was named after the commander of HMS *Glory*. But Richards departed slightly from this pattern to name Keats Island after Admiral Sir Richard Goodwin Keats, who is famous for having sailed his ship, HMS *Superb*, through a Spanish blockade in 1801.

Just west of Halfmoon Bay, Richards abandoned Royal Navy names because it was there that he received the welcome news that the horse Thormanby had just won the 1860 Epsom Derby. He promptly named the two large islands to the west of his position North and South Thormanby. He honoured the horse's owner, a man named Merry, by bestowing his name on the small island south of them. The channel that passes between these islands and the mainland he named Welcome Passage. (History does not tell how much of Richards' money was riding on Thormanby.)

Richards named Pender Harbour after his second-in-command. When Pender returned there in the *Beaver* in 1867 to resurvey the numerous rocks and islets within the harbour, he named Gunboat Bay, which forms Pender's inner harbour, after HM Gunboats *Grappler* and *Forward*, which were then stationed on this coast.

In Jervis Inlet, Richards selected names from Admiral Horatio Nelson's era and named the two islands in the mouth of the inlet Nelson and Hardy. The waters between the islands, Blind Bay and Telescope Passage, commemorate the incident in which Nelson held his telescope to his blind eye during the Battle of Copenhagen so that he would not have to see the withdrawal signal from his commander. Fearney Bluff on the southern tip of Nelson Island is named after Nelson's bargeman. The inspiration for Agamemnon Channel was the ship Nelson commanded during the battle in which he lost his arm. Nile Point at the most easterly tip of Nelson Island commemorates Nelson's victory over Napoleon's fleet at the mouth of the Nile in 1798. Captain Island at the north-eastern tip of Nelson Island is named after HMS *Captain,* Nelson's flagship at the Battle of St. Vincent in February 1797, and Vanguard Bay honours HMS *Vanguard,* Nelson's flagship at the Battle of the Nile. It was commanded by his close friend, Thomas Masterman Hardy, after whom Hardy Island was named. Hotham Sound and St. Vincent Bay were named for two of the admirals who commanded the British fleet during the Napoleonic Wars. Elephant Point, separating the two bodies of water, is named after Nelson's flagship in the Battle of Copenhagen. Nearby are Culloden Point and Mount Troubridge, named for HMS *Culloden* and her master, Captain Thomas Troubridge, Nelson's friend and a hero of the Battle of St. Vincent. Goliath Bay honours HMS *Goliath* which participated in both the Battle of the Nile and the Battle of St. Vincent, and the point immediately to the east of the bay is named for Vice-Admiral James Richard Dacres who commanded HMS *Barfleur* in the latter battle.

Richards and Pender would undoubtedly have continued working their way through the whole British navy and the entire fleet for place names, but fortunately, the three reaches of Jervis Inlet—Prince of Wales, Princess Royal and Queen's—had already been named during the 1840s. The names were intended to honour Queen Victoria and her two eldest children: Victoria, who was born in 1840 and given the title Princess Royal, and Edward, born in 1841 and titled the Prince of Wales. The name Princess Louisa Inlet first appeared on Admiralty charts in 1861, presumably placed there by either Richards or Pender, and although it is often assumed that the name was chosen for Queen Victoria's sixth child, Louise, who came to Canada in 1878 as the wife of the Marquis of Lorne, Canada's governor general from 1878 to 1883, the inlet's name most likely honours the Queen's mother, Princess Mary Louisa Victoria of Saxe-Cobourg-Gotha. She died on March 16, 1861, just as the new charts were being drawn up.

NATIVE PLACE NAMES

Although the Native Sechelt and Squamish people had names for every head-land, bay and mountain on the Sunshine Coast, few of these names have remained in common use among people of non-Native descent. Attempts by early European visitors to make literal translations of them only resulted in approximations since a number of the sounds used in these languages are unfamiliar to speakers of English. In the few cases where Native names have become accepted, they generally designate sites for which they were not intended. As a result, the community of Tuwanek on the east side of Sechelt Inlet takes its name from the *Tahw-ahn-kwuh* people who once lived at the head of Narrows Inlet; Skaikos Point in Sechelt Inlet is derived from *Sqaia-quos,* the name of the people of Pender Harbour, and the Kunechin Islets at the mouth of Salmon Inlet commemorate the village of *Hunae-chin* at the head of Jervis Inlet.

Most of the remaining place names on the Sunshine Coast are local names used to designate family homesites or the booming grounds used by specific logging outfits. Thus the pioneers referred to Grantham's Landing, Andy's Bay, Carlson's Point and Wilson's Creek. In time these names lost their possessive form and were entered into the gazetteer.

PART THREE
THE NATIVE PEOPLES

The history of the Native peoples of the Sunshine Coast may begin as early as a thousand years after the final retreat of the Pleistocene ice, that is, somewhere around 9,000 or 10,000 BCE. It is a complicated history that has come down to the present Native population in an intricate interleaving of legend and genealogy, ceremonies and privileges, each giving unique structure and significance to the facts of their past and to the social structure of their present lives.

No attempt will be made to recount this history here. On the other hand, the story of the interface between the Native and non-Native communities is vital to an understanding of the entire history of the Sunshine Coast and that story will be told here.

NATIVE TERRITORIES

Before contact with Europeans, the traditional lands of the Coast Salish nation known as the Sechelt or *Shishalh* took up the major portion of the Sunshine Coast. Anthropologists who came here in the early years of the 20th century believed that they could identify four main groups or septs of the Sechelt living within this area: the Klay-ah-Kwohss or *Sqaia-quos* who made their chief home at Pender Harbour, the Ts'unay or *Tsonai* at Deserted Bay, the Xenichen or *Klam-am-klatc* at the head of Jervis Inlet, and the Tewankw or *Tahw-ahn-kwuh* at the head of Narrows Inlet. In addition, they reported seeing numerous small groups in temporary or seasonal settlements throughout the area and estimated that more than 30 sites were occupied.

To the east of the Sechelts' lands were those of the Squamish people, another Coast Salish tribe. The line separating their lands ran due north from a point on the shore approximately halfway between the present-day settlements of Roberts Creek and Gibsons. Interestingly, scientists have recently discovered that this line coincides very closely with the dividing line between two distinct areas of plant and animal life. To the west of the line in the Sechelt people's traditional territory is the Gulf Islands Biotic Area; to the east in Squamish territory is the Coast Forest Biotic Area.

In general the differences between these two areas—and the reason there are variations in the plant and animal life—can be summed up in one word: rain. A comparison of weather statistics in the present-day towns of Sechelt and Gibsons, the main centres of the two areas, shows that while they have roughly the same number of hours of sunshine per year—somewhere between 1,600 and 1,800 hours—Sechelt registers a mean annual rainfall of 1,060.6 millimetres, while Gibsons—just inside Howe Sound—registers 1,293.2 millimetres of rain. And just another 20 miles up Howe Sound at Port Mellon, the difference increases dramatically; there the estimated annual sunshine decreases to between 1,400 and 1,600 hours and the rainfall increases to 3,213.9 millimetres. The heavy rainfall east of the dividing line produces a "climax forest" of dense conifers with fallen trees and a jungle of undergrowth that makes it almost impenetrable. The food potential for animals is low so only species that can adapt to this rank growth survive. The Squamish people living in this area therefore depended more heavily on the harvest from the sea than the land.

The Sechelts also gathered shellfish and netted or speared fish, but they had the advantage of a rich selection of plants and animals for food because there were more open areas and sparser undergrowth in their territory. They dined on the roots of Pacific hemlock parsley, sea milkwort, Pacific cinquefoil, spiny wood ferns and sword ferns, the bulbs of nodding onions, rice root, tiger lilies, chocolate lilies and blue camas, and the stalks and/or leaves of arrow-grass, fireweed, stinging nettles, and bracken fern fiddleheads. But the real bonanza came in the variety of fruits available: highbush cranberries, crabapples, mountain blueberries, saskatoons, huckleberries, salal berries, Oregon grapes, red currants, blackcaps, thimbleberries, salmonberries, and trailing wild blackberries. And since there was such a profusion of food for man, herbivorous animals also flourished.

PRE-CONTACT VILLAGE LIFE

Most of the permanent villages of the Native peoples of the Sunshine Coast were established near reliable sources of fresh water, generally in sheltered saltwater bays that gave some protection from the violent storms that rage down the narrow inlets in winter and from raids by hostile tribes from the outer coast. Because there is a limited number of such sites, over the thousands of years in which these people had made their home here, the same locations were repeatedly occupied, abandoned and reoccupied. One of the largest villages was at Deserted Bay, far enough from the mouth of Jervis Inlet to discourage all but the most determined raiders. Other villages were located within the Sechelt-Salmon-Narrows Inlet system, known as the inland sea, where the Skookumchuck (or Sechelt) Rapids at the north end of Sechelt Inlet provided a barrier. Of all the Sechelts' permanent settlements, only the one at the head of Pender Harbour was vulnerable to attack, but this village was mainly a winter retreat, a time when raiding parties seldom ventured down the coast.

Neither Vancouver nor Puget described the buildings they saw on the Sunshine Coast, but Puget filled a page of his log with construction details of houses he saw in a deserted village near Point Roberts, and it is very similar to descriptions of Sechelt longhouses that turn up in later church documents. Of the Point Roberts' village he wrote, "This must by its size have formerly been the habitation of near four hundred people. . . . The body of the village consists of three rows of houses, each row divided by a narrow lane and partitioned off into four or six square houses and every one large and capacious. This frame, the only remnant of the village [still in existence], must have [caused] the Native inhabitants an infinite trouble in the construction, and it still remains a mystery to me by what powers of machinism they have been able to lift up the heavy and long logs of timber which are placed on the top of the standards. These last are two and a half feet in circumference and erected perpendicular about fourteen feet from the ground. On the top of these standards or posts is a notch cut to receive the rafter which from its length will serve for two houses or perhaps more, each side and end of the house having three standards to support it. Besides the rafters going lengthways, they are likewise laid across and with their standards partition off the different habitations. I have no doubt that when occupied, the sides and tops are boarded in as large smoke-dried planks were found contiguous to the village."[1]

A Sechelt dugout canoe on the beach at Porpoise Bay c. 1904. In the background, running parallel to the beach, is Herbert Whitaker's dock. The building is the Yamamoto Boat Works, later used as the second Sechelt schoolhouse.
COURTESY OF THE SUNSHINE COAST MUSEUM AND ARCHIVES. PHOTO #98.

While the Sechelt people are not well known as totem or rock carvers as the more northerly tribes of the BC coast are, they did practise an art form that is still visible today: painting on the smooth, perpendicular rock faces overlooking the water, usually about 10 or 15 feet above the high tide mark—many of them along the upper reaches of Jervis Inlet. The colours used in the paintings have been dimmed by time and the elements so that most are difficult to locate today without a guide, but during the 1930s when their colours were brighter, they were mapped, sketched and photographed by Amy and Francis Barrow during summer-long cruises on their boat, the *Toketie*. In *Upcoast Summers*, Beth Hill's resurrection of the *Toketie's* logs, a dozen pictograph sites are noted in Jervis, Sechelt and Narrows inlets, in Pender Harbour and on Sakinaw Lake. The Barrows' records as well as their collection of artifacts are in the provincial archives and the National Museum.

WHITE MAN'S DISEASES

Although the population of the Sechelts and Squamish must have numbered in the thousands in early pre-contact times, their ranks had dwindled considerably by the time Captain Vancouver surveyed the coast in June 1792. Lieutenant Puget, returning to the *Discovery*, told Archibald Menzies, the ship's botanist and general scientific recorder, that the expedition had "found but few inhabitants in the northern branches [the inlets of the Sunshine Coast], but if they might judge from the deserted villages they met in this excursion, the country appeared to be formerly much more numerously inhabited than at present."[2] As Puget did not tell Menzies how long the villages appeared to have been vacant, and the expedition members never asked the Natives they met later any questions about the deserted villages, it is possible that the people were only away fishing or gathering berries or other foods. Puget, however, was apparently convinced that something calamitous had happened to the population.

In a 1965 CBC interview, Sechelt member Clarence Joe seemed to corroborate Puget's conviction when he explained that his people had formerly avoided the site of present-day Sechelt because it had been inhabited for a long time by a tribe "that was always at war."[3] He said that it was only after these people had been wiped out by smallpox that the Sechelts claimed the site. Anthropologists are divided on who these warring people were and when they lived there. While they could have been victims of an early 19th century epidemic, it is more likely that they were killed by a much earlier plague, and that their village was one of the deserted ones that Puget saw, since the first smallpox epidemic to sweep North America occurred in the 1770s, about 20 years before Vancouver's expedition. It had moved up the coast from the Spanish settlements in Mexico, then, through commerce between tribes, it was carried to the Natives of the Columbia valley and westward to the coast. Captain Vancouver's log records encounters with pock-marked Natives in Puget Sound, the San Juan Islands and Boundary Bay, and the Spaniards, Quadra and Valdez, reported seeing pock-marked Natives near Nanaimo. It is estimated that the populations of the affected tribes were reduced by at least 30 percent during the decade in which that epidemic raged.

In the years that followed Vancouver's brief 1792 visit, the only Europeans to come in contact with the Native people of the Sunshine Coast were surveyors and occasional traders who came looking for furs. Partly as a result of this lack of contact, for nearly 70 years the Sechelts were unaffected by the white man's diseases, including the smallpox epidemic of 1800 and 1801, which ravaged the populations of the Fraser and Thompson valleys. The smallpox epidemics of 1836–1837 were limited to the tribes south of the 44th parallel and north of the 52nd, but even in these places the results were not as devastating as the previous epidemics since most of the Natives, having survived earlier infection, had developed a degree of immunity. In 1848 the Hudson's Bay Company steamer *Beaver* carried measles to many of the coastal tribes. Syphilis and typhus were also introduced to many of the Native peoples during this period, but there is no documentation to show if or how seriously the Sunshine Coast peoples were affected by these diseases.

But while the Native people saw little of the white man during the first half of the 19th century, there were other disruptions in their lives. Probably in the first or second decade of this period, a rock slide in Narrows Inlet destroyed part of the main village of the Tewankw group of the Sechelts. Some of the Tewankws stayed to rebuild, but many resettled at Slahlt between Burnet and Angus creeks on Porpoise Bay, making this their new main village.

Legend tells of another village called *Qua-Ma-Meen* or Qualmamine beside Chatterbox Falls at the head of Princess Louisa Inlet that was also obliterated by a slide, although the date of this event is not known. Unfortunately, the site had been used by campers before Simon Fraser University archaeologists Neelley and Stewart investigated it in 1967, so most of the artifacts had probably been already taken, but the ones they did find were sent to the provincial museum. They included fragments of wooden burial boxes and charred skull fragments found in a rock shelter. In the slide debris they found clam and abalone shells, charcoal and miscellaneous wood and iron objects. The slide area has since been declared an archaeological site to protect it from souvenir hunters.

THE ARRIVAL OF THE OBLATE FATHERS

The year 1862 brought irrevocable changes to the lives of the Sechelt people. On March 13 of that year the *Brother Jonathan*, a sailing ship out of San

Francisco, docked in Victoria carrying a passenger suffering from varioloid smallpox, the most virulent strain of the disease. Although the authorities were aware of his condition, the man was not quarantined, and within a month the whole settlement was in the grip of an epidemic. Fortunately for the white population, a primitive form of smallpox vaccination had been invented a century earlier and was fairly widely practised even in such outposts of the empire. The Natives living on the outskirts of Victoria were not protected by vaccination, however, and since most of them were Haidas from the Queen Charlottes, which had been bypassed by previous smallpox epidemics, they had no immunity from earlier exposure.

Victoria's authorities, who had been under pressure by the white population for many years to evict the Natives because they were camped on prime real estate, used fear of greater infection from the Natives as an excuse to order them evicted and their huts burned. Throughout May and June, the Natives moved north, accompanied part of the way by government boats to make sure that they did not return. When they became too ill to travel, they stopped in the territory of other Native peoples along the way, infecting their hosts and leaving many of their dead on the beaches.

Among the Coast Salish tribes of the Fraser Valley and Burrard Inlet areas, the oldest members had acquired some immunity by surviving the earlier epidemics. As a result when the epidemic of 1862 struck, only the young people were at risk, and many of these had come under the influence of missionaries who had seen to it that they were vaccinated. The Sechelts, however, were unprotected because they had not accepted missionaries into their territory and they had no natural immunity as they had not been touched by an epidemic for close to 90 years.

In 1860 Father Leon Fouquet of the Oblate Order of Mary Immaculate had come to the Sechelts' Pender Harbour village in an effort to convert them, but he was driven away after only two months. It was probably right after this rebuff that the Oblates built a mission at the mouth of Chapman Creek in Davis Bay. Writer Dick Hammond recalled that as a child in the 1930s he had played near the remains of an old mission building "on the flat part near the mouth of the creek, halfway between the bridge and the salt water. I remember there was a white cross on the peak of the building."[4] As a result of the existence of this derelict church, the creek was known locally for many years as Mission Creek and the land adjacent to it is still known as Mission Point.

When the Sechelt people began to fall sick from the white man's disease in 1862, two chiefs were sent as emissaries from the Pender Harbour settlement to the Oblates at St. Charles Mission in New Westminster to persuade the fathers to come back. The Oblates agreed and appointed Father Paul Durieu to head a new mission to the Sechelts. A Frenchman, he had arrived in the Crown Colony of Vancouver Island on December 12, 1859, after five years' work among the Natives of Oregon. He was a superb organizer and a tireless worker but also a perfectionist, a combination destined to make him one of the Catholic Church's more controversial figures.

Father Durieu's appointment gave him the opportunity to try out a system he had devised for creating a model Native Christian community, a system that was often criticized—both in his own time and in retrospect—for its strictness. Although he began his mission at Pender Harbour, he intended this to be only a temporary base since an important feature of his system was the removal of the people from their old villages and the establishment of a new community at an entirely fresh location. For his new village Durieu chose the narrow neck of land, then sparsely inhabited, that ties the Sechelt peninsula to the mainland. Although the Sechelt people knew this place where the "warring tribe" had lived as *Chataleech,* Durieu named his new community Sechelt.

His flock was not a large one because only a fraction of the nearly 5,000 Sechelts who had lived on the Sunshine Coast in the early years of the 19th century remained after the 1862 epidemic was over. In a letter to the *Mainland Guardian* in 1875, Durieu stated that between the Sechelts and the Sliammons of the Powell River area, "they do not muster much more than 370 souls."[5] Indian Commissioner Gilbert M. Sproat, who inspected Sechelt village in 1876, counted a total of 167 people: 55 men, 56 women, 14 adolescents, and 42 children.

In order to be accepted into Durieu's system, the Sechelt survivors, although of different septs, had to be willing to abandon their traditional villages except during the hunting and gathering seasons and to make their permanent home together in Sechelt. Under his supervision, the new village was a tightly knit community. To administer it, he ignored the traditional chieftainships and appointed four new "chiefs." Reporting to them on the conduct of the villagers were a number of "watchmen." "Soldiers" policed the village and dealt out penances and punishments. The Sechelts living in the new village were no longer allowed to gamble, potlatch, dance or practise shamanism.

That they embraced the new lifestyle with little resistance is suggested by the fact that all the Sechelts were administered the sacrament of confirmation in the spring of 1871 in the little wooden church that they had built on the Sechelt waterfront three years earlier. By the following year they had constructed five traditional timber lodges beside it, each of them capable of holding 15 to 20 families. Having secured his congregation, Durieu immediately laid plans for a new and larger church. It was officially opened with Durieu's blessing on April 15, 1873, and named SS Redempteur or the Church of the

Holy Redeemer. It had been constructed from milled lumber purchased in New Westminster by the bishop, but the Sechelts were levied six dollars per family to pay for it.

This money came from logging. The Sechelts, who had only cut trees in the past in order to make canoes or build lodges, were now encouraged by Father Durieu—who firmly believed that idleness led inevitably to evil ways—to begin logging the adjacent forests in order to sell the timber to the sawmills on Burrard Inlet. Some Sechelts took out handlogging licences, others formed small co-operative logging companies. And although they had been primarily a hunting and gathering society, Durieu also set them to fishing for profit and cultivating gardens. By 1876 most had been encouraged to construct one-family frame houses, each with its own garden, and within a few years they demolished their traditional lodges. Durieu had, according to Bishop E.M. Bunoz in the *Etudes Oblats* published in 1942, "the unique power of making the Indians work."[6]

Although Durieu left the Sunshine Coast in 1875 to become coadjutor bishop of New Westminster, he retained a special interest in the people of Sechelt. According to Bishop Bunoz, on one return visit, Durieu called a meeting and learned from the watchmen that the young men of the village had bought a football and were trying to purchase uniforms so that they could play against the Nanaimos. Durieu forbade the game and confiscated the football.

"You are poor, ignorant Indians," he told them. "You think only of playing, of squandering your money and time. The right tool for people like you is the pick, the shovel, the axe, the saw." After mass, he marched them out to the marshland that lay parallel to the Trail Bay waterfront and set them to work digging a drain from the swamp to the inlet. When in time the swamp dried up, Durieu sent them fruit trees and berries to plant over the area. Bishop Bunoz' story concludes, "Later on when they picked the fruits on the old swamp, they realized how much better they were than the frogs and mosquitos. They appreciated the work imposed on them by their wise and loving 'papa'."[7]

LAND CLAIMS

Although a royal proclamation in 1763 had acknowledged the Native peoples' continuing ownership of all the lands they had traditionally used and occupied, in 1859 the colonial government under Governor James Douglas had begun allocating limited reserve lands to the Natives of British Columbia and Vancouver Island so that the remaining land could be opened to white settlement. Douglas had started the process with those who were already organized around church missions, and although he made it known that he expected them to turn to agriculture for their livelihood, the designated lands averaged only 10 acres per family, far too little for a self-supporting farm. Apparently, it was also his intention that they should pre-empt additional land as they required it, but in 1866, just two years after he retired from office, the colonies of Vancouver Island and British Columbia were amalgamated, and one of the new legislature's earliest acts was an amendment to the pre-emption ordinance to specifically exclude Native people from the right to pre-empt land.

Joseph Trutch, chief commissioner of lands and works during this period, then began a systematic reduction of the acreage that had already been allocated to the Natives in an attempt to make them all conform to a formula of ten acres per family of five. He enforced this allotment despite the fact that on the prairies each Aboriginal family received an average of 160 acres and those in Ontario received 80 acres. When BC became part of Canada in 1871, the Ottawa politicians, ignoring the fact that there had been no treaties to extinguish the land titles of the west coast Natives and also the fact that the colony's government had only been allowing 10 acres per family, signed an act of union in which it was agreed that the provincial government would set aside land for reserves only to the "extent that it has hitherto been the practice of the British Columbia Government to appropriate for that purpose . . ."[8] Under the new act the reserve lands were transferred to the federal government and the administration and welfare of their inhabitants fell to the Department of Indian Affairs. As soon as this was finalized, the BC legislature passed an act denying the Aboriginal people in this province the right to vote in provincial or municipal elections.

The man designated by Ottawa to administer the Indian Act in BC was Israel Wood Powell, a Victoria doctor, who was appalled to find out that many of the reserves actually contained not ten acres but less than five acres per family. In March 1873, after he reported this to his superiors, the government in Ottawa demanded that BC adopt the 80-acre-per-family standard. Powell, apparently believing that the federal government's will would prevail, met with a huge delegation of Natives, including members of the Sechelt people, at New Westminster in May 1873 to tell them that the reserves would be enlarged. But the BC government refused to be dictated to by Ottawa and agreed instead to 20 acres. Accordingly, Powell met again with the Natives on June 4 and informed them that they could expect only 20 acres. In the end, however, the BC government never implemented the new agreement, and Powell's response was to stop laying out reserves altogether on the grounds that he feared that the continuing injustice would increase the Natives' discontent and result in violence.

Meanwhile on the Sunshine Coast, where only the 45-acre Indian Reserve #1 at the mouth of Wilson Creek (Tsawcome) had been designated, the white population had begun to make serious encroachments on the Sechelts' traditional lands. On May 25, 1869, John Scales, late of the Royal Engineers of New Westminster, had marked out a 150-acre military land grant lying between Porpoise Bay and Trail Bay, right next to the Oblates' new settlement for the Sechelts. At the same time, prospectors looking for gold in the rivers and streams that flow into Salmon and Narrows inlets were staking mineral claims on the Sechelts' lands. The Moodyville Sawmill Company of Burrard Inlet was already cutting in the Gibsons area and had been granted rights to timber on Jervis Inlet.

The first clash came in the summer of 1874 when Chief Schelle and a delegation of Sechelts met with Sewell Moody at his Moodyville Sawmill to object to his company's logging on Sechelt land. Moody responded that since his timber lease had come from the government of BC, he had no obligation to the Sechelts, but he placated Schelle with the promise that the Sechelts could sell any trees they cut on their own land to his mill. The Sechelts went away from the meeting apparently satisfied and by the following spring they had 173 logs ready to be taken to the Moodyville mill.

In the meantime, a pre-emptor named Jabez A. Culver had set up camp on the site of the former Tewankw settlement in Narrows Inlet to cut spars for the Moodyville Sawmill, and a party of Sechelts, armed with muskets, arrived to order his loggers off the land. Culver and his men left without resisting, but his complaints once he was back in Victoria prompted the government to send the man-of-war HMS *Myrmidon* to Sechelt with a Magistrate Bushby and the superintendent of police on board. After the tribe was assembled and the culprits identified, Bushby proceeded to explain "the serious and unwarrantable nature of their high-handed conduct." The chief, who admitted he had instigated the attack, pointed out that his people had only been assigned one small reserve of land and that they feared "lest all the land which they most desired would be claimed and occupied by the whites."[9] In the end, the Sechelts promised not to molest any more whites in exchange for a promise that their land claims would receive attention.

In June 1875, when no further action had been taken on reserve lands, Chief Schelle, accompanied by a chief of the Sliammon people, visited the editor of the *Mainland Guardian* in New Westminster to ask him to make their grievances known to the public. In response, the *Guardian* published an editorial on June 9 under the headline: "A Great Injustice." According to the editorial, the Sechelts had recently learned that they were to receive only two acres per person. The editorial continued, "The dissatisfaction and discontent is growing very serious among them and Schelle looks for trouble if the reservations as promised is [sic] not secured to them . . . They bitterly resent any interference with their land, and the sense of wrong is deeply impressed on their minds. It is a matter calling for immediate investigation, otherwise we may have serious trouble. The Walkem government has persistently ignored this danger and have *[sic]* been granting timber leases and pre-emptions which encroach upon these people. Some settlement must be made without delay; common humanity requires it."[10]

A week later the newspaper published a letter from Father Durieu in which he restated the very real injustice being served to the Sechelts. "Schelle says," Durieu wrote, "that if the white men are coming one after the other before their reserves have been marked out, they will take the best of the land and encroach on the Indians until they have not sufficient land left them on which to produce food for the people."[11]

Durieu's warning took on more urgency a month later when William S. Jemmett, who was employed by the provincial government, arrived to survey Scales' military land grant of District Lot 303 and discovered that the former engineer had actually marked out 260 acres for himself. Since his grant could not exceed 150 acres, the government simply invited Scales to buy the additional acreage as District Lot 304 for one dollar per acre. Scales, who never occupied the land, accepted the offer, waited another 16 years before he applied for crown grant status, then promptly sold both lots to Lieutenant Governor Hugh Nelson, who also became an absentee landowner.

The joint federal-provincial Reserve Commission finally visited the territory of the Sechelts in December 1876. They travelled along the coast from Howe Sound as far as Sechelt village, then crossed over to Sechelt Inlet and continued on to Jervis Inlet. On their return journey, they worked their way down as far as Pender Harbour, then crossed the Strait Georgia. As a result of the commission's visit, Sechelt Indian Reserve #2, a parcel of 607 acres lying just east of Scales' land, was confirmed later that month. Added to the tract at Tsawcome, this allotment meant that, if Sproat's census was correct, the Sechelts now possessed less than four acres per person. Having anticipated that their earlier protests would correct this inequity, the Sechelts now became even more determined to have legal title to all of the lands that had been their people's territory before Europeans came. For the next 40 years they waged a running battle with the provincial government to have it returned to them. In the meantime, since most of the Sechelts now made Reserve #2 their principal residence, the confirmation of the reserve brought them all under the jurisdiction of the federal Indian Act. Although a further allocation of lands in 1884 preserved the Sechelts' rights to such traditional sites as Deserted Bay, the mouth of the Hunaechin River and a little rectangle of land at the head of Pender Harbour, these represented only a small percentage of the land that they had traditionally held.

About this time the Squamish people were also allotted two reserves totalling 67.5 acres on the Sunshine Coast. Reserve #25, which the Squamish knew as *Kaikalahun,* is on Howe Sound opposite Woolridge Island. Used primarily as a fishing station, it was only intermittently occupied. Number 26, known as *Chekwelp,* lies between Gibsons and Grantham's Landing.

OUR LADY OF THE ROSARY

Although the Sechelts had been forced by the government and the church to give up most of their traditional customs and ceremonies, the Oblates were wise enough to fill the void with religious pageantry. One of the most spectacular celebrations in the village was held in June 1890 for the dedication of a new and much larger church, Our Lady of the Rosary. For this event, more than a thousand Natives arrived in Vancouver by train from Catholic mission centres as far away as the Chilcotin. On June 3 they boarded the steamer *Yosemite,* chartered by the bishop for their trip to Sechelt. Five of the Native groups brought their own brass bands—all of them, according to newspaper accounts, "fantastically uniformed"—to join the Sechelts' own band (organized two years earlier), which waited on the steps of the new church to greet them with music.

The *Yosemite* then returned to Vancouver to bring two loads of excursionists to the mission to "see the charming little village and to witness the fireworks in the evening. The mission village" reported the Vancouver *World,* "is a most

*The members of the Sechelt brass band assemble for their photograph in front of
Our Lady of the Rosary Church on the occasion of its dedication, June 10, 1890.*
COURTESY OF SUNSHINE COAST MUSEUM AND ARCHIVES. PHOTO #255.

delightful place in which to spend a few hours, and those who took the trip yesterday were highly delighted with it. Sechelt Mission is situated on the southern shore of the island [sic]. The land slopes gradually down to the water's edge, and the view obtained from the water of the little village of neat white houses with the large and handsome church in the centre with a neat little graveyard to the eastern end, with the rising ground and forest as a background, was pretty in the extreme."

According to the *World*, the delegation of Squamish Natives waited until after dark to arrive "off the eastern point of the harbour. There the canoes, 50 in number, were tied in line, and the Chinese lanterns, of which they had a good supply, were lighted up. The tug *Leonora* then took the vessels in tow, and led the procession slowly across the harbour and back again. During the procession the band, stationed in the centre canoes, played several pieces in very passable style, while between these selections, songs were given by the companies in the other canoes. Rockets were sent off in abundance from several of the canoes in the procession, while from each end of the harbour and from the village miniature cannon added their share to the jollification. About 10 o'clock the processionists made their way to shore."[12]

The next day's celebrations were postponed owing to the death of Bishop Louis D'Herbomez, Oblate superior of the missions of the Pacific Northwest, and most of the Sechelts and their guests accompanied Bishop Durieu to New Westminster for the funeral. They returned on June 5 in time to join the solemn procession of robed church dignitaries who led the congregation and visitors through the village of white cottages to the new church. Built and furnished entirely by the Sechelt people, Our Lady of the Rosary Church was an imposing, twin-spired structure "with elaborate and tasteful decorations. The interior is still more beautifully and elaborately furnished than the exterior. The walls are hung with pictures of events in sacred history set in elaborately carved frames, and the altar and chancel fitted up with perfect taste . . ."[13] It had 2,240 square feet of floor space, but because it could seat only 400 people, the service, on the occasion of its dedication, was held in a huge tent set up beside the church. Inside was an improvised altar and on the floor were cedar boughs for the congregation to sit on.

For the next 16 years Our Lady of the Rosary was the centre of the Sechelts' community life; unfortunately, all of its fine craftmanship disappeared when it burned to the ground on January 14, 1906. Afterwards, the Sechelts built a new church on the same site. The new building, Our Lady of Lourdes, designed with a single spire, was dedicated in April 1907. Services were held in this beautiful structure until October 25, 1970, when it, too, was destroyed by fire.

THE DURIEU SYSTEM BEGINS TO WEAKEN

In 1894 a major depression hit Canada—triggered by a financial panic in the United States—and it lasted for nearly five years with a devastating impact on BC's lumbering industry. The Hastings and Moodyville sawmills closed many of their outlying camps and refused to buy from independent loggers. Hardest hit among the industry's workers were the Native handloggers and small co-op logging outfits who relied on the big mills for a market; as a result, most of the Sechelts' independent forest operations folded. Although conditions for the industry as a whole improved after the turn of the century, the Moodyville mill closed permanently in 1901, and the Sechelts lost one of their primary markets.

As new mills opened over the next few years, the Sechelts resumed logging, but in 1908 the provincial government, in an attempt to begin regulating the forest industry, passed a law that only persons named on the provincial voters' list could stake handlogging claims. This law was intended to exclude Americans, but since BC's legislature had already disenfranchised the Native people in 1871, the new regulation also excluded them from handlogging. While they were still allowed to cut on their reserve lands, most of the timber remaining to them on reserves such as Deserted Bay was not accessible without heavy equipment. Their independent logging operations were effectively at an end.

However, by this time, the Sechelts had experience in the industry, and many found work with white men's handlogging and gyppo outfits and even with the big timber companies in jobs that ranged from skid greaser and chokerman to high rigger and sawyer. As a result, by 1910 many of the Sechelts were leaving Sechelt and moving back to their old villages because they were closer to the logging camps. Here they began to re-establish a semblance of their people's former way of life, only now expediency demanded that they combine their traditional hunting and gathering tasks with jobs as loggers, cutting trees for white entrepreneurs on land that had been their traditional territory.

NATIVE EDUCATION

Although outside economic forces caused some of the Catholic clergy's influence over the Sechelt people to falter in the early years of this century, in one important area the church's influence was only beginning. The federal government, having decided that the education of the children was the key to the assimilation of the Native people into the white world, offered to provide operating funds to religious orders that would construct residential schools. The purpose of this partnership was to separate the children from their parents and divorce them from the language and traditions of their people. As a result, in 1904 the Sechelt people were persuaded by the Oblates to construct a three-storey school building on the height of land behind their church, approximately on the site where the House of Chiefs complex is located today. The school was dedicated on June 29 of that year by Father Augustine Dontenwill, Bishop of New Westminster, and named St. Augustine's School after the bishop's patron saint. Designed to accommodate 60 students plus staff, it included a chapel, a service building to house the laundry and workshops, and a stable for the school animals.

All children between 7 and 17 years of age were required to live at the school from September to June each year. The Indian Act permitted the police and Indian agents to track down children who did not attend willingly and remove them forcibly from their homes. Even when their families lived within sight of the school, the children could not live at home. Theresa Jeffries, who attended St. Augustine's school for eight years and lived there for another two years while attending the public high school, explained, "We were only allowed to come home on Sundays for a couple of hours. Allowed, mind you. We weren't allowed to communicate with our families [any other time]. And when they came to visit—we had a waiting room up at the school—one of the nuns had to be around. I don't know what they were afraid of, but they had to be around to chaperone when your parents came to visit with you."[14]

The Sechelt Indian Band celebrates the opening of the first St. Augustine's School on June 29, 1904.
On the left Our Lady of the Rosary Church which was destroyed by fire on January 14, 1906.
The flags of the four hereditary Sechelt chiefs fly atop the arch of greenery.
COURTESY OF SUNSHINE COAST MUSEUM AND ARCHIVES. PHOTO #99.

The second St. Augustine's School, opened about 1922, replaced the first school that was destroyed by fire on May 29, 1917. Both schools were surrounded with orchards and gardens, which the children cultivated.
COURTESY OF SUNSHINE COAST MUSEUM AND ARCHIVES. PHOTO #0192.

Although the mother tongue of the Sisters of the Child Jesus who came to teach at St. Augustine's was French, by law the language used in the classroom was English. The Sechelts' own language was strictly forbidden. Theresa Jeffries recalled having her mouth washed out with soap and being struck on the head and arms for uttering a word in the language in which she had been raised. When the children forgot and spoke in Sechelt, "We were told we were nothing but savages, that's all we'd ever be."[15] Even on parental visits, not a word of the Sechelt language was allowed so that in time the language was largely erased from the children's minds, and the parents had to learn English in order to be understood by their children. A revival of the language had to wait until the 1970s when Ronald Beaumont of the University of British Columbia began to make tape recordings of the last Sechelt language speakers, gradually creating the basis for a grammar that could be used to reteach it to the generations that had been forced to renounce it.

St. Augustine's Residential School burned to the ground early on the morning of May 29, 1917. Athough all the possessions of the sisters and students were lost, there were no casualties, and the homeless nuns were given lodging in the Sechelt Hotel. Classes were held in two temporary buildings for almost four years while a new school was constructed. The second St. Augustine's School, a solid brick structure, was opened about 1922 and continued in operation until the 1960s when the Department of Indian Affairs, intent on a new scheme for integrating Native people into the white community, began to encourage parents on reserves to send their children to public schools. The second St. Augustine's was demolished in 1975.

By the beginning of the 21st century the Sechelt School District was working closely with the Sechelt Indian Band to provide a special Native Studies program for First Nations students and Sechelt language classes in both elementary and high schools. In addition, there was a move to bring Aboriginal content into the general curriculum. By 2008 there were approximately 100 students living on band lands who were attending district schools and a total of 160 children with a Sechelt heritage within the district school system.

In 1988 the Sechelt Band opened an outward-bound type of school in a former logging camp at Deserted Bay, later converting it to a drug and alcohol rehabilitation facility. Then in June 1993 the Band acquired a 13-acre property, including a lodge and a small fish hatchery, at Vancouver Bay from International Forest Products (Interfor) in exchange for the right to establish a logging road and bridge on band land farther up Jervis Inlet. This new site was renamed the Skwakwee-em Healing Centre in honour of a beloved elder who was renowned for his work with dysfunctional children, and plans were made to use it as a healing centre for band members with drug or alcohol problems.

THE INDIAN AFFAIRS SETTLEMENT ACT

In 1912, after a half-century delay, the BC government under pressure from Ottawa agreed to set up a commission to study the question of Native reserves and make recommendations on their size. No mention was made of land titles or treaties. After four years of hearings and examination of reserves around the province, a report was brought down that allocated reserve lands. The Sechelts, who by the government commissioners' head count now numbered 290 people, were allotted 23 parcels of land totalling 2,092 acres. No more than 800 acres of this could have been considered arable. Of the remainder, 304 acres had been alienated to a company operating the slate quarry on Native land at Deserted Bay, 15 acres had been given to the Catholic Church for the benefit of the school, and the rest was composed of fishing stations and gravesites.

As well as confirming Chekwelp and Kaikalahun as Squamish reserves, the report recognized the Squamish people's rights to 33-acre Defence Island and two old burial grounds of half an acre each. One of the burial grounds, about 600 yards northeast of Chekwelp, had been the subject of a small controversy in the early years of the century when Gibsons pioneer George Glassford, who regarded this half acre as part of his pre-emption, attempted to evict a Native man who was camped on the land, even giving him money to camp elsewhere. Glassford made two trips to the land registry office in New Westminster only to find out that the land was designated "a reserved burial site," but he was promised that after the Native's death, he could appeal this designation and have it returned to his pre-emption. However, it remained the property of the Squamish people, even though their physical presence on the Sunshine Coast ended in the 1920s with the death of the last inhabitants of Chekwelp—an elderly couple known locally as Sally and Jimmy. In March 1925 the Department of Lands granted foreshore rights to the vacant Kaikalahun reserve to the Hastings Sawmill Company for a booming ground.

The Sechelts, dissatisfied with the results of the commission, accepted the suggestion of the Oblate fathers that they take advantage of a provision in the federal-provincial agreement that allowed for appeals. They flooded the commission with 66 separate applications for increased acreage of designated reserves and reconsideration of other traditional hunting grounds, campsites, graveyards and fishing stations that the commission had denied them. Fifty-eight of the applications were "not entertained" on the grounds that the land was not available, having been already staked and crown granted to settlers, miners or logging companies.

Among the rejected applications was one asking for the enlargement of Reserve #2 at Sechelt by the inclusion of the area staked by John Scales. Another rejected claim asked for the enlargement of Reserve #1 from Wilson Creek west to Reserve #2. "Chief Paul Policeman" applied for the Trail Islands, where for centuries the Sechelts had lived, fished and collected shellfish, but since the 1876 Joint Reserve Commission had not surveyed along the strait south of Pender Harbour, the islands had not been considered for designation as reserve lands in 1884. This was not Paul's first attempt to regain title to them; he had even tried to pre-empt the land but been told that provincial law denied this right to Natives. He then wrote to the Indian agent asking to buy the islands and was rejected as the right to buy property was also a privilege reserved for white men. The islands, with a total area of 111 acres, had been bought on September 22, 1892, for one dollar an acre by Arthur Prichard. Paul had then appealed this sale on the grounds that the islands provided pasture for his sheep, but his appeal was denied. He was not surprised when the government also said no to his 1916 application.

Of the eight applications accepted by the commission, in no case was the entire amount of land asked for received. However, by their determined assault on the government, the Sechelts did win title to 406.75 additional acres, of which 340 were steep, logged-off lands that even the commissioners deemed unsuitable for agriculture of any kind. One new reserve was added, a 14-acre parcel in Bargain Harbour.

Exasperated with the continuing appeals, in March 1919 the provincial government passed the Indian Affairs Settlement Act, which was supposed to permanently dispose of the "Indian problem" by making the boundaries of the designated reserve lands final and unalterable. In spite of this legislation, the Sechelts, along with the other Native people of BC, believed that the clause in the Act that required them to consent to these allotments would stall implementation of the Act indefinitely. Unfortunately, at this time the Liberal government in Ottawa, which had shown some sympathy for the rights of the Native people, lost power, and the new Conservative government appointed Duncan Campbell Scott to the job of deputy superintendent of Indian Affairs. Although better known to Canadians as a poet, Scott had made a career in Indian Affairs, and he was committed to a policy of Native assimilation into the white community. He believed that giving them adequate lands on which to make a living would only discourage them from entering white society. Scott campaigned for the passage of a bill in Parliament giving assent to BC's Settlement Act without the consent of the Native people, and it was passed on July 1, 1920.

Further agitation by Native peoples for consideration of their land claims was forestalled in 1924 by the passage of the Anti-Agitation Act as an amendment to the federal Indian Act. Section 141 of this amendment prohibited the prosecution of any land claim without the written permission of the Department of Indian Affairs and in addition prevented anyone from accepting payment from a Native person in return for legal advice, advertising, research or anything else that would promote a claim. For the next 27 years, the Sechelts were effectively silenced, forced to accept the lands designated for them with no regard for the justice of their claims.

During these years the Sechelt Native community became involved in the fishing industry. Until 1923 they had been denied commercial ocean-fishing licences, but when this restriction was removed, they began fishing for the canneries. The fishing week began Sunday when they rowed their skiffs out to the fishing grounds or had them towed there by the cannery packers. The week ended on Friday when the packers returned to collect the fish and tow the skiffs back to port. By the end of the 1920s some of the Sechelts had begun leasing gillnetters and seine boats from BC Packers, Nelson Brothers and other large cannery owners. Each summer, whole families would make the journey up the coast to Rivers Inlet or Prince Rupert; here the women worked in the fish canneries while the men fished. When the fishing season ended, the families returned to Sechelt so that the men could find work as loggers for the companies operating in Jervis, Sechelt, Salmon and Narrows inlets.

With the conclusion of World War II and the establishment of the United

Nations, the federal government became concerned with Canada's international image in relation to Native rights, and the Department of Indian Affairs began pressuring BC's legislators to amend some of the most glaring inequities on their books. The worst of these were disenfranchisement in provincial and municipal elections and the exclusion of Natives from the right to pre-empt Crown land. The provincial response was the removal in 1947 of all racial restrictions from the provincial franchise, but it was not until 1953, when all the prime land on the Sunshine Coast had long been alienated, that the law against Native pre-emption was struck down.

It remained, however, for the federal government to repeal the so-called Anti-Agitation Act before the Native people could return to the battle over land title. This occurred with little fanfare in 1951 as a result of international pressure. Over the next 20 years the Sechelts organized and decided what form of independence they would pursue; it took another 17 years before they could make it a reality.

SELF-GOVERNMENT

In 1971, when Minister of Indian Affairs and Northern Development Jean Chretien visited Sechelt to open the band's new administration offices, he urged them to escape the Indian Act forever by seeking self-government. The Sechelts took his advice, and under the leadership of Chief Henry Paull, allied themselves with the Musqueam, Squamish and Kamloops bands in order to be more effective in their negotiations with the federal government. They met with five successive ministers of Indian Affairs and a string of ministers of Justice, but the bureaucracy defeated them at every turn.

In the late 1970s the Sechelts broke with the alliance to begin negotiations on their own, but still the impasse with the government continued. They appealed to the Human Rights Commission in 1981, their brief saying in part: "We have committed no crimes . . . our one apparent offence is to be of indigenous origin in a country where the Native people are a small minority. For this we have been imprisoned. Our jailers are the bureaucrats at the Department of Indian Affairs, our cell is the Federal Indian Act, its bars created from the legal interpretations of the Act's provisions by the Department of Justice lawyers."[16] The commission members made representations to the federal government on the Sechelts' behalf with no effect.

The tide began to turn in November 1984 when Chief Stanley Dixon of the Sechelts met with Minister of Indian Affairs David Crombie in Vancouver. "Under the Indian Act, you are my father," Chief Dixon told him. "As my father, I ask you—let me go. I want to have the same rights as you do."[17] Crombie set up a 12-man transition team that would steer the Sechelts through the process of developing self-government enabling legislation and then implementing the final bill. Bill C-93 was ready for enactment in July 1986 but was stalled when the Treasury Board objected to two sections of the agreement. There was no help to be had this time from Indian Affairs as Crombie had been replaced by Bill McKnight who was not fully committed to the Sechelts' cause. The problem was resolved in last-minute negotiations between the Treasury Board, Chief Dixon and the band's financial advisor, Gordon Anderson, by setting up a referendum that would ask the band's members if they accepted a constitution that would accompany Bill C-93. Passage of the referendum was dependent on a yes vote from 50 percent plus one of the registered voters rather than the usual 50 percent plus one of those voting. However, the vote was 193 yes to 8 no out of a possible 220 voters. Bill C-93 became law on October 9, 1986.

Another year and a half passed in negotiations with the provincial government before the Sechelt Indian District Government was signed into existence on June 24, 1988. With the signature of BC's Premier Bill Vander Zalm and Chief Tom Paul, the Sechelt Native community became a legal entity with the same right to own its lands in fee simple, enter into legal contracts, invest money and make laws as any other municipality. From this time the Sechelts referred to themselves as the Sechelt Nation.

There was still the question of the alienation of the Sechelts' traditional lands to be considered, however. Rejected in 1988 because of the government's narrow interpretation of the term "traditional use," the Sechelt Indian District's comprehensive land claim was not accepted for negotiation by the federal government until April 1991, after a Supreme Court decision had forced the government to re-evaluate its interpretation. Although the Sechelts' claim covers 5,700 square kilometres of land—most of it settled by the non-Native community—the band was not asking for the actual land but cash compensation, including a retroactive 50/50 split of resource revenues on traditional lands and reinstatement of their hunting and trapping rights. They also asked for a partnership with government in the re-establishment of salmon runs in the streams emptying into Jervis, Salmon, Narrows and Sechelt inlets.

Treaty negotiations with British Columbia and Canada began in 1994 and an Agreement in Principle (AIP) was completed in April 1999 that included an offer of land, $40 million in cash, hunting, fishing and gathering rights (including a fishing quota and a proposed wildlife harvest area) and the phasing out of tax exemptions. It was considered inadequate by the Sechelt Nation's membership. For example, the land settlement, which was for 0.6 percent of the territory, represented the smallest offer of land to a Native band on a hectare-per-person basis in Canada. The cash compensation was to be paid out over 20 years, but its financial benefit would be offset by taxes that would result in a net loss to the Nation. The AIP also had no provision for an increased decision-making role for the Sechelt Nation. In March 2003 the Sechelt leadership submitted a set of conditions required for the resumption of treaty negotiations, which have yet to be met. In a 2004 referendum the Sechelt people gave their leadership a mandate to proceed with litigation if necessary.

PART FOUR
SETTLERS AND TOURISTS

It was 1884 before the first large blocks of land along the shores of the Sunshine Coast were thrown open for pre-emption. The provincial government's Pre-Emption Act of that year—a restatement of the original pre-emption ordinance of the combined colonies of Vancouver Island and British Columbia—allowed white British subjects over 18 to stake up to a quarter section (160 acres) of land for farming purposes. Lots were surveyed in chains, each equal to 66 feet, and recommended layouts were either 40 chains by 40 chains or 20 chains by 80 chains. In order to earn Crown grant status to his property, each pre-emptor was required to improve it to the equivalent of $2.50 per acre. These improvements must include a "dwelling house" as well as cleared and cultivated fields.

Provincial pre-emption records show that almost 90 percent of first claims staked on the Sunshine Coast before 1920 were abandoned as soon as clearing was complete, leaving the land for second and even third claimants to turn into farms. Most of these abandoned claims had been registered, not by farmers, but by loggers who found pre-empting a much easier way to acquire a block of timber than complying with the terms of a handlogger's licence. For bona fide farmers, the pre-emption terms were no hardship, although finding reasonably level arable land on the Sunshine Coast was a problem. Much of the area opened for pre-emption was bedrock, the rest of it deep layers of glacial till and marine sediments overlain with only a thin layer of soil.

GIBSON'S LANDING

Tradition has it that it was young men who came west in the 19th century "to grow up with the country." While this may have been true for those looking for gold or a fortune in lumbering, many of those who came to settle the West Coast were long past their youth. George Gibson (1828–1913) was 58 years old when he arrived. An ex-British Navy lieutenant, he had retired from the sea in 1878 to settle in Ontario where he had become a successful market gardener. Then in 1886 he and his two eldest sons, George Jr. and Ralph, left Ontario to come to Vancouver, built the little sloop *Swamp Angel* and set out to find suitable pre-emptions. Their search took them as far as Nanaimo, but on the return trip they found themselves off course and were forced to spend the night on Keats Island. In the morning they investigated the mainland nearby and found it promising. In August Gibson sent for his wife, Charlotte, and the rest of his family, and they appear to have spent the following winter in Vancouver.

On May 2, 1887, Gibson went to the government land office in Victoria and registered Lot 686 on the waterfront northeast of Gower Point. This square quarter section was right in the middle of a tract of recently burned-over land, and in the charred shell of a small log barn on the property he had found the blackened remains of several oxen. He learned from tugboat operators that the animals had belonged to a group of men who had begun logging there just a few years earlier. The summer had been extremely hot and dry, and a flash fire had wiped out all the timber they planned to cut as well as their equipment and draft animals.

George William Gibson and Mrs. Charlotte Gibson in the garden of their Gibson's Landing home in August 1904.
COURTESY OF SUNSHINE COAST MUSEUM AND ARCHIVES. PHOTO #1726.

George Gibson Jr. pre-empted L.685 to the south of his father's land on the steep cliff overlooking Shoal Channel, and George Glassford, who had married Gibson's second daughter Mary, pre-empted L.687 to the northeast of 686. By luck the Gibson and Glassford men had chosen to locate on some of the deepest and richest soil in the area, and since fire had already cleared much of it, they were able to plant vegetables, berries and fruit trees with little delay. By midsummer, Gibson Sr. was able to load produce aboard the *Swamp Angel* and take it to Vancouver to sell from a stall on the corner of Westminster Avenue (Main Street) and Hastings Street.

By the time he received his Crown grant in November 1888, Gibson Sr. had constructed a two-storey, 18- by 28-foot frame house; he had four acres under cultivation and 100 fruit trees planted. His son-in-law earned his Crown grant on September 20, 1889, with a two-storey, 16- by 24-foot shake-roofed log house and two acres of fenced and cultivated land. George Gibson Jr.'s land was Crown granted on June 17, 1891; his two-storey frame house was surrounded by four acres of producing farmland.

In 1890, Gibson, his sons and son-in-law built a wharf—or landing as they were known in those days—on the shore of L.686 to provide dockage for the *Swamp Angel* and other freight vessels. The dock, and in time the settlement itself, became generally known as Gibson's Landing without any formal naming process taking place, although for the purposes of the dominion postal services, the new settlement was designated West Howe Sound.

During the half dozen years following the staking of the Gibson and Glassford claims, the land all around them was pre-empted and abandoned again and again, sometimes by loggers who simply cut the timber and left and sometimes by greenhorns who were unprepared for the backbreaking toil of farming. After the waterfront land was all gone, staking began on the plateau above the harbour, an area that came to be known as Gibson's Heights. The Payne brothers, George and John, registered their claims to L.690 (between Payne, Henry and Reed roads and Highway 101) and L.691 (between Cemetery and Reed roads) on April 21, 1888. A Berkshireman, James Fletcher, his wife and son claimed L.682, on the southwest side of Pratt Road between Highway 101 and Chaster Road. It was Crown granted on June 21, 1892. Fletcher had been farming in Saskatchewan's Qu'Appelle Valley before coming west, but in Gibson's Landing he became a logger, clearing his own lot and those adjoining it and taking the timber out on skid roads that wound down to the water at the point where Kinsmen's Park is located today.

Five days after Fletcher's arrival, an 18-year-old from Ontario, Charles "Chuck" Winegarden, docked his rowboat at the landing to find work as a logger. A year later, having fallen in love with Gibson's third daughter, Emma, he pre-empted land at Hopkins' Landing in order to prove himself a suitable husband. They married in 1897. William and George Soames registered claims on April 30, 1888. William's lot was number 683. George raised sheep on his pre-emption, L.694, east of George Glassford's pre-emption; it included beautiful Soames Point, but lost a corner to the tiny Squamish Indian Reserve of Chekwelp, which also took a corner out of Glassford's lot.

How quickly the community was growing during this period is demonstrated by the fact that it became necessary to build a temporary log cabin school in 1889, only two years after the arrival of the Gibsons. Then on June 12, 1890, a school district was organized with trustees George Gibson, James Fletcher, George Glassford and William J. Manning whose pre-emption, L.688, straddled North Road at Highway 101; a year later the district constructed a permanent school on the present site of Gibsons Elementary at School Road and Highway 101. Mrs. Lucy Smith held her first class in the new Howe Sound School on January 19, 1891, with 23 children enrolled. The West Howe Sound Post Office was officially recognized on October 1, 1892, and the first postmaster was George Gibson Sr.

In 1895 Ralph Gibson, who had pre-empted the north half of Pasley Island west of Bowen Island when his father was pre-empting in West Howe Sound, sold his property to the Bell-Irving family and joined the family in Gibson's Landing to build the first general store. Unfortunately, British Columbia had just plunged into a depression that was to last for the next five years, and the store soon failed. Once again the settlers were forced to order their few necessities from Vancouver, either collecting them in their own boats or having them sent by steamship. As the depression eased, community agitation began again for a store, and George Gibson Sr. reopened his son's shop as an interim measure while he built one of his own beside the entrance to his wharf. His new business opened in 1900 and continued in operation until 1910 when it was destroyed by fire. In 1906 Ralph Gibson's building was bought and reopened for business by the James S. Chaster family who also took over as postmasters.

It had been a forest fire shortly before 1886 that cleared the waterfront slopes on which the Gibson and Glassford families began farming, and it was a forest fire that burned off the pre-empted flatlands above them 20 years later. In the hot, dry spring of 1906 a clearing fire on the Madden property at the north end of Leek Road quickly became a roaring forest fire, rising into the canopy. A brisk wind from the west drove it toward the settled areas. Some families fled before it; others stayed to save their buildings, forming bucket brigades and damping down sacks to put on the roofs of their houses and barns. Only one life was lost and very few buildings destroyed, but the fire burned both old- and second-growth timber as far as West Howe Sound, a distance of some five miles. Eighty years later a few of the blackened snags it left behind were still standing. The settlers had reaped one benefit from the fire: land they would have had to clear arduously tree by tree to make it available for farming had been cleared in a matter of hours.

Almost all of the burned land had been pre-empted, yet much of it lay empty. While pioneer families such as the Gibsons, Fletchers, Glassfords and Soames still persevered in the difficult life of the new settlement, many others had given up. Some sold their lands and the buildings on them to newcomers; others simply abandoned them to be pre-empted all over again by settlers with more stamina.

The second wave of Sunshine Coast pre-emptions had begun slowly around

1903 with farmers like Hugh Burns who staked the west half of L.691, which had been abandoned by George Payne during the depression years, but it was not until after the 1906 fire that new settlers began to arrive in substantial numbers. They included John Hicks who was to become a pillar of the little community, Francis Ward Shaw after whom Shaw Road was named, and William George Fletcher, whose father had claimed L.682 20 years earlier.

Logging near the junction of Highway 101 and Shaw Road in 1906. The timber snags are left from the fire earlier that year that began at the north end of Leek Road. Joe Shaw of Roberts Creek on left, John Hicks Jr. with hat, Wilbur Hicks (son of John Hicks Sr.) seated on log.
COURTESY OF SUNSHINE COAST MUSEUM AND ARCHIVES. PHOTO #979.

But the Gibson's community gained its largest group of settlers at this time as a result of problems in another settlement. In the early years of this century hundreds of Finnish immigrants had come west to join a communal society that had been established at Sointula on Malcolm Island, but a number of them soon became disillusioned with the experiment. In an effort to relocate their families, a few came to Gibson's Landing in 1905 searching for farmland, and they liked what they saw. The following year, much of Sointula was destroyed by fire, and this helped to decide another group of Finnish families to follow the first contingent to Gibson's Landing. With little free land left, the newcomers were forced to purchase property, and because they were farmers, most chose the flatland on Gibson's Heights.

Finlanders Karl Heino and Andy Wilander brought their families to share the former Leckie pre-emption (L.1657) on Cemetery Road. The old White pre-emption (L.902) was split between the Ruise, Gus Hintsa and Jake Hintsa families. Malkias Kyto and his family bought part of the Herb Smith pre-emption (L.914) on North Road. Blacksmith Pete Sauri established his business just west of Payne Creek close to the road to Sechelt. Others who came included the Poikula, Weise, Nygren and Wilkman families.

Karl Wiren and his brother John bought half of the original George Payne pre-emption in 1906. In old age, Karl's eldest son, Wiljo, recalled helping to clear the stumps on their land by first burning them down below ground level, then attacking the roots with handloggers' tools. Karl later acquired an ox, and after that a horse, then with the help of his sons, he cleared even more land. By 1916 when the family had sufficient pasture for a small dairy herd, Wiljo and John's son Laurie were operating a milk delivery service. "Father used to say that to make a living here you've got to be shod with iron, fore and aft," Wiljo Wiren said. "We had one of the few farms in the area from which you could make a living . . . but the work was brutal and the hours long."[1]

The farms of the Finnish families prospered, while at the same time the Finns were contributing to the social life of the whole community. In 1910 they built a hall known locally as the Workmen's or Labour Hall on the north side of the Sechelt Road about 200 feet west of Payne (Chaster) Creek. A year later another group of Finns built a second hall at the northwest corner of Payne Road and the highway; it was generally known as the Socialist Hall. They invited their neighbours to their plays and dances, and established an annual May Day picnic. As well, they introduced their neighbours to the traditional Finnish sauna bath, and it quickly gained acceptance in the non-Finnish community.

In the summer of 1909, F.C. Grantham, a Vancouver beverage manufacturer, bought 75 acres of George Glassford's L.687. He subdivided part of it to sell for summer residences then brought in workmen to clear roads and build plank sidewalks on the portion closest to the beach where he planned to build a "summer camp." They also installed a water system, diverting water from Soames Creek, which Grantham advertised as "the finest water on Howe Sound." After a floating wharf and the first two dozen board-and-batten cottages were in place, the summer vacationers began arriving by the boatload, and Grantham's workmen built more cottages. He called his resort "Howe Sound Beach," but after the federal government built a wharf there, it became generally known as Grantham's Landing. The new camp provided income for local farmers who sold the campers fresh fruit and vegetables, and for the Wiren family who delivered milk to them. (The Wirens, realizing that the greatest demand for their dairy's milk was coming from the summer people, cannily arranged for most of their cows to freshen in spring.)

As befitted a steadily growing agricultural settlement, on October 4, 1911, just 25 years after the Gibsons' arrival, the settlers formed the West Howe

Sound Farmers' Institute. Because most of the original pre-emptions had been broken up and sold as smaller farming parcels, the new organization signed up 90 members within the first year. The institute's founding secretary was William Winn, a Yorkshireman who arrived in Gibson's in 1912; he held the post until 1922. He organized the first Institute Fall Fair held in the Socialist Hall in August 1918 with displays of fruits and vegetables in the hall and livestock tied to the trees outside.

Winn bought the Chasters' store building in 1915 and operated it as a store, post office and telegraph agency for the next four years. When he sold the store business to the Carter brothers, newcomers to the community, in 1919, he moved the post and telegraph businesses to a new building just north of the public wharf, where he set himself up as a confectioner and provided a hall where the community's first movies were shown. The general store business went through several owners in the next few years then was sold to J.H. Drummond in 1927. For the next 25 years Drummond's Howe Sound Trading Company served the community and provided a mobile service via Model-T truck as far west as Wilson Creek.

Gibson's Landing's first and most beloved doctor was Frederick Inglis who came to the community in 1913. A graduate of the University of Manitoba in both medicine and divinity, Dr. Inglis had been a medical missionary in northern BC when he answered Gibson's Landing's advertisement for a doctor. A year after his arrival Inglis constructed "Stonehurst" overlooking Gibson's harbour to be his clinic and a home for his wife Alice Kathleen, who had been trained as a nurse, and their six children. He remained the sole medical practitioner in the area between Halfmoon Bay and Port Mellon for the next 33 years, except for a brief period before World War II when Sechelt also had a doctor. Although Inglis had arrived on the Sunshine Coast as a deeply religious man, he was strongly influenced by the beliefs of the Finnish people of the community, and in time he turned against the organized church, and became a socialist. He retired in 1945 when his son Dr. Hugh Inglis was discharged from the army to take over his practice. Hugh was joined by his brother Dr. Alan Inglis until 1948, when Dr. Alan moved to Vancouver to pursue a specialty in orthopedic surgery. Dr. Frederick Inglis died in 1950, exactly 80 years to the day from his birth. Ill health forced Dr. Hugh to retire in 1975.

In 1917 a new Methodist minister came to Gibson's Landing. A former social worker and a pacifist, James Shaver Woodsworth arrived believing that through his church he could minister to people in need, even though he was profoundly disturbed by the Methodist Church's support for Canada's participation in the war. However, like his friend Dr. Inglis, he soon found himself influenced by the socialist philosophy of the Finnish community. When he expressed his growing belief in socialism, he was vehemently opposed by postmaster William Winn, who was a highly vocal supporter of the war effort and a director of the church. As a result, Woodsworth resigned from the ministry and went to Vancouver where he found work as a longshoreman. His family of six children and his schoolteacher wife, forced to leave the manse, moved into Stonehurst with the doctor's family. Winn, not content with ridding the community of J.S. Woodsworth, next tried to have his wife fired as senior teacher in the Gibson's school, but he was not successful.

In 1919, Woodsworth accepted an invitation to lecture across the prairies, and he arrived in Winnipeg in time to speak to—and be cheered by—10,000 workmen involved in the great Winnipeg General Strike. On June 23 he was arrested for seditious libel along with many of the strike leaders; he was bailed out and later granted a stay of proceedings. The next year a royal commission report vindicated the strikers. Woodsworth returned to Gibson's in 1920 but left soon afterwards to organize the Commonwealth Co-operative Federation (CCF), and on December 6, 1921, he was elected Member of Parliament for Winnipeg Centre. Three of his children, including his daughter Grace MacInnis who also served as an MP, later returned to live on the Sunshine Coast.

Inglis and Woodsworth were not the only people in Gibson's Landing to be influenced by the socialist and pacifist beliefs of the Finnish community during World War I, so it was not surprising that a number of local young men refused to be recruited into the army. However, in June 1917 the federal government enacted the Military Service Bill which allowed conscription, and fearing that they would be dragged off to fight, a group of them chose to become "evaders,"

The remains of the World War I draft evaders' camp on Mount Elphinstone.
In this picture, taken in 1936, Bob Clarkson and his dog sit in front of one of the cabins.
COURTESY OF SUNSHINE COAST MUSEUM AND ARCHIVES. PHOTO #773.

going into hiding on Mount Elphinstone. They lived in log houses in the forest, surviving on foodstuffs smuggled to them by family and friends. Although they remained undetected until the war was over, there was a tragic end to their story. A local boy, Al Fletcher, who was on leave from the army, went AWOL, and when the military police came after him, he headed for the evaders' camp on Mount Elphinstone. Unhappily, he was wearing his uniform, and one of the evaders, not recognizing him and fearing that he was part of an armed force coming to capture them, shot him. For years the Fletcher family, when asked where their son was, simply said that he had "moved away." As a result, no one was ever tried for causing his death.

From the earliest days of the Gibson's Landing settlement, the best soil was always reserved for cash crops such as strawberries and raspberries, and gradually berries became the most important product of the area. When the fresh fruit markets of Vancouver became glutted after World War I, the berry farmers formed the Howe Sound Cooperative Canning Association under the auspices of the Farmers' Institute. Since a capital investment of $500 was needed to start their canning enterprise, they put shares on sale at $25 each, and within a year a total of 158 had been sold. The new organization's one-storey Howe Sound Cannery was completed in 1921 on land adjacent to Chaster Creek at Henry Road that was leased from John Wiren at one dollar a year; it was purchased outright in 1925 for $150.

Four large copper jam kettles were installed in the new cannery, and although the system used was extremely primitive, the first year's product, sold under the "Four Square" brand label, was exhibited and won the cannery the British Empire Trophy. A year later, when the little cannery began contracting its output to the W.H. Malkin Company of Vancouver, the Four Square label was retired. From that time on, it was sold as "Malkin's Best," but the label also carried a notice at the bottom that read "Gibson's Landing Pack." It sold for $1.25 a tin while Malkin's regular pack sold for a dollar.

Within five years of the cannery's first run the amount of land in the Gibson's area devoted to berry growing had doubled. Peder "Pete" Berdahl, who farmed where Highway 101 meets the Lower Road, and J. Kullander, who had bought property on Pratt Road, owned the largest acreages, but the Rhodes and Benns families on Reed Road were also big growers. As production increased, the cannery was forced to put on two shifts during berry season to keep up with the crop, but not long after this expansion, a government inspector paid a visit and announced that since the cannery had been in the practice of adding fruit pectin to the product, their label claiming that it was "pure jam" was illegal. Since the loss of the word "pure" on the label meant substantially reduced profits, the management responded by installing new steam equipment to increase output. It was used for the first time for the record harvest of 1931, but unfortunately, because no one at the cannery fully understood how to use the equipment, the jam was undercooked. Most of it was returned from stores and warehouses in the city for reprocessing and the loss to the co-op was enormous.

Although berry acreage fell off in the next two decades as farms were replaced by residential developments, the cannery remained in operation until 1952. Three years later the boilers and kettles were sold as scrap metal and the building, which had been enlarged and generally rebuilt in 1950, was sold for $4,000. For a number of years it was used by a soft drink distributor but today it is a private home.

Many of the Gibson's berry farmers also raised chickens and pigs successfully as a sideline, but other farming ventures were not as successful. A piggery established at the mouth of Twin Creeks early in the century failed after one year. George Lockett's attempt to raise turkeys on his Cemetery Road property before World War I lasted only three years. In 1915 two Americans from Washington state arrived unexpectedly in Gibson's with 700 sheep, which they herded into corrals on the former Henry property at the head of Gibson's Creek. They reassured the local farmers that the sheep would be pastured on the logged-over slopes of Mount Elphinstone rather than on the limited pastureland, but unfortunately, the mountainside had nothing but salal to offer, and the sheep began dying of starvation. The project ended as suddenly as it had begun when the provincial police arrived to take the new sheep farmers away in handcuffs for undisclosed crimes. The sheep were removed a short time later.

Several other farmers, among them Dan Steinbrunner—who had pre-empted first at Roberts Creek and then in 1903 closer to Gibson's—and Alf Wyngaert, raised sheep by pasturing them along the roadsides, but they faced strong opposition from dairy farmers who worried about their animals sharing the limited natural grasses with sheep. In the end, however, it was the constant inroads of cougars on the flocks that forced the sheep ranchers out of business a few years later.

In 1929 the Village of Gibson's Landing was incorporated within the boundaries of L.686 and L.685, the two quarter sections which George Gibson Sr. and his son had pre-empted in 1887, but construction of the first municipal hall had to wait until 1947. The boundaries were extended several more times after that, and in 1950 the name was amended to the Village of Gibsons. It became the Town of Gibsons in 1983.

The tourist industry remained more or less a summer cabin rental business in Gibsons until after World War II. Changes began in 1957 with the relocation of the ferry terminus to Langdale and the start of commercial development in upper Gibsons near the newly constructed Elphinstone Secondary School on the former Manning property. The next year SuperValu became the nucleus of Sunnycrest Plaza on the Hyde pre-emption and it was transformed into a mall 10 years later, providing more services for tourists. Motel and hotel construction followed in both upper and lower Gibsons, but it was not until 1962, when BC Ferries took over Black Ball and improved ferry service to the Sunshine Coast that the town gained real credibility as a tourist destination. The arrival in 1973 of CBC Television's *Beachcombers* crew to begin 19 years of filming provided a lure for visitors from all over the world. In 1992–93 Gibsons was also the venue for the filming of the Hollywood movie, *Needful Things*, adapted from a novel by Stephen King, directed by Fraser Heston and starring Max von Sydow. As with *Beachcombers*, many local residents were employed as "extras" and as crew. Today, although private boats account for a high percentage of Gibsons' visitors, more than 90 percent of tourists to the area arrive by car and ferry.

As the 20th century came to a close, the commercial corridor in upper Gibsons continued to expand dramatically, while in Lower Gibsons, generally known as "The Landing," efforts were concentrated on preserving local heritage. Among the most useful initiatives was the establishment of the Gibsons Heritage Theatre in the former Women's Institute Hall at the corner of North Road and Highway 101. Built in 1929 by volunteer labour, this building had served as a cultural centre for the community for many years but had fallen into disrepair. The Gibsons Landing Heritage Society took on the nine-year task of restoring it and creating a 150-seat theatre, which opened in April 2000. Another of the important heritage initiatives was Winegarden Waterfront Park on the site that was once occupied by Fred LePage's glue factory. Arnold "Chuck" Winegarden and his wife, Emma, the daughter of George and Charlotte Gibson, had made their home in the factory caretaker's cottage, and later it became home to the Winegardens' daughter Gertie and her husband, John Corlett. The Corletts then bought the old factory and converted it into apartments, but the building was demolished by new owners in 1970. The site sat vacant until 1994 when the Town of Gibsons bought it, but it was not until July 1, 2001, that it was officially opened as a park.

LANGDALE

The settlement at Langdale derives its name from the pioneer family of Robinson H. Langdale who on December 11, 1893, pre-empted L.1508, which is bisected by the stream that also bears the family name. To earn his Crown grant on August 29, 1899, Langdale built a one-storey house of dressed lumber and shingles, cleared three acres, planted it with timothy and clover, and fenced it to prevent deer from enjoying his fruit trees. Langdale, his wife, Emma, and their family of seven sons and five daughters left the area just after the turn of the century when their house burned to the ground.

In 1907 the Vancouver Young Men's Christian Association (YMCA) established Camp Elphinstone, a 110-acre youth camp, on the waterfront north of Robinson Langdale's pre-emption. This camp still provides two-week vacations for up to 300 children at a time. Camp Sunrise, located south of Langdale's pre-emption, was built by the Salvation Army in 1925 to provide summer programs for underprivileged children. In June 1957 the terminus of the Black Ball Ferry line, the forerunner of BC Ferries, was relocated from Gibsons to a site just north of Camp Sunrise, and gradually the area between the terminus and Camp Elphinstone has developed as a residential community.

SEASIDE AND PORT MELLON

Seaside, a resort at the mouth of the Rainy River in Howe Sound, had its origins in two pre-emptions on August 6, 1890. L.1364, straddling the river, was claimed by John T. Price, and L.1366, to the north of it, was claimed by Charles Henry Cates of the Vancouver tugboating family. Both lots were Crown granted the following summer, but Price sold his lot shortly afterwards to his neighbour's brother, Andrew Jackson Cates, who sold it in 1907 to his son George. The younger Cates then sold the southern 85 acres of the pre-emption to the British Canadian Wood Pulp & Paper Company in which he held shares, and on the remaining half he built the Seaside Hotel, surrounding it with gardens. Within a few years Seaside had become a popular holiday spot for boat excursionists and a regular destination for the Cates family's passenger steamer Britannia.

The British Canadian Wood Pulp & Paper Company constructed a mill on its portion of L.1364, and that area soon became known as Port Mellon in honour of the company's principal shareholder. Although for most of its existence Port Mellon has had fewer than 100 residents, during the early 1950s when the mill was running several shifts to keep up with the demand for kraft pulp, the settlement's population grew to almost 1,000. In 1953 Port Mellon had more clubs and organizations than any other town of its size in the province. However, two years later when a road was completed to Gibsons, an outward migration began until there was virtually no residential area left.

Meanwhile, in 1933, a year before George Cates' death, his hotel had burned during a "Squamish" storm, and the property was bought by a Mr. Story who rebuilt the hotel and operated it for a few years before selling it. In 1941 when the Sorg Paper Company of Ohio bought the Port Mellon mill, it acquired the hotel as well and operated it for 13 years through a subsidiary,

Seaside Park Limited. In March 1958 the top floor of the Seaside was gutted by fire and the hotel closed permanently. It was torn down a few years later. For many years the resort's existence was commemorated by Port Mellon's tiny waterfront public garden, Seaside Park, but it disappeared during the mill's most recent expansion.

GAMBIER ISLAND

Although Gambier Island is mostly solid bedrock, since the last ice age a fairly thick layer of fertile soil has accumulated at the heads of the three long bays that give the island its distinctive southern profile. In March 1886, more than a year before George Gibson established his farm near Gower Point, Henry Ross pre-empted 160 acres on the eastern side of the head of Long Bay. Ten months later he was joined to his west by Arthur Robert Davies on L.1653. Davies had cleared six acres, planted 332 fruit trees, and built a house, barn and chicken house before he received his Crown grant on May 14, 1895. Ross and Davies were joined by John Simpson on L.1259 in October 1888 and William Lawrence Johnson on a lot south of Simpson's in 1889. Ross abandoned his claim before completing his improvements and in 1908 Davies and Johnson sold out to Edward J. McFeely of the Vancouver hardware firm of McLennan, McFeely and Prior. McFeely increased the apple plantation to 1,100 trees and built a barn for his herd of purebred Jersey cows. In 1938 he rented the farm to William Warn who built up the dairy herd and established a daily milk route for the millworkers living in Port Mellon. When he could not make a profit on his apples on the Vancouver market, he sold these also in Port Mellon.

The pre-emptions on Gambier Island's West Bay and Centre Bay and along Thornbrough Channel were mainly claimed by loggers, and most of them were abandoned as soon as the timber had been taken off. A few, however, were Crown granted; Robert Leatherdale, Joseph H. Gill and William Girr staked a claim on the side of the island facing Thornbrough in May 1888, and although their main intention was logging, they did make improvements and received their Crown grant in October 1889. The northeastern end of Gambier, which is open to the storms coming down Howe Sound, was not pre-empted until after 1908, but most of the lots in this area, although Crown granted, were later abandoned.

In 1923 Camp Fircom, a retreat for mothers and children, was established by the First Presbyterian Church of Vancouver on 65 acres of a former homestead on the most southeasterly corner of Gambier. At first campers were required to row to the island, but today they arrive aboard the MV *Kona Winds* or water taxi from Horseshoe Bay. The Anglican Church's Camp

Artiban on Long Bay was begun as a summer resort for girls in 1924; its scope was broadened in later years to provide camping experiences for everyone from children to adults.

Gambier Island's recent history is one of peaceful solitude for a small year-round population, which includes many painters and ceramic artists, and for the owners of summer homes. Since only a foot-passenger ferry operates regularly to the island from Langdale, there are few roads or cars.

KEATS ISLAND

The first pre-emptors on 1,500-acre Keats Island were John Hooper and Lehannah Konderoy who arrived in 1888. They were followed by Harry White who homesteaded on the east side of the island. Soon the islanders had built a small sawmill and were making floats for fishnets; around the same time a logging outfit descended on the island and removed all the mature timber.

Roy Brown came to Keats early in the 20th century and claimed 440 acres on the southern part of the island. He built a house and barn on the island's long southwestern arm then imported Japanese workmen to clear the land for extensive gardens and meadows and create a series of rock walls at the top of the property as a rough reservoir that would provide irrigation water during dry periods. Unfortunately, Brown's house burned to the ground in 1920 and he left the island. Six years later an association of Baptist businessmen bought his abandoned property and, after setting aside 12 acres for a summer camp—which they named Keats Camp—formed the Keats Island Summer Home Company and subdivided the rest into recreational lots. Will Read, who was hired as caretaker for the property, built himself a sturdy house, Readhurst, and restored Brown's gardens to such productivity that he was soon supplying food to the other islanders. Later Keats Camp, which is still operated by the Convention of Baptist Churches of BC, bought Readhurst to use as a guesthouse. Although at first the camp offered only tent accommodation, in time neat white cottages were built on Brown's original meadow.

In 1930 the Presbyterian Church opened a camp for children on the east side of the island on property that had belonged to a homesteader named Johnson, but the camp closed in 1945. Meanwhile, the United Church had bought Harry White's former homestead and opened a camp there in 1940 but it, too, eventually closed. A camp run by the non-profit non-denominational Barnabas Family Ministries was established in 1986 on the 157-acre former Richard Corkum property, which had been operated unsuccessfully as an organic farm; the site faces Gambier Island and is viewed daily by thousands of BC Ferries passengers. The organization, which caters to family groups, began with tents for sleeping quarters and a construction trailer as a kitchen, but by the turn of the century they had constructed two large guesthouses, an administration building and caretaker's cottage.

In 1959 the BC government acquired 78 acres of the former MacDonald farm on the most northerly point of Keats Island in order to create Plumper Cove Marine Provincial Park. The original farmhouse and orchard still remain, but a wharf, mooring buoys and camping facilities were installed and a small pebble beach offers kayaking, swimming and beachcombing possibilities. By the 21st century Keats had been subdivided into approximately 465 parcels of land ranging from fractional acreage to hundreds of acres, but most of the island's 50 full-time residents live near the two government wharves, one at Keats Landing, which faces Shoal Channel, the other at Eastbourne on the southeast coast. Regular foot-passenger ferry service is provided from Langdale to Keats Landing via Gambier Island.

ROBERTS CREEK

The story of the Roberts Creek settlement begins in January 1889 when Thomas William "Will" Roberts surveyed a square quarter section for himself just east of the creek that now bears the family name. Before he could register his claim it was pre-empted by a logger named J.W. Stoney, but when Stoney discovered that the best timber on it had already been pirated by the company working the timber limit to the northeast, he moved on, leaving L.809 to Will Roberts. He filed his pre-emption on April 13, 1889, and earned his Crown grant on June 23, 1890, by constructing two cedar shake cabins, a chicken house and stables on the flatland beside the creek, and clearing three acres on which he planted 150 fruit trees. He was joined later that summer by his father, Thomas Roberts, formerly the head gardener on the Wilward estate in Redditch, England, and his mother Charlotte; once settled, they bought their son's pre-emption for $500 so that Will could move on to other adventures. Two years later another son, John Francis "Frank" Roberts, arrived. A cabinet-maker and ship's carpenter by trade, he had been serving aboard a freighter and jumped ship when it arrived in Seattle. He stayed in Roberts Creek long enough to build his parents a large log house a quarter mile east of the creek.

The Roberts family was not alone in the wilderness around Roberts Creek because the same fishboat that brought Will Roberts to this coast brought three other men to stake land nearby. On January 31, 1889, William Campbell staked L.810, a long narrow block with 20 chains of waterfrontage to the west of Roberts Creek. Although he was primarily interested in the timber on the property, he fulfilled the conditions of his Crown grant by April 18, 1891. The northern half of this property is now the Sunshine Coast Golf and Country Club. James Mitchell claimed the next stretch of waterfront, L. 1317, on the same day that Campbell pre-empted and received his Crown grant on December 1, 1892. On February 18, 1889, James Ross pre-empted L.1318, which is bisected diagonally by Flume Creek; it is bounded on the east today by Marlene Road. Thomas Moscrop pre-empted next to Ross on September 30, 1892; L.1321 included the mouth of Flume Creek. Today it is bounded on the north by Doris Road and is the site of Park, Henderson and Hunter avenues.

William P. Baker and his sons Malcolm and Frederick took advantage of the pre-emption clause that allowed families to claim land as a unit, and on September 3, 1891, they pre-empted L.1316, 480 acres running southeastward along the shoreline from the Roberts claim almost as far as the present-day Boy Scout camp. To the east of their claim, William Slater pre-empted L.1315, which is diagonally bisected by Joe Smith Creek.

After seven years at Roberts Creek, Thomas and Charlotte Roberts moved to Vancouver to retire, leaving their homestead vacant until 1900 when their son Frank, whose wife had died shortly after he returned to England, arrived back in Roberts Creek to take up the pre-emption. He and three of his children moved into the house he had built for his parents, while his married son Francis Thomas "Tom" Roberts and wife Nancy moved into the cabin built by Will Roberts. At first in order to support the family, Frank and his second son Louis Harry Roberts (known to history by his second name) were forced to find work in the mills and shipyards of Vancouver, leaving the two younger members of the family in the care of relatives. By 1903, however, Frank and 19-year-old Harry had returned to set up a shingle bolt camp along the creek, using a Chinese crew to load the bolts onto scows docked at a rock-crib landing they constructed on the west side of the creek.

Never one to stick long at any job, the following year Frank sold Harry the 40 acres east of the creek then took on the job of Roberts Creek's first post-master, rowing an Indian dugout canoe out into the bay on mail days to pick up the bag of letters from the Union Steamships' *Comox*. Four years later, he gave the postmaster's job to his eldest son, Tom, and headed for the Yukon to seek his fortune, although the gold rush there was over.

With all the waterfront alienated in the first staking rush, future pre-emptions were restricted to the upland areas. In 1891 Frank Roberts' sister Alice and her husband, W.H. "Dan" Steinbrunner, arrived to farm L.1319, lying on both sides of Flume Creek where Highway 101 now intersects with Flume and Lockyer roads. By the time they received their Crown grant on October 7, 1901, they had six acres cleared, fenced and cultivated, an acre of orchard, a log house worth $50 and two barns worth $100. Edward H. Lye staked L.1320 to the east of the Steinbrunners in October 1890; the present-day Lockyer Road crosses his pre-emption. He was still farming there in March

1908 when Roger McNutt, Willie Tom Lockyer, and Albert, Jack and Frank Reeves became his neighbours.

The Reeves were among the most successful of the early Roberts Creek farmers. Originally from England, the family had settled in Saskatchewan before moving on to British Columbia. Albert Reeves' first pre-emption choice was the same plot of land that Lockyer had filed on so his claim was disallowed, but in August 1910 he applied again, this time for L.3381, a 20-acre parcel squeezed between William Campbell's L.810 and Edward Lye's pre-emption. Jack Reeves' pre-emption, registered on March 12, 1908, was L.3376 to the northeast of the Lye pre-emption. After building a house and barn out of the shingle bolts left behind by Japanese loggers, he cleared 12 acres of the sandy loam and black muck for truck gardening. Within four years he had earned his Crown grant and was carrying his produce to Sechelt by horse and cart to sell it at the Indian residential school, resort hotels and summer cottages. In Sechelt he met Esther Gertrude Burch and three years later they were married. Besides their garden produce, they raised pigs, chickens and geese for market. Gertrude Reeves became widely known for her prize-winning woven products, which used the wool and hair of their farm animals.

Gertrude Reeves had one of the first cars in Roberts Creek, a three-wheeled

Jack Reeves with his delivery horse and cart. Reeves sold the produce of his Roberts Creek farm to the people of Sechelt from 1908 to the 1930s. On the left is John "Jack" Reeves Sr. with his horse Toby, which had belonged to the Sisters of the Child Jesus in Sechelt until its health deteriorated. On the right are John Reeves' brother, Albert "Bert" Reeves, and Bill Lockyer. The Reeves and Lockyers arrived from England together.
COURTESY OF SECHELT COMMUNITY ARCHIVES.

electric affair operated by six 6-volt batteries, which were charged on a Delco generator. When the batteries were fully charged, the car had a range of 20 miles and a top speed of 12 miles per hour. Once when the batteries were run down and the Reeves' son, Gordon, was driving, it began groaning on the way up the hill to the family farm. After he stepped out to reduce the weight, one of the rear wheels ran over his foot and the car rolled into the ditch. To get it out, he put it into reverse and began heaving on it, whereupon it bounced out of the ditch and down the hill again with Reeves in pursuit. Fortunately, there were no other vehicles or people on the road.

Mrs. Gertrude Reeves in her electric car at Roberts Creek about 1920. It was purchased in England and shipped around Cape Horn, arriving complete with the Delco generator that was used to charge its batteries.
COURTESY OF SUNSHINE COAST MUSEUM AND ARCHIVES.
PHOTO #1195.

The third member of the Reeves family, Frank, pre-empted L.3379, at the thousand-foot level on the mountainside. He had to build a half mile of wagon road and a 12-foot-long bridge in order to reach his property, but he qualified for his Crown grant with a house, a barn and cleared acreage on August 27, 1912.

By this time, many of the earlier pre-emptions had been abandoned, though a few had been reclaimed and subdivided. A portion of Edward Lye's pre-emption was settled by Mrs. Hanbury and her sons who planted an orchard and raised pigs and chickens. Joseph Smith, who bought part of the Baker claim on the waterfront east of the Roberts pre-emption, made his living growing artichokes for the Vancouver market; the creek running through his property received his name. William Pell pre-empted beside what is now Pell Road in upper Roberts Creek in 1907 then left the area to spend 15 years blacksmithing in the Enderby-Armstrong area. He returned with his wife in 1924 to farm his Roberts Creek property.

Meanwhile, each summer, in the absence of the owners of pre-emptions close to the waterfront, hordes of summer campers began to descend, having discovered that Roberts Creek could provide a convenient, inexpensive retreat for a tenting holiday. Harry Roberts turned this influx to his advantage by building a small store near the mouth of the creek where he catered to both farmers and transients. Two years later, having taken over the postmaster's job from his brother Tom, he moved the post office into his store as well.

An inventive, practical man with a multitude of talents, Harry Roberts set up a sawmill on the level land east of the creek mouth where his grandparents had planted their orchard. This mill provided lumber for most of the new settlers' houses, the timbers for the 13 bridges that had to be constructed when the Lower Road was built, and lumber for the first government wharf. Some of Roberts' lumber was also barged to customers as far away as Pender Harbour.

Harry Roberts' 36-foot yawl Chack Chack *moored at the mouth of Roberts Creek about 1920. Harry's sawmill is on the right and next to it part of the Robert McNair shingle bolt flume.*
COURTESY OF SUNSHINE COAST MUSEUM AND ARCHIVES. PHOTO #1027.

But perhaps the best-known use of the mill's timber output was for Roberts' own constructions: his landmark home, "The Castle," built east of the creek in 1917 for his bride, Effie "Birdie" Sissons; his 36-foot yawl, the *Chack Chack* and his combined work and pleasure boat, the *LHR*.

Tom Roberts had meanwhile become supervisor of the McNair Shingle Company's camp on the Campbell property on the west side of Roberts Creek, and it provided a good income while he was improving the farm he had established on the eastern half of the original Roberts pre-emption next to Stephens Creek. He sold milk, poultry and garden produce in Vancouver, rowing them out to the Union Steamship to get them to market. Unfortunately, both Tom and his wife died in 1912, Tom of a heart attack and Nancy in childbirth, leaving four young children.

When the shingle bolt camp finally closed and the Campbell property was abandoned, Harry Roberts and other settlers pre-empted and subdivided it, then built and furnished small cottages to rent to summer vacationers. Harry also built cottages on his own property for summer rentals. Then, as the demand for property grew, he subdivided the rest of his land, keeping only the portion needed for his home, mill and store.

The community of Roberts Creek was almost entirely dependent on water transport for supplies, but establishing any kind of ship landing there was extremely difficult because of the harsh southeasterly storms that pounded the shores every winter. For many years, passengers and freight were rowed out to the steamers, and boarding and loading took place directly from these small boats bobbing alongside in the water. When around 1909 the government anchored a float offshore, it was washed away in the storms of the following winter. The next summer a larger float was installed and it was washed away just as quickly. After that, Harry Roberts used his small launch, the *Midget*, to push a scow loaded with as many as 75 summer campers at a time plus a pile of freight out from the beach to meet passing steamships. Finally, in 1914 a government wharf was constructed, but because the builders had difficulty establishing footings, Harry was forced to move his store somewhat to the east to provide room for road allowance. When the new wharf was complete, however, the federal and provincial governments disagreed on who was responsible for the wharf approach, and it was Harry Roberts who organized the community to build and pay for it themselves.

In 1916 when McNair Logging needed to build a flume to get their shake bolts to the water, Harry Roberts agreed to let the structure cross his property in exchange for McNair financing a breakwater to protect the new wharf and creek mouth. After the flume was built, the company reneged, and Harry took them to court. Although he won, the amount he was awarded was not enough to build an adequate breakwater and it gradually disintegrated.

Since the wharf's relocation had left Harry's store far from his potential market, he built a new one, this time close to the east side of the wharf. By adding a spacious covered veranda onto the front and a ramp leading to the wharf, Harry provided travellers with a convenient waiting room and gave himself prime access to his market. Nearby he built a freight shed; always a cheerful non-conformist, he painted the words "Sunshine Belt" in large letters on its seaward side. A number of years later when Leonard Bailey (who had previously run a store at Egmont) leased Harry's store for a time, Bailey painted "Ye Olde Bailey" on the side of that building.

In these early years there were not enough children in Roberts Creek to warrant building a school, and families such as the Steinbrunners moved to

Gibson's in order to provide an education for their children. However, in 1919 two schools were opened in Roberts Creek: the Elphinstone Bay School at what is now the intersection of Lockyer Road and Highway 101, and the East Roberts Creek School at the intersection of Orange Road and Highway 101. Because the area was still so sparsely settled, in the first years of operation it was often difficult to find the six students required at each school to qualify for government funding, and underage children were enrolled to fill the quota.

In 1923 Harry Roberts leased out his mill and store and left the community for good. For a while he made his headquarters on Merry Island in the little house called "Bugaboo" that he had built as a base for cruising in the Gulf Islands, but around 1929 he pre-empted land on Nelson Island and made a home there for his second wife Cherry and their three children. His new house was known as "Sunray" or "The House of 10,000 Faces" because he had used 300 panes of glass in its windows. Here he also built a 32-foot, Chinese junk-style, three-masted schooner, the *Chack Chack III,* which was never launched.

Frank and Dulcie Downes, formerly managers of the Gibson's Co-op Store, became the new operators of the Roberts Creek store. They carried on business in Harry Roberts' old building until 1931 when they moved it closer to the wharf, enlarged and renovated it, and constructed new living quarters upstairs for themselves. Eventually they added electricity, refrigeration and the community's first hand-operated, gravity-flow gas pump.

The McNair flume ceased operating around 1922, and in the early 1930s Harry Roberts' mill, which the Downes had sublet to Charles Haslam and later to a Mr. Scriber, was also closed down and most of the machinery removed and sold. However, throughout the mid-1920s and 1930s the community of Roberts Creek still bustled with the summertime influx of vacationers and the regular activities of the farming community. Besides the Downes' store on the waterfront, there was by this time a small summer resort operated by Frederick and Johanna "Josie" Dunn, a general store opposite the present post office, a beauty parlour, shoe repair shop, barber shop, bakery, service station and cafe.

There were also three summer camps close by. The Kewpie Camp for girls was started in 1920 by Miss K. Brydon on property she had bought from Harry Roberts just east of the creek. The 200-acre Camp Byng on the Lower Road, which still provides summer scout training for boys, was leased by the Vancouver District Scout Council in 1922 and officially opened by the Governor General and Chief Scout Lord Byng of Vimy. The property was purchased for the scouting movement in 1925 with funding provided by the Vancouver Rotary Club. The camp trail, known as the Baden-Powell Trail, which leads from the lodge to the beach, was once the main logging skid road for the turn-of-the-century logging operation of James Cassidy, who boomed his logs in Byng Bay (known in his day as Cassidy's Landing). Camp Olave, on Highway 101 at the foot of Rat Portage Hill, was purchased by the Girl Guide organization in 1927 to provide summer camping facilities for girls.

For many years Roberts Creek's two schools served as the centres of the community's social life, but by 1934 school enrollment had increased to the point where it was no longer feasible to share the buildings, and the whole community rallied to build the Roberts Creek Community Hall on land donated by John Roberts. All the labour and materials were also donated, with William Pell cutting the shakes for the roof on his farm in upper Roberts Creek.

In the early 1940s a third general store, called the Seaview Market, was built in Roberts Creek beside the present post office and library. When Frank Downes retired a decade later, a local co-op took over the old store on the wharf, but by then Union Steamships had ceased to run and the wharf store was no longer a profitable business. It closed a few years later. The wharf had been badly damaged by storms in 1933 and rebuilt, but in the early 1960s a portion of it was stripped out and replaced with fill to form a new breakwater, which was leased in 1964 by Rockgas Propane Ltd., a forerunner of ICG Propane, for the installation of storage tanks. The remainder of the wharf slowly decayed until in 1970 it was declared unsafe and torn down. The propane storage tanks were removed in the early 1990s after the Hillside Industrial Park was established near Port Mellon.

Elphinstone Bay School closed in 1945, and East Roberts Creek School was replaced in 1952 by the Roberts Creek Elementary School on Hall Road (now called Roberts Creek Road). The new building was destroyed by fire in 1962, rebuilt in enlarged form immediately and enlarged twice again in the 1980s and '90s.

In the years after World War II, competition from the large-scale farms of the Fraser Valley and from produce imported from the United States gradually made it more and more difficult for the farmers of Roberts Creek to find markets. Much of the farmland was allowed to lie fallow; some of it was subdivided for homes. Then in the early 1960s, "the Creek" was rediscovered by the "hippie" generation. Many settled on the old farms, transforming them into communes. Although by the end of the 1970s many of these new "Creekers" had drifted back to the cities and others had moved farther into the backwoods, those who stayed on in Roberts Creek have been a powerful influence on the philosophy of the community and have led the fight to preserve its rural character. In more recent times the construction of a new block of stores in "downtown" Roberts Creek has continued the "Creek style" with board and batten siding, and the establishment of the internationally acclaimed Inside Passage School of Fine Woodworking there has underlined local values.

In 1987 Block 1 of L.809 at the mouth of Roberts Creek was purchased by the Sunshine Coast Regional District (SCRD). Once the site of the orchard planted by Thomas and Charlotte Roberts, and later that of Harry Roberts' mill, this block is now a regional district park. Cliff Gilker Regional District Park, with its playing fields and nature trails is just a short distance to the south on Highway 101, and Roberts Creek Provincial Park, designated in 1954, lies along the shore to the northwest.

WILSON CREEK AND DAVIS BAY

West of Roberts Creek, pre-emptions were staked around Tsawcome, Sechelt Indian Reserve #1, where Narvaez and the crew of the *Santa Saturnina* had replenished their fresh water supplies from the "*Rio de la Aguada*" in 1791. The first pre-emption here was made by William Simpson on L.1028, which bordered the north side of the reserve; its eastern boundary coincided with the present-day Field Road. To the east of this line is L.1029 which was filed on first by Beecher Hungerford in 1888 and abandoned then pre-empted by Donald J.R. Cameron on April 23, 1891. However, the creek which passes through this lot was not named after either of them; instead, it is known as Wilson Creek after James Wilson who was a blacksmith for Burns and Jackson Logging and lived northeast of Cameron. Next to it on the east side, L.1491 was claimed by John Fraser and Crown granted on August 4, 1892.

To the west of Indian Reserve #1, Loren Chapman, whose name is com-memorated in the creek that is a primary fresh water source for the western half of the Sunshine Coast, pre-empted L.1356, which stretched from Mission Point north along Davis Bay to the present Chapman Road. Lot 1329, on which most of the houses of Selma Park sit today, was claimed by Thomas R. Harvey on August 11, 1891, and Crown granted on November 6, 1891.

In the 1930s the main channel of Chapman Creek was dredged and the secondary creek mouth that had flowed east through Indian Reserve #1 was cut off. The increased flow of water in the main channel picked up much more sand from the creek bed, depositing it beyond the mouth to form the extensive sand spit that exists today at the south end of Davis Bay. In recent years the shore along the bay has been stabilized with a rock- and concrete-fronted seawalk and more parkland has been acquired between the beach and the creekmouth. This beach attracts hundreds of sun-worshippers and beach-walkers on fine days throughout the year and dozens of kelp and seaweed gatherers after every storm.

SECHELT

The pattern of development for the village of Sechelt was established in 1875 when the provincial government registered the military land grant of John Scales, recently retired from the Royal Engineers. When the limits of Scales' grant of L.303 and his purchase of L.304 were being confirmed, the federal government established their eastern boundaries to coincide with the western boundary of Sechelt Indian Reserve #2. Since Scales' western boundaries coincided with the present Shorncliffe Street, all of the level land that forms the isthmus between the Strait of Georgia and Sechelt Inlet was now claimed, and latecomers had to make do with the rocky coastal shelf lying to the northwest of Scales' property.

Although this land became available for pre-emption in 1884, it was another five years before anyone registered a claim. The first was Joseph Bouillon, a Belgian "architect" or building contractor who arrived in Sechelt with Father Paul Durieu on October 26, 1889, to begin construction of Our Lady of the Rosary Church on Sechelt Indian Reserve #2. Two months later he registered a claim for L.1310, 80 chains long and 20 wide, running from the ocean right up the bed of the creek that the Sechelt Native people called Chascom; he received title in 1893 and the creek became known as Bouillon's Creek. However, after William Jackson Wakefield pre-empted L.2406 higher up the creek on March 12, 1908, and began raising chickens and pigs there, the local people gradually began to call it Wakefield Creek.

After Bouillon pre-empted, another year and a half passed before the Sechelt waterfront attracted its next pre-emptors, a group of seven enterprising young men. The entire group, all but one of them French or Belgian, registered claims on August 13, 1891, on land lying between the claims of Bouillon and Scales. The single Englishman in the group was Thomas John Cook who claimed L.1331 adjoining L.303. In less than a year all of them had made enough improvements to qualify for their Crown grants, but only Cook stayed to settle on his land. A ship's steward, he made his pre-emption improvements between voyages on various shipping lines, including Canadian Pacific Steamships, and when the steam tug *Tepic* landed Cook, his wife Sara and their baby daughter Ada at Trail Bay in 1893, they became the first European family to take up residence in Sechelt. Cook called his property "Shorncliffe" in honour of the place where he had grown up in Kent, England, and the name was eventually attached to both a street and an extended-care centre located there. When in time he subdivided his land, he donated a block of it as a site for St. Hilda's Anglican Church and parish hall. After Cook's neighbours abandoned their lands, a new round of pre-emptions began. Lot 1384 which had been first claimed by Adolphus Giguere was pre-empted by John Reginald Nickson on June 6, 1912. Two years later when he qualified for his Crown title, he had built a $1,500 house for his family and had 4 1/2 acres under cultivation. Nickson's daughter Rene married Major T. Douglas Sutherland, who had been a tea planter in Ceylon before his service in World War I. In 1928, after Sutherland became a provincial police officer, he and his wife bought the waterfront portion of the former Bouillon property and employed Hector McDonald to build them a beautiful log home there; in 1940 Charles F. Reda converted it into the Wakefield Inn—a hotel with three rooms upstairs and a "beer parlour" on the main floor. In the 1970s it became a neighbourhood pub and remained a popular local haunt until 2005 when it was razed to make way for a housing development.

The Wakefield Inn, built in 1928, was a community landmark. It was demolished in 2005.
COURTESY OF ROSELLA LESLIE.

John Scales' L.303 and L.304, sold in 1891 to BC's Lieutenant-Governor Hugh Nelson, were finally settled after 1895 when Herbert "Bert" Whitaker bought them from Nelson's widow. The Whitakers, Bert and his father Alfred, had come to the Sunshine Coast from England via California early in 1892 and pre-empted 320 acres (L.1473) on the west side of Porpoise Bay, just south of Indian Reserve #4 at Snake Bay. While logging it and building a cabin, they camped in an abandoned logging bunkhouse on L.303; it stood where Wharf Avenue now connects with the Boulevard. The rest of the Whitaker family—Bert's four brothers, three sisters and his mother, Henrietta—joined them in the spring of 1894.

Bert Whitaker—just 20 years old when he acquired Nelson's land—was not slow to realize the potential of his situation. He now owned three-quarters of a mile of waterfront on Trail Bay and as much again on the Porpoise Bay shoreline, and he could see that, for miners and loggers working in the forests of Sechelt Inlet and its tributaries, the shortest route back to Vancouver was right through his lands. Within a year after receiving title, he converted the old logging bunkhouse into a store, the only one between Gibson's Landing and Pender Harbour, and quickly obtained a monopoly on provisioning all the logging and mining camps in the area. When he was appointed postmaster on March 1, 1896, the store also became the Sechelt post office. Two years later, business had grown so much that he transferred both operations to a new and much bigger general store building immediately west of the old one.

The interior of Bert Whitaker's first Sechelt store about 1904.
COURTESY OF SUNSHINE COAST MUSEUM AND ARCHIVES. PHOTO #1182.

Whitaker's next project was the construction of a 10-room hotel on the northeast corner of Inlet Avenue and the Boulevard. To avoid the strip of peat bog running parallel to the waterfront and just 100 feet inland, he built his hotel on the berm of land facing the sea. It was officially opened for business on July 1, 1899, with a band playing to welcome the S.S. *Cutch's* arrival with an excursion party coming from Vancouver for the celebrations. By 1901 Whitaker was looking for money to finance the construction of waterfront rental cottages. His prospectus advised potential investors that his Sechelt Hotel was "filled to overflowing during the summer months, and many intending visitors have been refused. With a very small increased expenditure, it is estimated that double the amount could easily be accommodated, and increase the profit very materially."[2] Over the next three years he built a number of cottages west of his Sechelt Hotel, two of which—Rock Cottage, next to Snickett Park, and Green Cottage, a block to the east—are still standing.

In 1902 Whitaker constructed a wharf at Porpoise Bay, siting it parallel to the shore just west of the present government wharf. This improved docking considerably, although boats berthed there were sometimes stranded on the mud flats at low tide. Within two years he had also completed a wharf at Trail Bay, and to guarantee that his hotel would be properly served, he invested in a small fleet of passenger vessels, beginning with the *New Era*, then the *Sechelt*, the *Tartar* and the *Belcarra*.

In spite of his new cottages and the construction of a small hotel annex, by 1906 Whitaker could not meet the demand for rooms, and he undertook an 18-room, three-storey addition to the Sechelt Hotel, achieving a certain elegance with its rambling style and elaborate verandas. He followed this with the construction of another store on the east side of Porpoise Bay (Wharf) Road at the Boulevard; three storeys high, it housed hardware, groceries and the post office. The former store then became the hotel's "bull pen" for logger guests.

It was also in 1906 that Beach House, the Whitaker family home, was completed. A gracious, three-storey, seven-bedroom house, it stood on a waterfront lot on the east side of Trail Avenue at the Boulevard. At this time it was home to Alfred and Henrietta Whitaker and all their family, but after Bert's younger brothers and sisters married and his parents retired to the city, the house became the home of Bert, his wife Mae and their children, Kenneth (1909–1954) and Isabel (1910–1976).

Bert Whitaker's reputation as a businessman was not an unblemished one. Joe Gregson, who logged in Jervis Inlet, reported coming down from the bush to find all the rooms in Whitaker's hotel full. He was allowed the privilege of sleeping on the beach for a payment of 25 cents. Others remembered him watering the milk that was sold in his store and faking breakdowns on his Porpoise Bay launch that serviced the Inlet's logging camps so that the loggers on board would miss their connection with the Vancouver-bound boat and be forced to pay for a night in his hotel. Even in an era when the standard of business ethics was considerably more flexible than today, Whitaker appears to have been a markedly devious man.

When a schoolhouse was needed in 1912, Whitaker was persuaded to let the children use a small building that he owned on the west side of Wharf Avenue, but in May 1913 he ordered them out because he had been offered seven dollars a month from the federal government to use the building as a telegraph office. The only other building available for the 18 children and their teacher, Grace Kent, was a boat repair shed at the head of Porpoise Bay. It had been established by a Japanese Canadian named Yamamoto around the turn of the century, but by this time he had moved on. At high tide the children could see the water lapping below them through the gaps between the floorboards, but it had to suffice until the community constructed a more substantial building at the corner of Osprey and Wharf streets. It was 1939 before a new school to house both elementary and secondary students was built at Cowrie and Shorncliffe streets, the site of the present Sechelt Elementary School.

The three years from 1906 to 1909 were extremely profitable ones for Whitaker: both of his lumber mills and his five logging camps flourished, and his steamship business thrived. He collected wharfage from ships arriving in both Porpoise Bay and Trail Bay, charged for handling their freight, and charged again for transporting their goods with his team from one dock to the other. His hotel was filled with loggers in winter and vacationers in summer.

But beginning in 1909 he suffered reverses with both his steamship company and his logging interests, and around 1911 he sold his holdings on both sides of Porpoise Bay to Angus Crowston. In 1913 he found a buyer willing to take his Sechelt Townsite holdings: the Canadian European Investment Syndicate headed by a German baron named von Lutwitz. With this sale, Whitaker, just 39 years of age, became an extremely wealthy man, and since he still owned a logging empire, he expected to become even wealthier. Early the following year the baron arrived to visit his new property, but by that time relations between Germany and the British Empire had become strained and in the climate of suspicion that reigned, the baron's every move was interpreted as a threat to the country's security.

On June 1, 1914, fire broke out at the Sechelt Hotel. Volunteers rushed to help and most of the furniture was saved, but the structure was a total loss. Six weeks later war broke out between Germany and the British Empire, the syndicate ceased payments on the mortgage Whitaker was holding and he was forced to resume ownership. Since a hotel was absolutely essential to the whole Sechelt enterprise, he set carpenters to work transforming his general store at the end of the wharf into a hotel, adding kitchens and more bedrooms on the shoreward side and a parlour on the side facing the road that led to the wharf. A new dining room seated 150 people. At the same time he converted the "bull pen" across the street into a new general store, later adding a second storey and attic to create a hotel annex.

There were few cars in Sechelt during this period, but W.J. "Joe" Marten operated an open-sided truck, known to everyone as "The Galloping Goose," to carry tourists and loggers from Porpoise Bay to Trail Bay and around the village. Passengers sat sideways in the truck while Joe, who was reputed to be the world's worst driver, drove at breakneck speed over boulders and potholes, braking at the last minute when he came to the wharf. On at least one occasion, he nearly took all his passengers into the bay, but a ride in the Galloping Goose remained one of the tourist highpoints for many years.

The second Sechelt Hotel in the late 1920s. It had been built as a general store in 1898, and then enlarged and renovated to become a hotel in 1914 after the first hotel burned. In 1936 this second hotel was also destroyed by fire.
COURTESY OF SUNSHINE COAST MUSEUM AND ARCHIVES. PHOTO #667 BY E.S. CLAYTON

While Whitaker was occupied with rebuilding, the All Red Steamship Line bought Thomas Harvey's Lot 1329 at Selma Park and began building a wharf there to provide access to their planned picnic park. By the next summer their ships were operating at capacity to bring in one-day excursionists. Meanwhile, Whitaker's Porpoise Bay wharf had been allowed to fall into disrepair and it collapsed on July 29, 1915; since it was also an integral part of his little empire, he had to hire carpenters to replace it early the following year, this time extending it farther into the bay to avoid the worst of the mud flats.

Business picked up after this series of calamities and misfortunes, with holidayers arriving at Whitaker's resort in record numbers. But the numbers were also increasing at Selma Park, and in October 1917 the owners of the All Red Line took advantage of the market to sell out to Union Steamships, a much more formidable rival than the All Red had ever been. Union enlarged Selma Park by building a new store on the wharf, a dozen waterfront cottages and a huge dance hall with a veranda that had a magnificent view of Trail Bay and the Strait of Georgia. A few years later they improved the picnic grounds with covered tables and cooking facilities.

Whitaker responded by constructing a tea room on the site of his first hotel. Here a Miss Blackburn, who had been a housekeeper for the Whitakers but was a confectioner by trade, provided teas each afternoon. By enlarging it a year or two later, Whitaker was able to use it as a dance hall in the evenings. Admission was 50 cents. His next innovation was to install tennis courts behind the tea room on the edge of the Sechelt swamp with its yellow pines, cranberry and labrador tea bushes.

The next round of calamities to befall Whitaker's Sechelt resort began with the destruction of the Trail Bay wharf during a fierce storm on the night of January 30, 1921. Before the winds died the following afternoon, most of the shoreward timbers and pilings had been washed away and the rest of the structure badly damaged. Repairs began immediately. Two years later his Porpoise Bay wharf fell into disrepair again, but this time the logging companies up the inlet petitioned the federal government to take over, and they installed a new dock to the east of Whitaker's old one. Its timbers have been renewed from time to time since then but it still stands on its original site.

After 1920, when Whitaker's health began to decline, he came to rely more and more on George Aman who had come to work for him in 1902, and on his cousin Edric Sidney Clayton who had come to Sechelt after overseas service in World War I. Aman had become company superintendent and in 1920 Clayton was appointed hotel and cottages manager. Four years later accountant Robert S. Hackett was hired to run the offices of the now seriously ailing company, but he was unable to save it. When the 50-year-old Whitaker died in 1925, his estate went into receivership. For more than a year it was operated by the Credit Men's Trust Association before it was purchased by Union Estates, a branch of Union Steamships. George Aman, Edric Clayton and Robert Hackett stayed on to work for the new owners, and when Aman retired in 1928, Hackett became superintendent and Clayton the store manager.

Competition between Selma Park and Sechelt ended with the acquisition of Whitaker's holdings by Union Estates. A new dance pavilion was built in Sechelt and dances were held in the two pavilions on alternate Saturdays. Whitaker's tea room was enlarged again and turned into a bathhouse with an adjoining coffee shop and ice cream parlour called the Barbecue. Beach House, the Whitaker family home, became a hotel annex. In 1928 three totem poles, carved by Rivers Inlet Native artist Paul Weenah and members of the Sechelt band, were raised on the Boulevard between the bathhouse and the store. They remained there until 1955 when, because of continuing vandalism, the company moved them to Bowen Island.

Herbert Whitaker with his family and staff on the steps of Beach House, the family home, about 1924. Herbert Whitaker is in a dark business suit upper left; his mother, Mrs. Henrietta Whitaker, is the woman in the dark dress beside him. Whitaker's cousin, Edric S. Clayton, is seated on the middle step on the far right.
COURTESY OF SUNSHINE COAST MUSEUM AND ARCHIVES. PHOTO #102.

In 1933 Union Estates, exasperated by the need for constant repairs to the Trail Bay wharf, sold it to the federal government, which built a new one on the same site. Union successfully weathered the Depression years by cutting back on the staff at its resorts and on the number of runs made by its ships, but on July 26, 1936, the company sustained a serious loss when fire struck the second Sechelt Hotel. With no fire equipment available, it burned to the ground. Beach House now became the only hotel, but since this cut the resort's available accommodation in half, the company constructed more rental cottages along the waterfront and in the orchard around the tennis courts.

Union Estates did not have a monopoly on the tourist industry in Sechelt during this period. Opeongo Lodge, built in 1926 at the corner of Teredo Street and Shorncliffe Avenue on former Cook property, was operated by Bryce and Gertrude Fleck. With its tennis courts and waterfront location, it was a very popular destination. William A. Youngson, who came to Sechelt to work for the Flecks, built Rockwood Lodge in 1936 at the intersection of Cowrie Street and Shorncliffe Avenue. (In 1988 the lodge and its grounds became a centre for cultural and educational activities; it is the home of the nationally renowned Sunshine Coast Festival of the Written Arts founded in 1983.) Glendalough, the home of Jack and Carrie Mayne, on the northwest corner of Cowrie and Inlet, also provided tourist accommodation.

Because Sechelt's economy was oriented toward logging and tourism from its earliest days, farming was never as important as it was in Gibson's Landing and Roberts Creek. Although gardens were cultivated as early as the 1870s by the Sechelt Natives under the supervision of the Oblate fathers, the first cultivation of land by non-Natives waited until necessity prompted the Whitakers and Cooks to plant kitchen gardens and orchards. Whitaker eventually enlarged his family's gardens and dairy herd in order to feed his hotel guests; produce that was left over was sold in his store to his cottagers. After 1913 the primary commercial sources of produce in this area were Jack Reeves of Roberts Creek and

Pacific Airways Ltd. photo of Sechelt, about 1925. On the left,
the Trail Bay wharf extends into the bay. St. Augustine's School is centre right.
Sechelt Inlet, centred by Poise Island, extends into the distance.
COURTESY OF SUNSHINE COAST MUSEUM AND ARCHIVES. PHOTO #825.

Jiro "Jim" Konishi, his wife, three sons and one daughter who farmed 32 acres of L.1437 on the west shore of Porpoise Bay. Konishi, a Japanese Canadian, established a dairy farm and grew fruits and vegetables that the family delivered by horse and cart. At the time of his death, a month after Pearl Harbour, Jiro Konishi had operated the farm for nearly 30 years. On March 15, 1942, the remaining eight members of his family were "evacuated" by federal government order; they were required to live outside the coastal area for the duration of World War II and never returned to the Sunshine Coast. The government sold off their land and equipment and the farm deteriorated until the 1960s when it was taken over by a hippie commune.

By the mid-1940s, although Sechelt was still oriented toward tourists arriving from the water, the business section was beginning to expand past the waterfront. Jack and Lee Redman with partners Stuart and Nellie Killick were operating the thriving Sechelt Service Store, established by Joe Spangler, on the east side of Cowrie Street between Inlet and Trail. Although initially they offered general merchandise including hardware and groceries, in time they came to specialize in foodstuffs. In 1963 when they moved their business to the Lang Block, also on the east side of Cowrie, they changed the name to Redman's Red and White Store.

Edric Clayton left Union Estates in 1949 and a year later he and his wife Florence opened their own store on the west side of Cowrie Street between Inlet and Trail avenues. Clayton was by this time 59, late in life for a new venture, but the store prospered and a year later they were able to afford a 17-cubic-foot refrigeration unit to keep the dairy products cold.

Sechelt waterfront in the late 1930s. The large building in the centre of the picture is the Sechelt Inn, formerly the Whitaker family home, Beach House, built in 1906. The two cottages to the left and the two on the extreme right were built as rentals by Bert Whitaker, the remainder by Union Steamships. The Trail Bay wharf is just out of the picture on the right.
COURTESY OF SUNSHINE COAST MUSEUM AND ARCHIVES. PHOTO #1233.

On November 16, 1948, with plans underway to completely rebuild the government-owned Trail Bay wharf, it was seriously damaged when the freighter *Bevin*, attempting to dock during a storm, broadsided it. Shipping was diverted to Roberts Creek and Gibson's while reconstruction took place. The new wharf opened for business in March 1950, its approach lined with lamp standards to avert damage to the dock by ships berthing after dark with only the help of their searchlights. Union Steamships, which benefited most by this addition, paid the light bill. The wharf was out of commission again after storms that occurred on November 30, 1950, and January 4, 1951, ripped out pilings and stripped planking and stringers from the deck. Repairs were made, and during the next few years Union's ships and those of Gulf Lines docked regularly, side by side with smaller pleasure craft and even seaplanes. In 1956 the British American Oil Company was granted a permit to construct a short pipeline from its plant on the site of the second Sechelt Hotel (on the waterfront at Wharf Road) to the head of the wharf to allow them to load and unload oil and gas.

By 1952 the Sunshine Coast Highway had been completed and paved as far as Sechelt, and the community began to shift its orientation from water to road transportation. Although Union had installed a gas pump beside the store in the early 1930s and a gas station had been operating on the northeast corner of Inlet and Cowrie since 1937, it took the arrival of the paving crew to make it a profitable business. Paving the road also brought a small real estate boom and more prosperity to the shops on Cowrie Street. The Claytons enlarged their store in 1956, then doubled its size six years later. Edric Clayton died in 1965, but the next generation of the family, led by his elder son, Richard "Dick" Clayton, moved the business to its present site in 1970 and made it the hub of the prosperous Trail Bay Centre.

The empire of Union Steamships and Union Estates had begun to crumble before World War II ended. In 1944, the Selma Park property was sold and the dance pavilion was remodelled and reopened as the Totem Lodge. Fire claimed it on April 6, 1952. The Selma Park wharf was demolished shortly afterwards. The Sechelt dance pavilion was sold in 1954 to Morgan Thompson and Bill Parsons, and in November of that year they celebrated the grand opening of their Sechelt Men's Wear in the centre section of the building. But within two years Union Estates' general store, which had been the main attraction for trade on the Boulevard, closed, and Thompson and Parsons moved their business to Cowrie Street. The old general store was demolished in 1965; the Royal Terraces condominiums stand on that site today. On May 27, 1971, the dance pavilion, like so many of Sechelt's landmarks, was destroyed by fire.

Sechelt became a municipality in February 1956. The vote had been close: 86 in favour of incorporation and 71 against. In the election on April 14, five commissioners were elected: Christine Johnston, Bernel Gordon, Sam Dawe, Alex Lamb and Frank Parker. Mrs. Johnston, who topped the polls, became chairman. A small building that had been used by the Bank of Montreal was moved onto municipal property at Inlet and Mermaid and on November 24, the same day that power was switched on for Cowrie Street's new street lights, it was formally opened as the Sechelt Municipal Hall. It was replaced in 1966 and enlarged in 1981. The municipality was increased in size in 1990 by including Sandy Hook, Tuwanek, Selma Park and Davis Bay. After Sechelt voters approved the construction of a new library on Block 7 of L.303 in 1993, the plan was adapted to add a new municipal hall above the library; the library and new municipal hall were officially opened in November 1996.

During the later 1950s when the condition of the Trail Bay wharf had deteriorated again, government officials decided that a wharf was no longer necessary in Trail Bay because the Black Ball Ferry Service had made other scheduled water transport to the Sunshine Coast obsolete. They suggested the Trail Bay wharf should be put up for sale, but before that could happen, it was badly damaged in a storm in April 1960 and closed to all traffic except that of the oil company whose pipeline still snaked its way to the end of the wharf. During the next decade it suffered the regular battering of winter storms but continued to stand, a gaunt reminder of a bygone era. Then on June 10, 1970, vandals set it on fire, and although the fire was put out before the flames reached the oil pipes, the wharf was now both an eyesore and a hazard to the community. A year later it was sold to Sechelt Marina Resort Limited, a joint venture of Vic Walters and Rivtow Marine Limited, which intended to demolish it and construct a new wharf in collaboration with the oil company. Before it could be torn down, vandals again set it on fire. As a result, Rivtow barged in a crane in December 1971 and removed the entire wharf, including the pilings. By this time the oil company had made other arrangements and no new wharf was built. The lease for the water lot was cancelled in June 1976. In 2000 the Sechelt Downtown Business Association (SDBA) spearheaded a drive for a new Sechelt pier close to the site of the original wharf. Construction Aggregates Ltd., which was enlarging its loading facility in Trail Bay at this time, funded most of the construction costs for a foot-traffic pier, which was then enhanced by the establishment of a park on the site of Whitaker's second hotel.

SECHELT INLET

Although the village of Sechelt was from the first primarily tourist-oriented, a good portion of its prosperity always came from the logging industry, especially from the handlogging and timber leases that bordered the inland sea. In the Porpoise Bay area, however, much of the timber taken out actually came from pre-emptions. Only months before Alfred and Bert Whitaker filed on their L.1473 pre-emption south of Snake Bay in 1892, Edward R. Taylor had pre-empted L.1509 to the southwest of it and just north of the small Indian Reserve #3. Taylor quickly built a log hut and began taking off the timber, rafting it out to mills in Vancouver through the Skookumchuck. In six months he had cleared enough land to qualify for his Crown grant. To Taylor's west on L.1472, James Young was logging at the same rate. Albert Parsons filed on L.1437 to the south of Taylor and Indian Reserve #3 and built a wharf there in order to berth the boat that he used to boom the logs taken off his property. L.1437 later became the site of Jiro Konishi's farm. In the 1930s the portion of L.1437 lying within the southwest corner of Shoal and Reef roads became the farm of an elderly couple, E.J. Scattergood and his wife Isabella. The Scattergoods had raised goats in the northern town of McBride, and having decided to retire to the coast, solved the problem of transporting their goats to their new home by herding them all the way south to Kamloops then west through the Pemberton valley to Squamish. They became known to their new neighbours as the Scattergoats.

Herman Carlson was an exception to the general run of pre-emptors on Porpoise Bay because the land he chose on August 28, 1909—L.3047 lying on the west side of the inlet between "Little Rocky Point" (Piper Point) and the outcrop that is today known as Carlson Point—had already been designated as someone else's timber lease. But Carlson, who had lived in the Sechelt area for some five years at this point, chose his land, not for its timber, but as a homesite for himself, his wife Otilie, and his five sons—Ellis, Ivar, Eric, Gustaf and Axel. All of the men of the family were in demand for their carpentry and boatbuilding skills, but Ellis, the eldest, (also known in the Swedish tradition as Ellis Hermanson rather than Carlson) is remembered best for building the Whitakers' Beach House and for supervising the construction of Our Lady of Lourdes Church on the Sechelt Indian Reserve. Herman Carlson died in 1911 and his pre-emption was taken over by his wife. When she received her Crown grant on September 22, 1913, the family house was valued at $950, with workshops, storerooms, stables, haybarns and chicken houses at $450; 14 acres were under cultivation. The family was very popular locally, and their friends often boated out to visit them for afternoon tea. The entire family, however, left the Sunshine Coast for the United States when Canada introduced conscription during World War I and they never returned. Years later the handlogging Solberg family took over the Carlson's homesite, and it was inhabited until 2002 by Bergliot "Bergie" Solberg, a well-known local eccentric.

On September 8, 1890, a pre-emption for a lot on the east side of Porpoise Bay was filed by Arthur M. Bouillon, the draftsman son of Joseph Bouillon, the architect for the Sechelt people's Our Lady of the Rosary Church. His claim was listed as L.1410, and his description placed it at the mouth of a small creek "known to the Indians as Aqualac Creek." In fact, the lot actually included the homes of Michael Paul of the Sechelt band and several of his relatives as well as 10 acres of cleared and cultivated land. Unfortunately, the site had not been designated a reserve by the commissions of 1876 or 1884. Bouillon burned the houses, built his own 16- by 20-foot log cabin and qualified for his Crown grant in September 1892 by claiming two cleared acres and two slashed acres. A few years later he abandoned it. It was pre-empted again on November 18, 1904, by David Stewart Gray who earned his Crown grant with two dwelling houses (presumably one of them had been built by Bouillon) and five cleared acres. As the result of this pre-emption, the creek became known as Gray Creek. In 1915, Michael Paul appealed to the royal commission for the restitution of his property but his appeal was denied.

In the 1960s Gray Creek became the water source for two small, water-access-only settlements, Sandy Hook at Four-Mile Point, which was subdivided into recreational lots in 1963, and Tuwanek, one mile farther up the inlet, sub-divided in 1960. The creek was designated as an alternate source of fresh water for the Sechelt municipal district around 1981, but it was not until 1985 that an intake was installed and a water main attached to integrate it into the fresh-water system for the district. In the 1980s the lower creek became the site of an important hatchery for the fish-farming industry, and in 1999 the hatchery was approved for the culture of sturgeon.

After Sechelt Inlet Road reached Sandy Hook and Tuwanek in the late 1960s, these settlements began attracting full-time residents; both were absorbed into the District Municipality of Sechelt in 1990. In 1993 members of the Sandy Hook Community Association, led by Gertrude Pacific, began pushing for protection for a portion of the second-growth hemlock and cedar forest on L.7148 that straddles the Inlet Road adjacent to Sandy Hook. In 1996 the BC government recognized it as a Heritage Interpretative Forest site, and since that time the community association has built and maintained bridges and walking trails there.

Except where it had been alienated for timber leases or Indian reserves, all of the land between Bouillon's L.1410 and Sechelt Indian Reserve #2 was pre-empted by loggers between 1890 and 1892. L.1557 which is crossed by Angus Creek was claimed by Joseph Gendron and crown granted on September 14, 1892. Gendron cut some of the timber but did not clear-cut it, and then sold it to Bert Whitaker. When Whitaker was suffering financial reverses around 1911, he sold the lot, as well as several more on the west side of Porpoise Bay, to Angus Crowston who was interested in the mineral potential of the upland area. But when Crowston was about to lose the property in 1945 for non-payment of taxes, it was his son Bruce and his daughter-in-law Doris who provided the money to save it. They also bought the lot next door, L.1558, established their home and a sawmill on it, then around 1956 leased the small Native reserve between the two lots in order to start a tourist campsite along the waterfronts of the reserve and L.1557 and L.1558. In 1966 the provincial government bought L.1557 from the Crowstons and it became Porpoise Bay Provincial Park five years later.

William Burch Smith filed on L.1652 north of Gendron's lot; it includes the gravel pit operated for many years by Pacific Rim Aggregates and then by Renco Concrete. L.1438 which today accommodates a row of light industrial enterprises was pre-empted by Jean Sirais and Crown granted on April 30, 1892. The site of the Sechelts' former village of Slahlt between Burnet and Angus creeks was a timber lease at this time, but it eventually became a subdivision called Porpoise Bay Estates.

SARGEANT BAY

Approximately three and a half miles northwest of the village of Sechelt lies a small bay known to old-time mariners as Norwest Bay but generally known to local people as Sargeant Bay in honour of its first pre-emptor, Frederick Sargeant, who filed at the head of the bay on L.1324 in May 1887, the same month that George Gibson registered his pre-emption in West Howe Sound. Much of his acreage was marshland that attracted a wide variety of bird and animal life, but Sargeant was determined to farm it and all his efforts went into clearing the timber, constructing dikes, a dam and floodgates, then into ditching and draining the land. By the time he received his Crown grant on October 21, 1890, he and his family were still living in a log hut worth just $20.

During the next 20 years the property was logged and a steam-driven sawmill was set up at the mouth of Colvin Creek, which empties into the bay. The next owners, the Fords, established a hunting and fishing lodge there with four small cabins for their visitors. Vancouver businessman Art Angell bought the lot in 1961 and laid out a subdivision called Welcome Woods on the upland, but when he began dredging the marsh and diverting the creek mouth to construct a marina, the Sunshine Coast Regional District refused him a permit to continue. Angell sold to the Sargeant Bay Marina Corporation in 1983, and this company developed a sophisticated plan for a high-density subdivision. The project was thwarted by the determined opposition of the Sargeant Bay Society, and on October 16, 1989, the provincial Ministry of Parks bought the lot for a park. Since that time the Society has worked to return the property to its original state and encourage natural plant and animal life.

HALFMOON BAY

North of Sargeant Bay on the mainland opposite the Thormanby Islands, on August 11, 1891, James Rawding arrived to pre-empt L.1327, along with his friend, Ephraim Walker, who filed on L.1326, securing for themselves the beautiful shore that is now known as Welcome Beach. In a very astute move, Rawding then promptly purchased a further 160 acres in a long narrow lot (1427) along the coast to the north, adjoining his L.1327, thereby acquiring the entire Redrooffs shoreline from Welcome Beach to Halfmoon Bay.

In 1909 James Rawding sold L.1427 to the partnership of B.G. Wolfe-Merton and Hubert Kitchin who constructed the summer resort known as Redrooffs, the name deriving from the fact that all their cabins had red roofs. (The double "ff" comes from the old English spelling of the word.) They built six log houses and a road as far as Halfmoon Bay the first year then later built another half-dozen cabins in the adjoining Arbutus Bay area. By 1912 they were also operating a store called the Redrooffs Trading Post. The new resort's dock became a regular stopping place for the Union Steamships passenger boats that were now providing competition for Whitaker's Sechelt Steamship Line. In 1914 the dock was washed away in a storm, and until it was replaced by a government wharf in 1920, residents were forced to row out in small boats to meet the coastal steamers. The Halfmoon Bay area was not connected to the rest of the peninsula by road until 1928.

After Hubert Kitchin died around 1930, his widow married Peter Millan, and Millan added a recreation hall to the Redrooffs complex. The Millans sold the property in 1937, but it reverted to them when the buyer, Tom McKay, was unable to keep up the payments. A few years later, they sold it again, this time to Karl S. Bell who brought in Frank Lyons as cottages manager and his wife as dining-room manager; in 1942 he began subdividing and selling off the property. The part that held the old Kitchin-Millan house was acquired in 1955 by Jim Cooper of Vancouver, and he ran the property as a trailer court until the SCRD bought it. When the buildings were razed, the new park created in their place was christened Cooper's Green.

Just north of Halfmoon Bay lies Smuggler Cove, so-named because a smuggler of Chinese immigrants named Kelly, also known as the King of Smugglers, is rumoured to have evaded arrest by hiding there. The cove was also used as a storage area for liquor manufactured on Texada Island during the US Prohibition years. From there it was loaded into fast boats and smuggled across the border. In 1971 Smuggler Cove became a Class A provincial marine park.

MERRY ISLAND

Merry Island lies three nautical miles from Halfmoon Bay between Welcome Passage and Malaspina Strait, both of them major arteries for seagoing commerce. In November 1902 the federal government established a lighthouse on the southeast point of the island, a 57-foot-high, square white building with a fixed white beacon on top. Will Franklin, the first lightkeeper, found it a labour-intensive job as he was given only a hand-held foghorn to warn passing ships of danger. As he was paid a mere $360 a year, he and his wife, Mary Ann, pre-empted the remainder of the island and farmed it with flocks of sheep, ducks, turkeys and chickens. He retired as lightkeeper in February 1932 but retained ownership of the island until 1954. His replacement as lightkeeper was World War I veteran E.J. Leclerc; when, seven years later, he became too ill to continue, his wife, Helen, and two teenaged sons took over the job. They were replaced a year later by W.C. Copeland followed by George Potts in 1950. In September 1954 Potts and his wife, Diana, launched their skiff into heavy seas to successfully rescue the crew of the American vessel *Neama*, which had struck a reef near Pender Harbour. Four months later Potts saved the crew of the motor vessel *Paige*, which had gone aground on a nearby islet during a raging southeast gale. Potts was honoured at a ceremony at Government House in Victoria where he was presented with a citation from the Royal Canadian Humane Society.

The first Merry Island lighthouse was replaced in 1966—this time with a square, white, 40-foot tower with a red lantern on top that produces a flash every 15 seconds. At the same time electrical and telephone cables were laid to the island. Statistics compiled in 1987 showed that between 1979 and the end of 1985 the station had provided visual searches for the Rescue Coordination Center 39 times, performed rescues or towed disabled craft 13 times, and provided repairs or fuel to disabled craft 11 times. The lightkeeper since 1985 has been Don Richards and the station is managed by the Canadian Coast Guard Pacific Region. Merry Island remains privately owned except for the light station.

PENDER HARBOUR

Pender Harbour has never been a single settlement like Sechelt or Roberts Creek or Gibsons. It is, instead, a collection of settlements bordering an intricately indented body of water, and for the first 50 years of their existence, the only means of communication between them was by boat and a few trails through the bush. As a result, the Harbour became locally known as "the Venice of the North."

When the first tourists arrived in Pender Harbour on a Union Steamships excursion boat on July 18, 1891, there was already a wharf, a store-cum-post office, and a hotel of sorts waiting for them. The proprietor was an Englishman named Charles Irvine, merchant and postmaster, and his place of business, known as Irvine's Landing, was on the point of land that guards the north side of the entrance to Pender Harbour. Irvine is reputed to have purchased the 160-acre property from "a Chinese trader" some five years earlier, which may be true since there is no record of a pre-emption in his name. He made a living at first by providing supplies for logging operations in Jervis Inlet, but the arrival of the Union Steamships excursion boats improved his prospects immediately. The ships paid docking fees to use his landing, and the picnickers bought drinks and candy before they hiked off to Hotel Lake to eat their picnic lunches, then dig clams on the Harbour's beaches.

Union Steamships' *Comox* began a regular logging camp run that same year, at first stopping occasionally at Irvine's Landing but within a few years making it a regular port of call. Irvine sold out shortly after the turn of the century to John and George West who in 1904 sold 80 acres of the land plus the buildings to Joe Gonsalves, a former sailor and fisherman from the Madeira Islands. Gonsalves had been living on Brockton Point in what is now Stanley Park, where he had met and married Susan Harris, a member of

The hotel and store belonging to Gonsalves and Dames at Irvine's Landing, Pender Harbour, about 1920. Theodore Dames' house on the far left, the hotel in the centre, and the store on the right at the head of the wharf.
COURTESY OF SUNSHINE COAST MUSEUM AND ARCHIVES. PHOTO #764.

the North Vancouver Salish nation, but a land dispute had prompted him to uproot his growing family and move them to Irvine's Landing. And it was the beauty of Gonsalves' daughter Matilda that prompted a Russian seaman named Theodore Dames to follow the family there and become Gonsalves' partner. Together Gonsalves and Dames built a large hotel, then a saloon at the head of the wharf. Afterwards they sent to Vancouver for Joe Perry, a huge black man whom Gonsalves had befriended, and they installed him as saloon bouncer and handyman. Ida (Donley) Higgs recalled Perry "special ordering" overalls from her father's store; when they arrived from the city, she and her young brother played hide and seek in them, using the legs for tunnels.

Gonsalves and Dames were not alone in Pender Harbour. A small colony of Scottish fishermen lived on Fishermen's or "Bolshevikie" Island in Gerrans Bay, one of the many branches of Pender Harbour. Each summer these men sailed north to Knight Inlet to fish, but in winter they fished within daily range of Pender Harbour, sometimes selling their catch to a floating cannery in Jervis Inlet and sometimes to the P.H. Alder Cannery in Bargain Bay, on the other side of Bargain Narrows. Gonsalves and Dames could count on them as customers during the winter, while in the summer the excursionists brought revenue into both store and hotel. When logging came to Pender Harbour a few years later, they acquired a fresh captive clientele, and among the loggers, the Harbour became known as the Land of Portuguese Joe in honour of Joe Gonsalves

By this time there were also a number of Japanese families and a colony of Scottish farmers and fishermen living on Francis Peninsula opposite Fishermen's Island. It was a hard life for them, scratching a living in difficult soil, with the result that the area acquired the name "Hardscratch." A 32-year-old ex-boxer and machine shop genius named Hiram Eugene Dusenbury arrived in the harbour in 1905 and bought an island in Gerrans Bay on which to set up a machine shop and boat repair business. The island soon became known as Dusenbury Island, and when local fishermen began equipping their boats with Easthope engines, they made regular trips there for repairs. Dusenbury also invented a direct-reverse, four-cycle boat engine that was used locally.

Meanwhile, in September 1907 a man named Robert Donley had pre-empted L.1866 in Bargain Bay just south of the unoccupied Bargain Harbour Indian Reserve and the by-now-vacant P.H. Alder Cannery building. A steam engineer from Detroit, he had come west after losing an arm when an engine exploded and spent nearly 10 years exploring the coast before he found the Harbour. Donley returned to Detroit to marry, and he and his bride, Margaret Scott Donley, spent their first winter together in a tent on their pre-emption. Their nearest neighbours were Japanese shingle bolt cutters working just northeast of the reserve. The bolt cutters' camp was not a large one and it lacked the customary Japanese *ofuru* or bathhouse, so every evening the loggers would rush naked down the hill to bathe in the ocean. As soon as he heard them coming, Donley would thrust his wife into their tent where she waited modestly until the coast was clear again.

When Donley's pre-emption was disallowed in the spring of 1908 because he was not a British citizen, he bought Edgecombe Island at the mouth of Bargain Bay and a small piece of land on the southeast corner of Francis

Peninsula, part of the 1889 pre-emption of Michael Schilke, Crown granted in April 1891. Donley and his wife settled there to raise chickens, and he marketed the eggs by paddling canoe-loads of them out to passing steamers for delivery to Vancouver. After six years on the farm, he moved his family—which now included daughter Ida and son William—to Pender Harbour where he built a store and a wharf at the point of land still remembered by old-timers as Donley's Landing (off Hassan Road). Donley became the agent for the All Red Line whose ships were now making daily runs between Powell River and Vancouver in competition with Union Steamships, which docked its ships across the Harbour at Irvine's Landing. He did a good business provisioning the fishermen and their families while at the same time serving as fish buyer for the Crown Fish Company of Vancouver. Around 1915 he built a smokehouse on pilings over the harbour and bought herring to make into kippers; for years he supplied them to Woodwards Stores in Vancouver. He held onto his fish-buying monopoly until 1920 when a man named Pope set up a buying station at a landing just west of his own.

William F. Rouse, who had been a smelter worker in Nanaimo, arrived on his little tugboat *May* in Earls Cove on July 4, 1909. With him were his wife Maryann and his eight children. They moved into a derelict cabin on a deserted pre-emption and homesteaded there for three years before hooking the *May* onto the floathouse they had built to tow it into Bargain Bay where they had bought 12 acres of the old Schilke pre-emption on Francis Peninsula. Here Rouse, who was now in his late 60s, beachcombed while his wife,

The Warnock family fleet of fishing vessels in Bargain Harbour. 1946. The larger craft are seiners.
COURTESY OF THE SUNSHINE COAST MUSEUM AND ARCHIVES. PHOTO #595.

who was a midwife, looked after birthing for the whole community. Their daughter Martha married Martin Warnock, an engineer and head loader for P.B. Anderson Logging, and in 1919 these two brought their young family to settle on the peninsula overlooking Bargain Bay. Warnock and his sons became fishermen, their first boats being the *Kerry W*, built by Harry Volmers of Nanaimo, and the *Kerry Jr.*, and eventually they developed the largest of the local fleets of fishboats. After they acquired a contract to provide Woodwards of Vancouver with fresh codfish on Fridays, they would fish all week using live tanks; then as the father drove the boat to the city, the sons would kill and clean the fish so that it arrived absolutely fresh.

The only major pocket of rich arable land in this area lies at the head of Pender Harbour where the Klein family lived. They had arrived from the American south as early as 1911 at which time they began filing pre-emptions, and although the sons of the family, John, Fred, Pete and Bill, were primarily loggers and miners, they took full advantage of the soil at "Kleindale" to grow family gardens. Today their land is occupied by Roosendale Farms, which markets hydroponically grown tomatoes and cucumbers.

As in Gibson's Landing, there were young men in Pender Harbour who fled when the Military Service Bill of June 1917 was enacted by Canada's parliament. They built cabins in the valley between Sakinaw and Ruby lakes and lived there until after the end of the war, only coming down into Pender Harbour in the dead of night to buy supplies. At Donley's store it was Mrs. Donley who served them, her husband having decided that if he knew nothing about them, he would not have to lie if questioned by the police. Donley had built a larger store at his landing in 1915 and donated the smaller one to the community for a school. Eight students were required to qualify for a teacher, and since there were only seven of the necessary age living in the Harbour, Donley's daughter Ida, still just five years of age, was enrolled to fill the quota. The first teacher was a Miss Gordon.

By 1920 the population had outgrown the school, and Donley donated land for a new and larger one. Martin Warnock beachcombed the logs, towed them to a sawmill on Texada, then towed the finished lumber back to the Harbour. A work bee that included the Warnocks, Kleins, Donleys and all the inhabitants of Hardscratch had the new schoolhouse ready for the fall term. Ida Donley and Cedric Meyers were the first graduates of the Pender Harbour School; she was 13, he was 15.

Pender Harbour was connected to Sechelt by telegraph as early as 1910, while the trail along the telegraph line was for many years the only land access to points south. The telegraph office was located at Irvine's Landing.

By the 1920s a new kind of tourist had come to Pender Harbour—private yacht owners. For nearly 20 years the 50-foot *Aquila,* owned by the Rogers family of sugar refinery fame, arrived in Pender Harbour every June and departed in September. Some of the yachters also built summer homes on sites around the Harbour; the Rogers home near Garden Bay was a magnet for half of Vancouver's society element. Novelist Bertrand "Bill" Sinclair first came to the Harbour as a tourist on his boat *Who Who* in 1917, then rented a cabin for the winter while he completed a new novel; in 1922 he bought property on Sinclair Bay and built a home of his own. His presence attracted writing and boating friends from California, including Stewart Edward White in the 60-foot *Dawn,* Robert and Kathrene Pinkerton in the *Triton,* Lee Peck and Erle Stanley Gardner.

Author Bertrand Sinclair c. 1908. Sinclair bought property on Pender Harbour in 1922 and his presence there attracted other writing and yachting friends like Erle Stanley Gardner.
FROM THE AUTHORS' COLLECTION.

The Depression years brought desperately bad times to the communities around Pender Harbour. Like many others, Robert Donley lost his store and all his property in 1934 because he had given credit to people who now were destitute. Prices for logs and fish had plummeted and most of the men were on relief. After 1932 some of them went to the federal government's relief camps at Wood Bay and Silver Sands where they were put to work completing the road from Sechelt to Pender Harbour. The road reached Garden Bay and Irvine's Landing about 1936, but it was not paved until 1957.

Until some time after World War I there was no medical help available in the Pender Harbour area except for the services of midwife Maryann Rouse and an American doctor named Howard who settled in 1913 at the point where the Harbour narrows to become Gunboat Bay. Unfortunately, he was practising illegally as he had lost his licence for earlier malpractice, but since he had the only medical knowledge for miles around, his services were constantly in demand. He left the community around 1920 after a patient died and he was once more charged with malpractice.

In those days, loggers injured in Jervis Inlet or even down the coast as far as Halfmoon Bay would be taken by small boat as far as Irvine's Landing where they would be left in the freight shed until the next steamer arrived, perhaps a day later, in order to get to hospital in Vancouver. Too many of them died before a ship arrived, and in 1930 the logging and fishing communities resolved that a hospital must be built in Pender Harbour.

The first attempt to get a hospital began when the Reverend John Antle of the Columbia Coast Mission offered the community an unused float hospital that was anchored in O'Brian Bay, north of Port Hardy; Hiram Dusenbury spearheaded the drive to raise money to hire a towboat to bring the hospital to the Harbour, but when the towboat hit a storm in Johnstone Strait, the hospital buildings were lost. Undaunted, Dusenbury began raising funds again through box socials and dances, and R. "Barney" Bryneldsen Sr. of Hospital Bay donated several acres of land on which to build it. The community rallied to the cause, donating labour and materials, but just as construction got underway, real estate agent Henry Darling appeared on the scene to demand what they were doing on his property. It seems that the land Bryneldsen had so kindly donated was actually on the adjoining Darling property, but Darling relented when he learned what the community was trying to do and deeded the land for the first St. Mary's Hospital. The 12-bed hospital was officially opened on the north side of Pender Harbour at Garden Bay on August 16, 1930, with Lieutenant-Governor R.R. Bruce cutting the ribbon. Although medical staff came and went from the new hospital at an alarming rate, there was seldom a gap between doctors. Wilfred "Tiffy' Wray recalled a Dr. Ployart being the first, followed by Drs. Martinoff, Johnson, Connell, Pierce and Corbett. After World War II there were Drs. Victor Rogers, Friessen, Warren, Volen, Cripp, Hitchen, John Playfair, Alan Swan, Peter Stonier, Eric Paetkau, Walter Burtnick and Masterson.

By 1954 when Dr. Alan Swan joined Dr. John Playfair in Pender Harbour, it was apparent that the building had outlived its usefulness. He recalled that "there was no elevator and if you had to move people from downstairs to upstairs, you had to carry them around [the building] and in the back door and up the stairs. It certainly helped to have a couple of young doctors because there was no orderly. The lab was a little hole in the basement and the X-ray room was grossly inadequate . . . There was a plebiscite and the community voted over 90 percent—including Pender Harbour—to construct a new hospital. The old one was not only antiquated, it was in the wrong place. The centre of population [by this time] was in Roberts Creek, though the centre of the area geographically is Halfmoon Bay. So they compromised with Sechelt and the land was donated by the Sechelt Indian Band, which must never be forgotten."[3] The Pender Harbour hospital closed when the new one opened in December 1964.

After World War II the number of yachts frequenting the Harbour grew, and so did the number of marinas. In time more than a dozen large yacht clubs and many small marinas began operating in the Harbour's small bays and coves, attracting so many visiting boaters that they often outnumber the tourists who arrive by car.

St. Mary's Hospital on Hospital Bay at Pender Harbour on its dedication day in August 1930.
COURTESY OF THE SUNSHINE COAST MUSEUM AND ARCHIVES. PHOTO #136.

EGMONT

The story of the settlement of Egmont, just north of the Skookumchuck Narrows on Sechelt Inlet, is the story of an amazing collection of rugged individualists, beginning with Joseph Sylvey, sometimes known as Joseph Silvia Simmonds, who was born around 1828 on Pico Island in the Azores and arrived on the West Coast around 1860. His second wife was a Sechelt Native woman, Lucy Kwatleematt. According to legend, sometime during the late 1880s, he spent several years living in one of the bays near Egmont Point and fishing in Jervis Inlet. After Joseph Silvey's time there, the story of the Egmont settlement straddles the Inlet because newcomers clustered first on one side of it, then the other. On the west side the first large parcel of land was purchased during the 1890s by a Captain Archibald who sailed on the Empress liners. In his absence his property—200 acres stretching from Secret Bay (later known as Co-op Bay) south to Waugh Lake—was managed by the brothers George and Percy Garrett. Shortly after the turn of the century, this property was acquired by an American, Miss Viola Fuller, who became Mrs. Waugh (hence the name of the lake) and finally Mrs. Points.

The first resident on the east side of the Skookumchuck was John Wray who arrived in 1903 after it was rumoured that a fish cold storage plant would be built there. Since Wray had pre-empted three years earlier on Nelson Island a mile north of Fearney Point and had not yet fulfilled his Crown grant requirements, he could be no more than a squatter on the new site. Meanwhile, his eldest son, Jack Wray, had pre-empted on the west side of the inlet; he and his father and brothers then made their living handlogging and fishing. When the fish plant had not materialized by 1906, John Wray moved back to Fearney Point where he received his Crown grant on October 19, 1910.

Joseph Silvey's second son, also Joseph, who was born in 1879 at Nanaimo, returned to Egmont in 1904 with his wife, Maria King, and two children and bought 40 acres on the Egmont waterfront next to Mrs. Points' property. He and his sons handlogged, seined for salmon and trolled for ling cod. Two years after the Silveys' arrival, George Vaughn, an American, moved into the cabin vacated by the Garrett brothers, and he became Silvey's handlogging partner. Six years later Vaughn married Mary Elizabeth Gaynor, and in 1914 their son Johnny was the first white child born in the community. When fire destroyed the homes of both the Silveys and the Vaughns, they moved to the east side of the Skookumchuck. The present-day Lafarge gravel pit at Earle Creek just outside the rapids is on the site of the Vaughn property. Silvey pre-empted just south of Indian Reserve #26 fronting the inlet. Alfred Jeffrey filed on the land east of Silvey so that the two properties surrounded the small reserve on three sides. Although Jeffrey's mother was a member of the Sechelt band, he was in constant conflict with the reserve's inhabitants and finally strung barbed wire to keep them out. Joseph Silvey died in Egmont in 1940 but his descendants still live in the Egmont area.

"Tug" Wilson and a man named Yungblundt, a pair of roughhewn loggers and ex-British cavalry officers who had seen service in the Gold Coast, India and South Africa, arrived in Agamemnon Channel in 1912 and took pre-emptions around Killarney Lake. They had built fine log homes and were horse logging the timber on their property when war was declared in 1914, and both left to join up again. Yungblundt's niece, Nelly, who had been part of his household, went to Vancouver where she met Tom Earl when she was visiting war wounded at Shaughnessy Hospital. They married and returned to Agamemnon Channel where they made their home in the little bay that came to be called Earls Cove. In time it became the southern terminus for the ferry to Powell River. Yungblundt was killed overseas, but his brother—Nelly's father—took over his pre-emption. Tug Wilson survived the war but spent his remaining days in Princeton, BC, as the proprietor of the pool hall.

In the spring of 1912 John Wray's brother Walter arrived at the Skookumchuck to pre-empt next to John's briefly held homesite. Walter Wray built four large chicken houses and a smokehouse, fenced his property against invasion by deer and was soon loading crates of eggs into his boat each week to row them the 16 miles to Pender Harbour to meet the Vancouver-bound boat. A third brother, George Wray, joined the Egmont community in 1914, and took up 80 acres between the Vaughns and his brother Walter.

A school was built in 1917 beside Joe Silvey's home on the east side of the inlet with a Miss King as the first teacher; however, the community had trouble keeping teachers since they boarded at Walter Wray's house next to the rapids and had to row to and from the schoolhouse against the strong tides. It was George Wray who finally took on the government contract to construct a mile of eight-foot-wide trail along the shore past the rapids so the teacher and others could get to the school on foot.

William Griffiths, his wife and six children came to Egmont in 1920 when his 25-foot sailboat was blown off course on a trip from his pre-emption on Cortes Island to Vancouver. The family took over a deserted cabin just east of Egmont Point on the east side of the inlet. The cabin had been built of unpeeled fir logs in 1914 and by this time colonies of ants had eaten half the wood away, but the Griffiths family stayed on, with William supporting them by fishing. Several of the local rowboat fishermen came to help him cut a trail through the bush to Joe Silvey's property so that the Griffiths children could attend school. However, by 1921 there were not enough children living on that side of the inlet and the school had to be closed.

The first store in Egmont had been a temporary one run by a Japanese Canadian named Nakashima who bought fish from the local fishermen and supplied them with groceries. The first permanent store was built in 1917 by Walter Wray and Alfred Jeffrey for Leonard Bailey on the foreshore of Joe Silvey's property near the school. Then Wray, who took over as store manager, applied for a post office, and although the area was generally known as the Skookumchuck, he listed its name as Egmont. When the post office was granted, the community also officially took the name. When Bailey sold the store to another Japanese Canadian, George Hatashita, in 1921, Walter

Wray convinced the government that no "alien Japanese" could hold public office, and he put the post office onto a float and towed it to his own place. That same year, after a telephone line was strung from tree to tree along the west shore of Sechelt Inlet all the way to Egmont, Wray also took over the job of operating the local telephone system. However, the line was constantly being cut by falling trees, and finally a deadhead sticking up from a boom of logs broke the line where it hung low over the rapids. This time the government refused to repair it. The local fishermen found a great many uses for the wire.

Walter Wray earned Crown grant status on his pre-emption in 1916 but left in 1925 for Nelson Island's Vanguard Bay where he became a justice of the peace. His Egmont property was bought by Colonel Codville who also took over the job of postmaster.

In 1921 government surveyors arrived in Egmont to map the available Crown lands in the hope of attracting returned soldiers; instead the survey prompted a general rearrangement of the existing inhabitants that saw the Vaughns and Griffiths moving to the west side of the inlet to make sure their children got an education. Volunteers then built a cedar-shake-clad schoolhouse, locating it behind the Vaughns' house because their children were the youngest.

Old Egmont on the east side of the inlet in 1922. The store on the left was built by Walter Wray in 1916 and sold to George Hatashita who installed a fish-buying station on floats with live fish tanks. Along the waterfront at the far right are Native cabins.
COURTESY OF THE SUNSHINE COAST MUSEUM AND ARCHIVES.
PHOTO #1212 BY E.S. CLAYTON.

Their teacher was Miss Vert Chesney who had previously taught at St. Vincent Bay in Jervis Inlet.

Meanwhile, Union Steamships had decided it was too risky to deliver the mail to Colonel Codville's post office because it was too close to the Skookumchuck, so mail delivery was made from Pender Harbour by gas-boat to the west side of the inlet, then by rowboat to the other side. This remained the situation until 1931 when George Hatashita at last became postmaster and returned the post office to the store building from which it had been taken 10 years earlier. By this time, he and his family had also established a successful fish-buying business there, despite the fact that two other Japanese fish buyers, Nobukichi Takai and a man named Maeda, had brought in another store on a float and installed it directly in front of his store. After a few years, Hatashita's daughter Kay took over his store and post office, and a young man named Ted Hyashi was sent to renovate the store and add living quarters upstairs. Takai's sons came to take over the other store and fish-buying business, and they became very popular with the local fishermen.

In January 1942 after Canada declared war on Japan, the local people petitioned to have the post office removed from Hatashita's store, and the job went to Imer Beamish who built a cabin for it on a float and tied it up near the store. Shortly after this the Canadian government began forcibly removing all Japanese from the coastal area, giving each family just 24-hours' notice to vacate. In early March, Nobukichi Takai, fearing that his store and fish-buying floats would be stolen or vandalized in his absence, sold them for $2,000 to Queen Charlotte Fisheries, although they had been assessed at $6,200. Then on the night of March 14 each household in Egmont was awakened by Ted Hyashi and the young Takai boys coming to ask their neighbours to settle their accounts with the store before eight the next morning as they were to be taken away at that time. But since the people of Egmont operated by the tides and not the time, they had ignored the introduction of daylight saving time, and when they arrived to pay their bills, the Japanese families had already been taken into custody. Mr. Nakashima, by now an old-timer in the community, had escaped in his boat to avoid internment, but he was found and arrested.

Queen Charlotte Fisheries, which acquired Hatashita's store from the Custodian of Enemy Alien Properties, hired two local fishermen, Herbert "Murphy" Madsen and Dave Mowat, to run both stores so that the local people could continue to get supplies. During a drinking bout one night, the two men ran out of booze and continued their party with the liquid in some interesting brown bottles they found in the store. It turned out to be bleach and Mowat, who had ulcers, died. After the war the fish-buying businesses and stores were sold and resold, finally ending up in the hands of Angus Lutz.

After the Japanese Canadian fish buyers left, Egmont's fishermen formed a co-op, choosing as their base seven acres of land at Secret Bay. It had belonged to Mrs. Points, but she had been unable to keep up with the taxes during the Depression and it had reverted to the government. LM & N Logging (Longacre, Moore and Neufeld), which held the timber rights on the remainder of the Points property, levelled the land in exchange for permission to build their crew quarters there, and the co-op then installed a scow and floats and an onshore cabin for their fish buyer. A consumers' co-op store was established nearby along with a house for the manager. About this time the government, having been petitioned by Angus Lutz for help in improving his floats on the east side of the inlet, instead installed a large float and pier in Co-op Bay. Home Oil followed by setting up its tanks beside the co-op store. Rivalry for the job of postmaster then developed between Imer Beamish and the co-op's manager, Percy Crowe-Swords; the co-op manager won and the post office moved to the west shore where most of the community now lived. This was, said postal authorities, *positively* the last time the post office would be moved. A new and larger school was built on the co-op property about this time. The co-op closed in 1954 and was sold to John and Lily Dunlop.

A road connecting the settlement of Egmont to the rest of the peninsula was finished in 1956, and a year later the provincial government set aside 35 hectares to preserve the wilderness area adjacent to Skookumchuck Narrows. This park was enlarged to 88 hectares in 1987, the same year that the salmon-farming company Scantech Ltd. established a 5,000-square-foot fish processing plant in Egmont. However, despite the resulting population influx, the character of the community has not altered appreciably.

DORISTON

The settlement of Doriston on the west side of Sechelt Inlet just inside Skookumchuck Narrows began when Bert Whitaker established a sawmill there at the turn of the century, but the first permanent settler was a man named Shaw who gave his name to the small cove there. It was after Shaw left in 1914 to join the army that Sam Lloyd brought his family to live in the cove and renamed the growing farming, logging and fishing community after his daughter Doris. As the community grew, Lloyd became postmaster, rowing to Sechelt and back once a week to collect the mail; he was paid $60 a year. His wife became the local telephone operator after the line was strung along the shore from Sechelt to Egmont. In 1923 the Jardine family arrived from Sweden with their young sons, Gunnar and Martin. Using only hand tools the family built themselves rowboats before they realized that they needed bigger boats for salmon fishing. The rails that they used to haul their boats up onto the beach for repairs and maintenance were still in place at the turn of the 21st century. After World War I, there were enough children in the settlement to start a school; the teacher was Gladys Rose. In the 1930s the four daughters of cod fisherman Bill Anderson were among the children in the school, although the family lived further inside the Skookumchuck, halfway between Doriston and Egmont. One summer day in 1938 three of the girls—teenagers Mary, Ruth and Betty—set out for Egmont in a small boat. Left behind at home was the second daughter, Doris. Later that day a fisherman coming through the rapids found a boat floating upside down in slack water and towed it home. The girls' bodies were never recovered; the only thing found was a pail with a smaller one sealed inside it that the girls had been taking to the store to buy ice cream. The family moved to Sechelt shortly afterwards.

When the Gilmour family arrived in 1934, the teacher was living in the house on the waterfront that they had come to buy. Since there was no other house available for her, they paid $200 to buy a 32-acre piece of nearby Crown land with 1,000 feet of waterfront and proceeded to scrounge home-building materials: bricks from an abandoned brickworks at Storm Bay just inside Narrows Inlet, lumber from an old logging bunkhouse, and plumbing pipe from an abandoned steam donkey they found in the woods of Narrows Inlet. A water wheel on a nearby creek provided electricity. The elder Gilmours died in the 1950s, but although the settlement became largely depopulated during the next decade, their two bachelor sons, Donald and George, remained for another 40 years, sometimes logging or fishing, but mostly busy with construction projects like George's 40-foot trailer and Don's massive electric organ.

HOTHAM SOUND

For the entire north end of the Sechelt peninsula, the epitome of civilized elegance was deemed to be in Hotham Sound. There a Kentuckian named Tacket had retired about 1895, built himself a rambling, split-cedar house, surrounded it with gardens and fruit trees and settled down to spend his remaining days in splendid isolation. His retirement was only slightly disturbed by the arrival of the Hollingsworth family around 1898. Robert Hollingsworth pre-empted in a cove south of Freil Falls, naming it Granville Bay in honour of his first son. The house he built for his family was the grandest one in the entire area with extensive gardens sloping down to the sea. There, Mrs. Hollingsworth served meals on linen tablecloths with a full silver service, including silver napkin rings, and provided her guests with white sheets on their beds—even when the guests were rough miners or loggers. And she entertained them by playing her piano, one of only two in the entire area.

All of the accessible, high quality, mature timber in Princess Louisa Inlet was logged during the first decade of the 20th century, so when writer Erle Stanley Gardner first visited it in the 1930s, most of the scars had healed, and he was enchanted with what he saw. "There is a calm tranquility," he wrote, "which stretches from the smooth surface of the reflecting waters straight into infinity. There is no scenery in the world that can beat it. Not that I've seen the rest of the world, but I don't need to. I've seen Princess Louisa."[4]

Only one pre-emptor ever established a home in the inlet. He was Charles Roscoe Johnstone who had been working at the slate quarry at Deserted Bay when he filed on L.4212 on the north shore of Princess Louisa in October 1910. Here he built a three-room house for his family and cleared two acres for a garden. He received his Crown grant in December 1916 but apparently lived there only until the end of World War I. The Johnstones' only neighbour was a deserter from the Prussian army named Herman Casper who had arrived in the early years of the century and built himself a cabin beside the rapids. Although he would later claim to own the land, Casper was a squatter, subsisting for close to 40 years on handlogging. His hobby was providing a home for stray cats and he is reputed to have had as many as 26 of them at one time. He was a well-educated man, an amateur musician and composer, and a clever mechanic and handyman, and although it might have been lonely there during winter's protracted storms, in summer Casper was visited by every boater, logger and fisherman who came up Jervis.

The summer of 1919 brought a friend from Germany who was accompanied by a 38-year-old Californian named James Frederick Macdonald. "Mac," as he is known in Jervis Inlet legends, had a shell marl mine in Nevada. He fell in love with Princess Louisa Inlet and in 1927, having amassed a fortune, filed for a Crown grant on the 45 acres of logged-off land beside Chatterbox Falls at the head of the inlet. However, since he was not a British subject, it cost him $420.

Macdonald hired the McNaughton family to build a home for him beside the waterfall. John McNaughton and his sons Bill and Don handlogged in Queen's Reach and had become expert axemen; the house they created for Macdonald with their axes in the next two summers was a work of art. "The whole thing, inside and out," wrote M. Wylie Blanchet in *The Curve of Time*, "was made of peeled cedar logs—fifteen and twenty inches in diameter."[5] The main room was 40 by 20 feet and featured an enormous granite fireplace. A kitchen, bedroom and bathroom were also on this ground floor. A stairway led up to a balcony that overlooked the living room, and led to two more bedrooms and another bathroom. All of the furniture, including a huge couch in front of the fireplace and a massive dining table, had been hand-hewn from logs.

It was here for the next 11 years that Macdonald entertained visiting yachtsmen, including actors John Barrymore, Ronald Colman, William Powell, and Mack Sennett. Unfortunately, Macdonald's beautiful home in the wilderness burned to the ground in 1940 and it was not rebuilt. Instead, since he always spent his winters in California, he chose to have a floathouse built and moored beside his Princess Louisa property for his summertime use. In the winter it was generally towed into Pender Harbour.

The third entrepreneur to fall under Princess Louisa's spell had more resources than either of his predecessors. Thomas F. Hamilton, the inventor of the variable pitch propellor and partner in Hamilton Beech Aircraft Limited, first saw Louisa in the mid-1930s, and the beauty of the little inlet inspired him to plan the most luxurious resort the BC coast has ever seen: the Malibu Club. He began working toward this goal by negotiating to buy all the old Crown grants surrounding the inlet. Herman Casper, who was ready to retire to the city, negotiated a deal for his squatter's rights with Hamilton. Macdonald, however, refused to sell.

On the point of land on the north side of Malibu Rapids Hamilton spent $2,000,000 to build a sprawling, rustic log chalet with its own power plant, nine-hole golf course, volleyball and tennis courts. Barge-loads of sand were brought in to create beaches. For $250 a day, guests were provided with accommodation, gourmet meals, and the use of an assortment of boats from canoes to small yachts. A ski lift to the 4,000-foot level of nearby Mount Helena never materialized, however, for after just two years' operation, the Malibu Club closed its doors. World War II had erupted and the millionaires that Hamilton had anticipated becoming his clientele were too preoccupied with making guns and planes to enjoy the tranquillity of Princess Louisa Inlet. In 1951 Hamilton advertised Malibu for sale and although the property excited enough interest among buyers that many came out to view it, his price was unacceptable.

From his floathouse at the head of the inlet, Macdonald watched the would-be buyers with growing anxiety. He was now in his 60s and feared that when he was gone, his property would fall into less caring hands, and the inlet would become a private playground. In 1953 he placed his land in trust with the Princess Louisa International Society, a yachtsmen's association formed to ensure that the property would always provide a free haven for boaters. Ten years later the society gave the land to the government of British Columbia on the condition that it would become a marine park; since June 1965 it has been supervised by the provincial parks service. In October 2003 the society gave the province another 2,200 acres surrounding the head of the inlet; the park is now 50 times larger than Macdonald's original grant.

Malibu Lodge was sold in 1954 to the Young Life Society, a religious organization dedicated to the Christian education of youth. The selling price was reported to be $300,000. During the summer months, 250 teenagers arrive each week on the society's cruise ship, the *Malibu Princess,* for religious studies and an outdoor vacation. They each pay $250 for a week's use of facilities for which Hamilton charged his 1940s' millionaires $250 per day.

CLOWHOM

The original resorts built at the head of Salmon Inlet were perhaps the most rugged of all those on the Sunshine Coast. Intended primarily as retreats for those who take their fishing seriously, they offered few other diversions.

Clowhom Resort, situated on the bridge of land between Clowhom Lake and Salmon Inlet, was developed side by side with both the logging and power industries. In 1927 American lumberman Frederick W. Leadbetter, who had purchased the ailing pulp mill at Port Mellon, began looking for a fly-fishing retreat in the vicinity of his new mill. On a cruise up Jervis Inlet on the *Dorothy Vose*, the 52-foot yacht that had come with the Port Mellon deal, Leadbetter ventured into Sechelt Inlet, then into Salmon Inlet and came at last to Clowhom Falls.

Walter Thicke, who managed the shingle mill beside the falls, introduced Leadbetter to the Clowhom trout which ran around 16 to 18 inches in those days, and Leadbetter was hooked. Thicke's company, which owned most of the property around the lakes and the falls, went bankrupt shortly afterwards, and on November 1, 1931, Leadbetter's Columbia Steamship Company Limited bought the mill property as well as the water rights to the Clowhom River for $5,000. Leadbetter turned the mill's employee accommodations to his own uses, making one of the smaller cottages into his private lodge, assigning another to his caretaker and using the mill's large bunkhouse for the dozen or so guests with whom he would generally arrive on the *Dorothy Vose,* stopping over in Pender Harbour en route. At other times, they would all arrive by seaplane.

After Leadbetter's death in 1948 his Swedish son-in-law, Nils G. Teren, took over the management of Columbia Steamships and Clowhom Lodge. A year after his father-in-law's death, Teren scuttled the aging *Dorothy Vose* in deep water near the head of the inlet. However, Teren and other directors of the Columbia River Paper Company went on trial in 1962 for unauthorized stock options and salary increases and the exercise of improper control of the company. The mill property was then claimed by Leadbetter's heirs, headed by his grandson, Ambrose "Bubby" Cronin, who had also inherited the two retail businesses that his paternal great grandfather, P.J. Cronin, had begun in 1878.

The Dorothy Vose in Salmon Inlet in 1936.
COURTESY OF AMBROSE CRONIN.

During the Teren years, Cronin had been denied access to the property, but when he finally owned it, he began offering holidays there to his top salesmen as a reward, then as more people learned about it, he developed it into a commercial resort.

The resort's caretaker since the early 1930s had been Godfriedus "Kim" Kyme, and when he died in 1962, Ed Laidlaw of Sechelt was hired to take his place and carry out renovations. Heavy snowfalls in 1964 destroyed two of the old mill buildings and three years later Laidlaw dismantled and burned the last of them. He retired in 1974 and the position was taken over by John Alvarez, a Portland man who had immigrated to Canada that same year. In 1980 Cronin had a two-storey, six-bedroom cedar lodge built at the top of the hill overlooking both Salmon Inlet and Clowhom Lake. The lodge was sold to Len and Myra Kwiakowski in December 2000 and they have operated it since that time as a commercial resort.

Clowhom Lodge was not the only resort at the head of Salmon Inlet. Around 1937 George S. Moore of Vancouver bought L.3796 near the northeastern end of Clowhom Lake. He built a fishing lodge in this remote spot with the intention of bringing his guests in by float plane, but by the time his Clowhom Lake Lodge opened, World War II gas rationing had grounded his plane. Heavily in debt, Moore paid off his account to Art Dawley, the New Westminster hotelier who had bankrolled him, by signing the lodge over to him.

Meanwhile, Fred Mansell, the owner of a small resort and a trapline on the opposite side of Clowhom Lake, placed an ad for an assistant in *The Vancouver Sun*. It was answered by another Vancouver man, Alfred Taylor. Over the winter of 1942 and '43, between treks to check the trapline, Taylor investigated the vacant lodge across the lake. When Mansell told him it was for sale and that he was considering buying it, Taylor wrote to Dawley and bought it himself.

From the arrival of the first guests—a group of Royal Canadian Air Force personnel who flew in on an air force plane in June 1946—the resort quickly became an oasis for sports fishermen. Taylor, however, nearly missed enjoying his success. Early in March 1948 he arrived in Sechelt via Union Steamships to reopen the lodge after the winter shutdown. He then caught a ride on the Universal Timber Company crew boat to that company's logging camp at Sechelt Creek where he kept a 10-foot boat to take him to the head of the inlet. In his small boat piled high with supplies and mail, he was halfway to the head of the inlet when his boat was swamped by the wake of the Clowhom Lodge launch driven by Kyme. Dressed in heavy winter clothes, Taylor swam for his life in the freezing water and managed to reach the shore and clamber up the steep bank onto a ledge. From there he fought his way through the salal toward the Universal camp. In the meantime, Kyme had discovered the semi-submerged boat and rushed back to Universal to tell the loggers that Taylor had drowned; Taylor, hearing Kyme shouting the news, realized through his exhaustion that if he could hear Kyme, then Kyme should be able to hear him, and he yelled until rescue arrived.

One afternoon in 1955, Sechelt logger Ted Osborne came to Taylor's Clowhom Lake Lodge with an offer. "BC Electric's going to be flooding this place," Osborne said. "They're building a big dam at the falls."[6] And he offered

Al Taylor of Clowhom Lake Lodge stands with a day's catch in front of one of the float planes at his dock. Taylor operated the lodge from 1943 until the Clowhom Lakes were dammed in 1950.
COURTESY OF AL TAYLOR.

to purchase the timber surrounding the lodge for $2,500. Taylor declined that offer and the one for $5,000 that followed. They settled for $10,000 and Osborne promptly wrote out a cheque.

A year later the BC Electric Company offered to purchase Taylor's land or move his buildings to higher ground. Believing that fluctuations in the level of the lake would ruin the fishing and create a muddy mess along the shore, Taylor accepted their purchase offer. The last guests came to the lodge on September 8, 1956. The timber was logged and the lodge burned; there was soon nothing to show that this was once a busy resort with up to six seaplanes tied to the dock at one time.

PART FIVE
LOGS AND LOGGERS

THE MOODYVILLE TIMBER LEASE

The first timber sent to a sawmill from the Sunshine Coast was cut on a lease that had been surveyed in 1874 at Gower Point. The order to map its boundaries had caught up to surveyor George Hargreaves at Pender Harbour where he was laying out timber leases for the provincial government, but the owner of the Gower Point lease—Sewell Moody of the Moodyville Sawmill Company—was much too important to be kept waiting. Hargreaves and his assistant packed their equipment into their skiff and sailed for Gower Point immediately.

According to Hargreaves' diary, they arrived on July 9 and set up camp on the beach two and a half miles west of the point; in fact, they were only one and a half miles west of it, just beyond the mouth of what would be called Payne's, then Pratt's, then Chaster Creek. The whole survey took three days because of the rough ground in the creek canyon and the fact that the north boundary of the claim lay on an old burned-off area overgrown with young evergreens, salmon-berry bushes and shoulder-height salal. Later that summer Moody sent in a crew with ox teams to start cutting timber. The main skid road that they developed began on the beach east of the company's lease (near the present-day Gibsons wharf) and swung wide to avoid the steepest part of the incline, crossing into the lease at the top of the hill, then fingering out into the company's timber.

With building booms underway in Australia, China, Hawaii and Chile during the 1870s, the Moodyville sawmill on the north shore of Burrard Inlet and the Hastings mill on the south shore were working to capacity, between them turning out 145,000 board feet per day. As timber on the slopes close to the mills was used up, they launched a number of small paddlewheel steamboats— the first tugboats—to tow log booms from leases like the one at Gower Point. So heavy was the demand for timber that by 1881 the Gower Point lease had been logged off, except for the gullies and creek beds which were too steep to log with oxen. Moodyville's men cut only the finest trees, and sometimes took only a log or two out of them, leaving the rest on the ground to rot. Douglas fir was the preferred species, and some of the trees they found here were as much as 1,000 years old and 200 feet tall. They also took the clear, knot-free portions of western red cedar trees, but left hemlock since there was no market for it at that time.

HANDLOGGING

While Gower Point provided the first Sunshine Coast logs for the Burrard Inlet mills, some of the largest booms to arrive there in the late 19th century originated in Jervis Inlet's Prince of Wales Reach where handloggers were cutting their first timber about the same time Moody began logging at Gibsons. At first they cut Douglas fir almost exclusively because it had a guaranteed market, but as the demand grew for cedar products, the handloggers took cedar as well. By the terms of their cutting licences, they were limited to the use of axes and saws to harvest their trees, and Gilchrist jacks and gravity to herd them into the saltchuck. The first handloggers had "roving licences" that allowed them to cut trees anywhere, so they looked for good stands along the shores of the inlets where they could fell their trees directly into the water. Within a decade, however, licensing terms had become stricter, reducing each handlogger to a staked-out square mile of trees, but of necessity the timber they staked and cut was still confined to that bordering the water. Who these earliest handloggers were or even how many there were is not known since the provincial government kept no records before the turn of the century. More is known about 20th century handloggers.

Charlie and Ethel Whittaker came from Chehalis County, Washington, at the beginning of World War I to handlog in Princess Louisa Inlet. Later they moved to Queen's Reach in Jervis Inlet where Charlie built a home for his family just north of Patrick Point; the Whittakers—father Charles and son Henry—logged there for more than 40 years. Later, Henry took out his own handlogging licence for the south side of Jervis Inlet between Glacial Creek and Vancouver River; he turned to machine logging only toward the end of his career in the 1950s.

The Fisher family operated from a floathouse in Vancouver Bay at the mouth of High Creek during the 1920s and 1930s. The father, whom Francis Barrow, skipper of the *Toketie,* described as having spent many years "in the Chinese customs" was married to a very large Chinese lady, and because of his dignified demeanour was known locally as "Lord Fisher." His part of the family logging operation was to wait in his rowboat just off Moorsam Bluff while his two sons felled trees; as each tree hit the water, he would secure it and tow it back to camp. Fisher was still handlogging as late as 1953 although by this time he had moved his floathouse to the northern side of Princess Royal Reach.

Brothers Donald A. McNaughton and John McNaughton were New Brunswick loggers who came to handlogging in Jervis Inlet via the Klondike gold rush and a few years of machine logging on Cracroft Island. By 1908 Donald McNaughton was handlogging at Jack Bay; then on December 29, 1915, he was granted a permit to cut at the mouth of Webster or Slane Creek in Queen's Reach. By that time John McNaughton was operating a 10-man high lead outfit with a steam donkey at Britain River, and he remained there until the forest fire of 1919 burned out his timber. By backfiring and pumping water up from the river, McNaughton's crew saved his camp and equipment, but afterwards he left Britain River, moved his family to the mouth of Ruby or Smamit Creek in Queen's Reach, and went back to handlogging.

Although John McNaughton remained primarily a handlogger after that, he and his sons, Don and Bill, who became two of the best axemen on the coast, are perhaps more widely known for creating the palatial Macdonald house in Princess Louisa Inlet. They constructed the log house itself and all its furnishings using only handlogging tools. When World War II broke out, Don and Bill McNaughton became part of the army's forestry corps, and when they returned to civilian life, they logged again, first with a gas donkey in Queen's Reach, then with a donkey and caterpillar outfit in Egmont. However, their first love was trapping, and for 25 years they tended traplines every winter in the Skwakwa and Vancouver valleys.

Jimmy Archibald cut the timber along the shoreline northeast of Slate Creek during the winters of the 1930s and prospected during the summers. Norwegian immigrant Herman Solberg handlogged the Sandy Hook area in 1928, while at the same time working a trapline on the east side of Porpoise Bay. His daughters, Bergliot "Bergie" and Minnie, in time both went to work in logging camps as whistle punks, and Bergliot carried on her father's trapline, eventually getting her permit changed to the west side of Sechelt Inlet from Snake Bay to Egmont.

Many a handlogger met death when he slipped off a cliff to disappear into the sea or when rough water swamped his open boat. In the mid-1930s one of the Pohl brothers who were logging four or five miles north of Britain River vanished, boat and all. He had called at the Boulder Creek camp of handlogger Oliver Larsen, and it was after dark when he left there. A search was carried out by all the boats in the area, but neither he nor his boat were found.

Although many of the early handloggers graduated in time to machine logging, their places were taken by a fresh tide of rugged individualists. Forestry records show that even during the 1960s there were as many as 20 handloggers at work on this coast, still bound by the restrictions of the original handloggers' licences with the one exception that they were now allowed to use power boats.

LOGGING WITH HORSES, OXEN, ROLLWAYS AND FLUMES

After Sewell Moody's company finished cutting on its Gower Point lease in 1881, smaller outfits moved in to log the adjoining blocks. In 1887 George Gibson found the remains of a barn belonging to an outfit that had attempted to log with oxen just east of the Moody block. Their timber, animals and equipment had been destroyed by fire.

Many of the smaller logging outfits continued to use oxen, or "bulls" as they were then known, up to World War I. A logging team was generally made up of eight or ten yoke or span of the animals, and while they could pull more than a horse team could, they were much slower. Logger L.S. Jackson, who came to Gibson's in 1909, recalled "the resigned look of mute despair that the critters had" and wondered how they ever got where they were going because "they surely called the turn in slow motion."[1]

The Pratt brothers—Roger B., Robert J., William I. and James L.—used ox teams in the 1890s to log their 640 acres of pre-empted land just west of the old Moodyville lease from Shepherd's Rock to the end of Gower Point Road. Their camp was just a cedar-shake shack, adequate for keeping out the rain but not the wind. The floor was made of split cedar and the loggers' bunks were rough planks covered with ferns and hay. "The crew, such as there was," wrote L.S. Jackson, "could swing their feet out over the side of the bunk and they were at the table. The fire was an open square of gravel built up with boards with a hole in the roof to let the smoke out. The chap who told me this said that they never thought much of it since most of them rarely stayed more than a few weeks."[2] When Jackson visited the Pratts' campsite in 1910, the remains of the shack were still there with the bones of two oxen nearby; rumour had it that they had been starved to death.

Logging with oxen on the Chekwelp Reserve between
Gibson's Landing and Grantham's Landing about 1905.
COURTESY OF THE SUNSHINE COAST MUSEUM AND ARCHIVES. PHOTO #1193.

Oxen were used as late as 1907 by Japanese shake cutters in Bargain Harbour, but Charles Dupres is believed to have worked the last ox team on the Sunshine Coast when he took out the timber on the ridge north of Highway 101 in Gibson's Heights just before World War I. The logs were skidded to the head of a chute near the present-day Gibsons Elementary School and they hit the beach just east of the wharf.

The majority of camps, however, brought in horses because they worked faster than oxen, were more agile on the slopes and had greater endurance. Both ox- and horse-logging outfits used skid roads laid with split cedar "skids" set crossways for the logs to ride on. The centre of each skid in this wooden road-way was grooved so that the logs would keep to the middle of the track as they were pulled along, and the logs themselves were barked on the side that would adapt best to this groove in the roadway. To prevent the leading edge of each log from hooking up on the skids as the teams dragged them along, the logs were all "sniped" or trimmed at an angle on the lower edge. By fastening them together in single file, as many as 5,000 feet of logs could be dragged out of the bush at one time. This log train was hooked to the team by "dogging" each side of the lead log to a chain that led to the team's single-tree, then attaching each succeeding log by dogging it on the top only. Enough slack was left between the logs so that the team could get the first one moving before the weight of the next one was added. To help the train of logs move more freely, a "greaser" went ahead of the horses to daub the skids with a mixture of beef fat and dogfish oil. At the water's edge the "dog-chains" were removed from the logs, loaded into a hollowed out log or "pig" that had been dragged along behind the last log of the train, and the team was then turned around so that it could pull the loaded pig back to its starting place.

Skid roads were used most effectively on flat or somewhat sloping land, but neither horses nor oxen could negotiate their loads of logs down the steep bedrock slopes at the water's edge. Rollways were the answer to this problem. Jim Leatherdale, who horse-logged west of the old Moodyville lease after 1890, dumped his logs at the top of a steep 50-foot incline above the beach at Mahon Road. To get them from there into the water, he built a rollway by laying cedar poles vertically side by side against the bank; when he was ready to make up a boom, the logs were released from their pile and allowed to roll down into the water.

Robert McNair, who logged the lower flank of Mount Elphinstone, approached his timber lease from the east via skid roads developed by earlier loggers who had worked their way up to that side of the mountain from Howe Sound. But to take his logs out, McNair ran a new skid road almost due south down the mountainside, through the fork where the Sunshine Coast Highway now meets Lower Road and from there straight down to a rollway below present-day Beach Avenue.

The remains of similar rollways can be found along all the waterways of the Sunshine Coast. A few, so decayed that they are almost unrecognizable, date back to horse-logging days, but because no one has ever come up with a better system of getting logs into the water, many of them are the by-products of more recent logging. For example, on the west side of Sechelt Inlet rollways have been in use right into the 21st century.

Open flumes were designed for use on longer slopes, some of them carrying logs or shake bolts downhill for as much as five miles before they reached the water. The heyday of the flume was the period between 1890 and the late 1930s, when they were the solution to logging the steep hillsides from Port Mellon to the head of Jervis Inlet. Some were greased to carry the logs downhill—these were often referred to as chutes—but most flumes were built where a water supply—a lake or a dammed creek—was available to flush the logs down. Like rollways, they were built of durable cedar planks and logs, and as a result, they remained intact decades after the loggers who used them were gone. The remains of one or two of them may still be seen on the high ridges between the creeks. On the northeast side of Glacial Creek in Jervis Inlet a 1933 forest survey found an intact flume that had been last used in 1908.

Most flumes were built by small, nameless logging outfits that spent a few years taking out timber then left with as little fanfare as they had come. Other flumes achieved some local fame because of incidents that happened there or because their owners stayed to become settlers. One of the earliest flumes on the Sunshine Coast was constructed by J. McMyn near Grantham's Landing to carry logs cut by his crew on the plateau area that is now crossed by Chamberlin Road. Teams of oxen skidded the logs to the brow of the hill where they were manoeuvred into the generously greased flume. McMyn's operation ended when he was killed after a large log bounced out of the flume, struck a nearby tree and fell back on him.

The largest and longest flume to be constructed in the Gibsons area in the early years of the 20th century ran in a straight line from a dam on Payne Creek on the side of Mount Elphinstone right down to Gibsons Bay. C.S. Battle and J. Drew built it to bring processed lumber from their steam-powered mill on the side of the mountain. The partners were under contract to the Canadian Pacific Railway to cut inch-and-a-half-thick planks 16 feet in length for railway water towers.

At Dakota Creek on Howe Sound a flume was installed in the late 1920s to streamline a yellow cedar and cypress operation that had previously been worked by moving the mill higher and higher up the creek as the lease was logged off, then hauling the cut lumber downhill on sleds. Construction of the flume allowed the mill owner, a man by the name of Taylor, to relocate his mill at tidewater and load lumber barges directly from the mill. In the early 1930s Taylor switched to making specialty products, chiefly battery separators, from yellow cedar, but even this move was not enough to save his operation in the Depression years, and it closed around 1935.

A four-mile-long flume beside McNab Creek, northeast of Port Mellon, which was built around the turn of the century for a shake bolt operation, was straightened and upgraded in the mid-1920s to accommodate the production of poles by the K & K Pole Company of Everett, Washington. By this time all the huge ancient cedars had been taken off the mountainside for shakes, leaving a mass of smaller cedars that were tall, straight and knot-free with only a crown of limbs on top, and the company could get two and sometimes three 20- or 25-foot poles out of each of them. K & K operated four camps beside the creek—Camp 1 on the beach accommodated the men who supervised the booming ground; at Camp 2, two miles up the creek, a sawmill provided the lumber to build and repair the flume; and camps 3 and 4 housed the loggers. Camp 4 was also the site of the dam that had been built across the creek to create a pond. To bring the poles to the flume, Chinese labourers constructed a network of skid roads, each road being about six feet wide and made of four-inch-thick split-cedar puncheon with a round skid laid down approximately every five feet. According to a man named Baxter, who lived with his parents in a one-room cedar shack at Camp 4 during 1926 and '27, that camp consisted of "three or four bunkhouses, a cookhouse, blacksmith shop and barn. There was 12 teams of horses [because] they ran five 'sides,' each consisting of one road team and one yarding team, two teamsters, one hooktender and one sniper. There was also one spare team and one freight team. I guess with the cook, the bullcook, blacksmith and [loggers], there was about 35 men" in the camp. All supplies were hauled up to the camps on sleds via a skid road on the west side of McNab Creek but "quite a ways from the creek at times to keep to the evener ground." The loggers, however, had a simpler method of coming down from the camps: they "would nail two 20-foot poles together and ride the flume to the beach where a platform had been made for them to jump off before the poles shot into the saltchuck." Baxter recalled his father saying that "although it was a perfect show as to time, ground, volume per acre, stumpage, low wages, et cetera, and thousands of poles were taken out, the K & K made no money on McNab Creek because of the cost of the miles of skid roads, even with cheap Chinese labour."[3] At the other end of the Sunshine Coast the Gustavson brothers installed a flume in the early 1920s to send their timber into the inlet from a lease at the head of Jervis Inlet on the east bank of Hunaechin Creek. And when

Bob Campbell moved a small outfit into the valley of Treat or Beaver Creek in Jervis Inlet around 1934, he used steam donkeys and a diesel caterpillar tractor to yard timber to the head of a 2,200-foot-long flume. When Campbell went broke after about two and a half years of logging there, the operation was taken over by John Klein of Pender Harbour who used the same flume and tractor combination until just before World War II.

DONKEY ENGINES

Steam-powered winches known as "donkey engines" eventually replaced horses and oxen for the job of "yarding" logs short distances to a point where they could be hauled out of the woods. The early machines were small and light-weight, often incapable of moving the enormous logs of the old-growth forests, and because of this, they were extremely dangerous to operate. One day in 1916 Robert Hollingsworth, who had an outfit in Granville Bay on Hotham Sound, was yarding with his steam donkey when one log hung up. He ordered the engineer to pull harder, but when the man said he was giving it all it would take, Hollingsworth took over the engine. The mainline broke and, flying back, wrapped around his head, decapitating him.

Good donkey engineers were a valuable asset to the camps fortunate enough to employ them, but poor ones could shut down the whole operation. The Union Steamships' *Cheakamus* stopped at a float camp near Glacial Creek in June 1929 to pick up two men heading for Vancouver; one was a Scottish

Empire Steam Donkey with double-extension firebox used as a trackside yarder and skyline machine. Far machine is an Empire Duplex Loader. Gustavson Bros. Camp, Deserted Bay, approx 1950. Man in centre bending over is woods foreman Adolph Swanson
COURTESY OF HAROLD AND BEA SWANSON.

engineer looking for another job, the other was his former boss looking for another engineer and another donkey engine. It seems the Scot had literally worn out his donkey engine in one day by running it without oil. The valves had been pounded so thin they could be broken with the fingers.

Since the donkey engines were wood-burners, each outfit had to employ a woodcutter to keep it fueled. Many of them were local eccentrics. In a turn-of-the-century St. Vincent Bay logging camp belonging to Phil Hiltz, the wood-cutter was an ex-logger named Robert Heard who was well known to the people of Egmont where he rowed once a week to buy his groceries. "Old Bobby" was very proud of his cabin stove, an oversized, castiron monster inherited from a logging camp. On the back of the stove sat a grey granite coffee pot into which he popped the occasional dogfish liver. To polish the stove, Bobby tipped out some of this oil and with a rag wiped it over the stovetop. The stench, according to his neighbours, was quite awe-inspiring.

RAILROAD LOGGING

Railway technology came to the forests of the Sunshine Coast around the turn of the century, putting within reach timber that had been considered inaccess-ible just a few years earlier. Many of the first locomotives used for logging were aged mainline engines that had been retired from service, although in time locomotives specifically designed for the woods were built. In the early days, the logs were simply hooked one behind the other as they had been for horse and ox teams and pulled behind the engine, sliding along between the tracks on the greased sleepers. Later, the logs were carried on cars, generally the type known as "skeleton" cars, which consisted of a pair of trucks (four-wheel sets) joined by a heavy timber drawbar.

The first documented railroad show on the Sunshine Coast began operating around the turn of the century at Pender Harbour on a timber lease belonging to the Hastings Sawmill Company of Burrard Inlet, and that operation took out approximately 50,000 board feet a year at a cost of ten dollars an acre in royalties. In 1912 an American named Peter Boward Anderson took over the lease; although American companies were prevented by law from leasing BC timberland directly from the government, there was nothing to stop them logging for or buying out legitimate leaseholders.

P.B. Anderson & Company, headquartered in Bellingham, Washington, had entered the BC industry in 1907 by buying out Duggan Logging's lease on Flat Island (now known as Harness Island), south of Pender Harbour. Anderson's son C. Dewey Anderson recalled in a 1957 interview that he had arrived in camp as a 14-year-old in 1909 to find 40 or 50 men, all of them "older, rough, old-time loggers" at work in a skid road outfit that used horses to haul the logs to "a fore and aft flume." It was more crudely constructed than most flumes, with two large logs forming the sides and a smaller one the bottom.

Duggan's lease was logged out by December 1911, and after the Christmas shutdown Anderson moved his crew to the head of Pender Harbour to work the Hastings Mill lease. He modernized the operation, putting in a high lead system and extending the railway from the Harbour up past Haslam Lake, which he named after his accountant, Charlie Haslam, who had logged earlier above Roberts Creek. Anderson's contract with the mill paid him about six dollars per thousand board feet for logs dumped into Pender Harbour; the mill company was responsible for towing them to Vancouver. "Dad did fairly well in there,"[4] Dewey Anderson said. P.B. Anderson's final camp on the Sunshine Coast was on the Skookumchuck south of Waugh Lake, with a rail line running into Secret (Co-op) Bay; that camp opened in 1915 and closed the following year at the same time as the Pender Harbour operation was also shut down.

A railroad logging outfit owned by the Gordon Development Company that operated in Halfmoon Bay c.1915. The steam engine is a Climax, which had fully sprung trucks that could handle the roughest track without derailing or losing traction.
COURTESY OF SUNSHINE COAST MUSEUM AND ARCHIVES. PHOTO #4218.

The Heaps Timber Company of Vancouver, one of three companies owned by James W. Heaps, and then by his son, alderman Edward Hewetson Heaps, moved into Narrows Inlet in 1907 with a standard-gauge railway show. Within a year the company had three miles of track under construction and had brought in a locomotive and eight flatcars, although most of the large logs were simply dragged along behind the locomotive. The camp's output for the next five years averaged 50,000 board feet a day. In 1913, about the time management was turned over to Heaps' son, the operation was modernized by bringing in a more powerful engine, a two-truck 45-ton Heisler, from the company's other camp at Ruskin. It operated in the rugged Narrows Inlet area until 1920 when all the accessible timber in the lease was exhausted. When the camp closed, Heaps moved the Heisler to his new timber lease above the handlogging line in Jervis Inlet's Queen's Reach.

CUTTING SHAKES

Shortly after the handloggers and horse loggers came to the inlets of the Sunshine Coast, shake cutters also arrived, looking for the enormous old cedar trees that would provide knot-free shakes and shingles. Unlike the regular outfits, they often worked logged-over land, taking cedar logs that had been discarded by previous outfits. When they worked in virgin timber, they logged selectively, for the most part taking only the huge cedar trees and leaving other species standing.

Many of the shake cutters on this coast were Japanese who worked under contract to the large Vancouver mills. Although most of their camps were exclusively male, the camp established on the William Campbell property just west of Roberts Creek in 1905 also included women and children. The focal point of their village of cedar shake houses was a bathhouse or *ofuru* built on posts over a large iron tub in which the women heated water each day to be ready for the men's evening communal bath. In other camps, such as the one operating in Bargain Harbour in 1907, the communal bath was the ocean.

Shake cutters could go farther from the water than handloggers for the trees they wanted because they cut their logs into four-foot bolt-lengths right in the woods and either dragged them down to the water on horse-drawn sleds or flushed them down flumes to be bag-boomed and towed to market. However, they could only make use of a flume where there was a good slope to the sea and a source of water at the head of the flume to wash the bolts downhill. To take cedar from the slopes of Mount Elphinstone, an operator by the name of Stoltz reconstructed the old Battle and Drew flume in 1914. When completed, it was seven miles long with a 2 percent grade, and Stoltz diverted the waters of both Payne and Langdale creeks into it to carry the cedar bolts to saltwater at the mouth of Langdale Creek. It remained in operation until 1922; a watchman maintained it for another two years, then it was abandoned, machinery and all. For another 10 years, it was used by hikers as the regular trail up the mountainside.

Flume Road at Roberts Creek commemorates the shake bolt flume built before the turn of the century beside the creek that drains Randall's Lake into Elphinstone Bay. At a point about a quarter mile north of Highway

Shingle bolts being flushed down the McNair Shingle Company's flume at Roberts Creek, about 1925.
COURTESY OF THE SUNSHINE COAST MUSEUM AND ARCHIVES. PHOTO #1112.

101, the stream was dammed to form a pond that would store enough water to flush the bolts down the flume. The shake cutters stockpiled the bolts until a scow arrived in the bay below, then pushed them into the pond and opened the flume gates.

From approximately 1904 to 1907 one of the Rat Portage Lumber Company's shake-cutting camps was located between Roberts Creek and Wilson Creek. The largest timber interest in eastern Canada, this company had weathered the depression of the 1890s by constantly diversifying its operations and its sources of timber. Early in the new century, when faced with stiff competition from lower-priced BC lumber products such as finished exterior and interior siding and shingles, they had solved the problem by buying into operations on the West Coast. In time the skid road that Rat Portage used to drag their bolts to the water at Wilson Creek became the most dangerous section of the Sunshine Coast's Highway 101—Rat Portage Hill.

One of the best known shake-cutting outfits was that operated by Roy Fleming after 1916 at three sites in Roberts Creek. These camps, however, were never known by the name of their owner but as McNair's Camps because the shakes were sold to the Robert McNair Shingle Company of Vancouver. At Fleming's largest camp, high on the mountainside, he used mules to haul the bolts to the pond he had created by damming the west fork of Roberts Creek. The flume, owned by McNair, ran for four miles downhill through the Reeves' property on Lockyer Road and out over Harry Roberts' shoreline sawmill where the lumber had been cut to construct the flume. The last shake-cutting camp in the Wilson Creek area operated during the late 1930s and into the early war years. All the cutters and the families who lived in camp with them were Japanese Canadians, and on March 15, 1942, all 44 inhabitants were sent by boat to Hastings Park in Vancouver and from there into internment camps in the Interior.

While the handloggers, horse loggers and shake cutters were establishing themselves close to the water, the big logging companies were laying claim to enormous tracts of timber farther inland. Unfortunately, forestry records are fragmentary before 1912, the year the Forest Service was formed, so it is difficult to trace all the grants, leases and licences held by the early giants of this industry. The facts are also confused because BC's timber policy changed almost year by year until that time. Yet the general historical outline of a few of these 19th century companies and the location of the tracts they logged is available in old archival documents and newspaper stories.

The Moodyville Sawmill Company that had been the first company to cut timber near Gower Point was also the first to acquire a lease on timber adjacent to Vancouver Bay in Jervis Inlet. The year was 1889, and although no more than 15 years had passed since the first handloggers had begun cutting there, all the timber that gravity and Gilchrist jacks could manoeuvre to the waterline was gone. What had attracted them to the area, besides the quality of the timber, was the bay itself. Although Captain Vancouver had been unable to anchor his survey boats there because of its depth, this bay provides one of the few booming grounds along the entire south shore of the inlet that is relatively safe from the weather.

The records show that Moodyville was assessed a royalty of 50 cents per 1,000 board feet on all the timber they took out of the Vancouver River watershed and an annual rent of ten cents per acre of timber land. This was an innovation on the part of the provincial government because before Moodyville acquired this Vancouver Bay lease, logging companies in this province had only been awarded their timber rights in two ways: as leases for which they paid an annual rent or, more often, as outright grants of Crown timber, sometimes including permanent ownership of the land as well. The Moodyville mill apparently received one of the first of a new type of lease, introduced in 1888, that required companies to pay both royalties on the timber they cut and rent on the land underneath it. In addition, the new regulations obliged the company to maintain a sawmill of a specific capacity, a ruling that virtually eliminated competition from small operators.

Moodyville's Vancouver Bay camp opened in September 1889 with about 100 men and a half dozen horse teams that were to be used to skid the timber down to the bay from the slopes above the Vancouver River. Their foreman was Big Billy Dineen, reputed to be one of the best axemen on the Pacific Coast. According to old-time logger Eustace Smith, Dineen once bet he could fall 40,000 board feet of timber in one day. There were plenty of takers since nobody believed he could do it, but Dineen picked out four big firs with an average size of 10,000 board feet, "all of them with a heavy lean,"[5] and began chopping. He won the bet and cleaned up.

In 1891 the Moodyville company was sold to a British consortium, and at a time when most of the big logging companies were making their camps more efficient by installing wood-burning steam donkey engines for yarding timber to their skid roads, the new owners elected to stay with horse logging on the Vancouver River. Two years later, western Canada followed the United States into a 10-year depression, and in the tight timber markets that developed, Moodyville was squeezed out. The camp at Vancouver Bay closed around 1895. When the company's mill on Burrard Inlet shut down in 1901, the Vancouver Bay leases were allowed to lapse.

A horse logger named Joe Gregson began taking timber from the valley of High Creek, which also flows into Vancouver Bay, sometime before 1905. This was the same year that Andrew Haslam, who had gone broke operating a saw-mill in Nanaimo, obtained a timber lease on the south side of the Vancouver River and installed a railway show. But Haslam brought in a narrow-gauge track system—just three feet between the rails—and an 0-4-0 saddle tank engine, and both were totally unsuitable for the rugged terrain. The narrow base made the loaded cars unstable, and the locomotive was so light that it could not handle the steep grades of the mountainside. Within two years Haslam switched to standard gauge, but the change came too late, and he went broke again about 1908. He had worked 200 acres of his lease.

By this time BC's timber lease policy had changed again, reducing the sawmill requirement so that small outfits could enter the game once more, and the Sunshine Coast's real logging boom began. Nearly 250 applications for timber leases for the stretch of coast from Howe Sound to the head of Jervis Inlet were delivered to the offices of the Ministry of Lands and Forests between the fall of 1905 and the end of 1908, some of them from handloggers, but the majority from small logging companies eager to become big ones. Among the accepted applications was one from the Vancouver Clear Cedar Mill Company for a lease south of Vancouver Bay and another from Ernest Crockford for two 640-acre leases north and east of the bay. By 1914 both companies had logged and were gone from Vancouver Bay.

Although several small companies seem to have taken timber out of this area during World War I, the next definite date in Vancouver Bay's history is 1926, when the Vancouver Bay Logging Company acquired a timber licence on an 8,000-acre tract that spanned the Vancouver River. The principal owner of this new company was David Jeremiason, a quiet, heavy-set, hard-working Swede, a pioneer of the Sunshine Coast logging industry. He had begun his career with a single horse team then later bought out Booth Logging and their operation at Dark Cove on Goliath Bay in Jervis Inlet, a railroad show with an inclined track down to the bay. The old locomotive he inherited for taking the loaded cars down the last steep slope to the water had been built by Washington Iron Works with a special 12-foot drum mounted on the front so the engine could be hauled back up the slope again by cable and pulley. Jeremiason lost two loaded skeleton cars one day when they became uncoupled as they were being shunted downhill by the locomotive; the logs popped to the surface but the cars were never salvaged.

In Vancouver Bay in 1926, Jeremiason put close to 700 men to work, mostly as fallers, and because many of them brought their wives and children to live at the camp, his company built a schoolhouse and hired a teacher. In three years of intensive logging, the company clear-cut over 1,000 acres of timber, and laid down seven and a half miles of railway line to bring the logs out to the inlet. But in the summer of 1930, when the lumber markets in eastern Canada and the United States suddenly dried up, Jeremiason was forced to close the camp and dismiss the men. A couple of caretakers remained behind to keep the buildings and equipment in repair, ready to operate again as soon as the "temporary market conditions" improved.

However, many years passed before conditions improved, so it was not until 1935 that Jeremiason moved a crew into Vancouver Bay again. In the early 1940s he sold out to the Jervis Inlet Timber Company, which in turn was bought by British Columbia Forest Products in 1946. About 150 men were employed here in these later years, most of them working as fallers. Even though chainsaws had been invented, few were in use at this camp because none had been designed that were compact and light enough to be carried up and down on the mountainsides. But as the design of chainsaws improved and two-man saws gave way to lighter one-man saws, the output of this camp increased while the number of men on the payroll decreased.

By the 1980s there was no logging in the valleys above Vancouver Bay. Instead, the slopes had become a patchwork of forests of different maturity. Some of them, including the high-elevation mature timber that was inaccessible in earlier years, could be ready to log again within a few years, but it will be an expensive project to renew the roads and to build a new bridge over the Vancouver River.

LOGGING PRINCESS LOUISA

In all of the Sechelt Forest District the area for which the most complete record of leases and licences is available is the timberland surrounding the little inlet off Queen's Reach that Captain Vancouver mistook for a river—Princess Louisa Inlet—although even here there are chapters missing in the story. The trees bordering the inlet were already gone when the first 20th century loggers appeared on the scene, and no record exists of the names of the handloggers who took them. On May 2, 1907, the Heaps Timber Company received Licence #11814 to log Princess Louisa's north shore; their 640-acre tract began two miles from the narrow entranceway at Queen's Reach. Two months later the Vancouver lumber company of Cook & Tait Limited was granted a licence to log the south bank from halfway up Princess Louisa to the inlet's head. Both companies found large sections of barren bedrock in their lease lands and their operations were handicapped by the steepness of the mountains that surround the little inlet. Both were gone by 1910 when Charles Roscoe Johnstone pre-empted in the inlet. Handloggers Charles Whittaker, Charles Tribett and two unnamed licence holders followed them in 1915. Anonymous loggers took the stand of enormous cedars at the head of the inlet on the other side of Chatterbox Falls from Qua-Ma-Meen. When M. Wylie Blanchet, author of *The Curve of Time*, visited the inlet around 1930, she found only their stumps and the remains of a switchback skid road that had been used to negotiate the huge timbers down the 600 feet of precipitous slope.

After all the easily accessible stands of timber were felled, the government allowed several more parcels of land on the shoreline to be pre-empted and some were in time Crown granted. After that, Princess Louisa's trees stood undisturbed until 1938 when the American, Thomas F. Hamilton, decided to build a luxury resort at the entrance to the inlet. To have complete privacy for his guests, he bought up all the old Crown land grants and the timber rights where possible. From the government he also acquired a tract of "wild land" on the slopes of Mount Helena to complete a block of 9,587 acres adjoining the inlet. He failed to negotiate a deal for the timber lying on the west side of Mount Helena and it later went to BC Forest Products, which clear-cut it in the 1970s.

When Hamilton's resort failed in 1951 he advertised all his timberland for sale, but it was five years before he attracted a buyer. Logger Cam Hudon of Mission, BC, bought 9,000 acres in 1956 for his three logging companies— C. Hudon Logging, Tommy Bay Logging and Louisa Bay Logging—but found that the only tract really worth harvesting was on the eastern slope of Mount Helena. However, Hudon lacked the resources to work it, and two years later the entire block was seized by Royal Trust, which had advanced Hudon the money.

In 1961 it was bought by MacMillan Bloedel Limited, which used con-ventional towers to log the accessible timber; the remainder was of dubious quality. For a time it was rumoured that MacMillan Bloedel was negotiating a "land swap" of this lease with the provincial government for better timber, with the Mount Helena acreage then being added to Princess Louisa Marine Park. However, in July 1999 MacMillan Bloedel was bought out by the American lumber giant Weyerhaeuser Limited, which in 2007 sold district lot 3524, 3525, 3515 and 3514 at the head of Princess Louisa Inlet to the Princess Louisa International Society and the Nature Conservancy of Canada. The remaining timber surrounding the inlet is owned by Island Timberlands Limited Partnership, which bought up Weyerhaeuser's remaining BC leases.

LOGGING THE INLAND SEA

Handloggers seem to have come to Sechelt, Salmon and Narrows inlets in the 1870s at the same time as handloggers first began working in Jervis Inlet. However, since booms assembled in the inland sea had to be taken to market through treacherous Skookumchuck Narrows, most of the timber there was still intact in 1893 when 18-year-old Herbert "Bert" Whitaker arrived from England to pre-empt land on Porpoise Bay. Before he was 30, he was operating two logging camps and two sawmills on Sechelt Inlet. One mill was at Doriston, just inside the Skookumchuck, while the other, operated by his younger brother Ronald, was built on piles over the shallow water at the head of Porpoise Bay just east of the limits of the present-day Sechelt Marsh. This latter mill provided the lumber for construction of Whitaker's hotels and stores. It was closed shortly after World War I, but the piles on which it was built were still standing as late as World War II. After timber leasing regulations were relaxed in 1906, Whitaker expanded his logging empire by acquiring leases to almost 10,000 acres of timber in the nearby inlets, including a wide strip of forest along the north shore of Salmon Inlet from the mouth to the mid-point and over the saddle of land into Storm Bay at the entrance to Narrows Inlet, all of the timber around that bay, a large tract on the west shore of Sechelt Inlet opposite the mouth of Salmon Inlet, and the timber on Poise Island in Porpoise Bay. However, Whitaker was financially over-extended when the business slump came after World War I, and by the time he died in 1925 he had lost both his mills, his logging companies and his timber leases.

Whitaker was not the only operator taking out timber along the shores of this inland sea in the early years of the century. Between 1900 and 1910, another 16 handloggers and small skid-road outfits staked timber along these waterways. They included Cecil A. Whitaker who logged the peninsula lying between his brother Herbert's Salmon Inlet and Storm Bay leases, Ernest Crockford and C.S. Battle who took the timber on the east side of Porpoise Bay, and seven separate outfits that logged on the south side of Salmon Inlet. They were followed by railroad shows in the 1920s, and truck and caterpillar tractor shows in the 1940s and much later by helicopter outfits.

EARLY LOGGING COMPANIES

The history of the forest industry on the Sunshine Coast is studded with the stories of men who arrived with a team and a little credit and then, according to logger L.S. Jackson, "just moved in where they thought they could log and went at it, something like picking a few apples."[6] In fact, so many logging outfits lined the shores of the Sunshine Coast in those early days that, if they had possessed modern logging technology, they would have taken every tree from the area within a decade or two. But most were small skid-road operations using horses or oxen, and since logging with oxen was not practicable for a pull longer than a mile and a half from the water, and horse logging was good for no more than a three-mile pull, they were unable to reach the best of the mature timber.

However, many of these early entrepreneurs stayed to build logging empires, transferring their camps from place to place as they logged out their leases. Almost all of these moves were made by water, and the operators became adept at skidding equipment, workers' housing, cookhouses, repair shops and bunkhouses onto floats. Sophie Brackett's 1947 experience was typical of these events. Her husband, Lloyd, worked for Eagle Bay Logging (later known as Logco), which was owned by Earl Lewis Laughlin and Charlie Philp and based in Pender Harbour, although they had been logging on Galiano Island. Now they were moving to a new lease at Halfmoon Bay. "We arrived on a beautiful April day. We came across the Gulf in . . . the houses we had been living in on Galiano. There wasn't a breath of wind and we cooked and played cards. There were 14 married couples and a crew of, I think, 50 single fellows . . . [The houses and cookhouse and shops] were all pulled up on the shore just above Redrooffs [resort]. We were like a little town. When we got to Halfmoon Bay there was no power but we had our own power [generators] . . . Nobody in Halfmoon Bay could understand this bunch that came in overnight and all of a sudden there was a little town."[7] Laughlin and Philp worked Halfmoon Bay until 1953 when the company was dissolved.

GUSTAVSON LOGGING

The four Gustavson brothers arrived on the West Coast from Sweden in 1914 and hired out as loggers on Vancouver Island. Their next jobs were with the Capilano Timber Company, a railroad show that was logging the watershed of the Capilano River in North Vancouver. One of the four brothers died in the 1919 flu epidemic, and another was incapacitated in a logging accident, but in 1920 the two remaining brothers, Eric and Thure, took out a handlogging licence for the west side of Porpoise Bay. When the timber ran out, they moved to the head of Jervis Inlet, east of the mouth of Hunaechin Creek, where they used horse teams to drag the logs to the head of a flume that led to the saltchuck.

In 1929 Eric and Thure Gustavson obtained financing from a distant cousin, miner A.J. Anderson—known to the family as "Old Man Anderson"—to buy the lease and equipment of the Regina Timber Company, which around 1920 had taken a lease at Misery Creek on Salmon Inlet. They had logged off the lower slopes, sending the logs down the final precipice via a flume to the little cove they had christened Regina Bay. Three years later, when their logging operation reached the 900-foot level of the sidehill, they had recognized the need for more modern equipment and obtained loans to install a railroad that would give them access to timber higher up the mountain. However, the final one and a quarter miles of track that they built to the water had a grade of approximately 45 percent, one of the longest and steepest inclined rail lines ever built in BC's forests. In fact, it was far too steep for any locomotive to negotiate, so the company bought an enormous "snubbing engine" from Smith & Watson Ironworks of Portland. This snubber had a water-cooled drum that measured 10 feet in diameter and both air and mechanical brakes. It was installed a mile and a half from the water where the loaded cars were unhooked from the locomotive and attached one at a time to the snubber's drum cable. Then as the cable was slowly released, each car rolled down the steeply inclined track and out onto a wharf set on pilings over the bay. Here the uprights holding the logs on the car were released and the logs tumbled into the water.

Gustavson Brothers Logging camp at Misery Creek, Salmon Inlet, 1932.
The "snubbing engine" on the right is beginning the process of snubbing the skeleton carload of logs on the left of the picture down the last one and a quarter miles of track to the booming ground. In the middle of the picture empty skeleton cars wait on a side track.
COURTESY OF HAROLD AND BEA SWANSON.

Unfortunately, the cost of setting up this complicated operation was so enormous that by 1928 the Regina Timber Company was in receivership. The beneficiaries of their misfortune were the Gustavsons, but within six months of their purchase, North America was plunged into the Great Depression and the brothers had to fight to keep their new operation rolling. "I can remember things were so tough," Eric's son Arnold Gustavson recalled, "that when we shut down just before Christmas that year, Dad had to go out as foreman for one of the companies over on Vancouver Island so he could make enough money to get started up again in the spring—just so he could buy groceries for the crew. I remember that because he wasn't home for Christmas."

But the camp reopened in the spring of 1930 with more than 60 men, and the loads of logs began rolling down the incline again to the bay, which

Johnny Joe of the Sechelt Indian Band, head loader for Gustavson Brothers Logging at Deserted Bay in 1947.
COURTESY OF HAROLD AND BEA SWANSON.

had been rechristened Gustavson Bay in honour of the camp's new owners. All freight and personnel were brought up to the camp on the skeleton cars on which the logs had come down the hill. "We didn't have a special boxcar or a covered car or anything like that when we brought in supplies," Arnold Gustavson explained, "just a long drawbar with two bunks on it to hold the logs. That's what we rode back up on."

By the time they had logged off the Misery Creek lease in 1934, the Gustavsons had laid seven miles of steel and were operating two locomotives with 17 skeleton cars. Their next move was to Jervis Inlet where they set up their railroad in the valley of Slate or Stakawus Creek, southwest of Deserted Bay.

According to Arnold Gustavson, this was the last railway logging show on BC's mainland. In 1938 the family switched to truck logging in Deserted Bay. "Quite a few people had tried logging on that site and gone broke on it," Arnold Gustavson recalled. "It was a real tough operation—hard logging because of the terrain—but after you got in there, the timber was good."[8]

Right from the beginning of their Misery Creek years, the foreman of the

Gustavsons' camp had been another Swede, Adolph Swanson, Eric's brother-in-law. The two men had married the Nordin sisters, also immigrant Swedes. While technically the language of the camp was English, only Swedish loggers were hired, so they generally spoke Swedish among themselves. Adolph Swanson's son, Harold, who came to work there in his early teens, claimed it was years before he discovered there were men of other nationalities out in the woods.

In Deserted Bay, the Gustavsons' camp was located on the north side of the Deserted River, directly across from a village used in summer by the Sechelt people, and as a result some of the Native loggers were hired onto the Gustavsons' crew. "Whenever we'd start up again in the spring, we'd go down to Sechelt and pick up the men right from the reserve there," Arnold Gustavson explained. "They were hard workers and good workers and they'd outperform everybody. I can remember some of them—Johnny Joe and Clarence Joe, August Joe and the Dixons—all of them worked for us at one time or another."[9]

A few individualists drifted in and out of the Gustavsons' camp at Deserted River. Steve Johnstone was a member of a handlogging family who had pre-empted in Princess Louisa Inlet in 1910, but Steve and his brothers took more naturally to trapping, only turning to logging when their traplines in the mountains beyond Princess Louisa were doing badly. At such times Steve Johnstone would cut firewood for the Gustavsons' camp or hire on as their winter watchman. Loggers recalled that he often went barefoot even in winter,

A two-man chainsaw in use, cutting firewood for the cookhouse, at Gustavson Brothers Logging camp at Deserted Bay, Jervis Inlet, 1947. Eric Gustavson is on the left end of the saw.
COURTESY OF HAROLD AND BEA SWANSON.

that on one occasion he shot a rat that had invaded his shack even though it meant blowing a hole in the floor, and that when he returned from his annual excursion to Vancouver he was often wearing nailpolish and lipstick. He died in Vancouver in the late 1960s after he was struck by a car.

Gustavson Logging remained at Deserted Bay until 1951 when the company was sold to North Shore Lumber. By this time, it was managed by Eric's son Arnold, and he remained with the operation until all the timber in the lease had been logged. After the sale of the company the older generation of the Gustavson-Swanson family retired and the younger ones invested in new businesses. Eric Gustavson died in 1961, his brother Thure 10 years later.

Truck logging at Oscar Niemi's Halfmoon Bay camp, 1930.
The truck, a chain-driven Mack with hard rubber tires, is shown tilted toward
the rollway in order to dump its load of two enormous cedars. To the rear of the
truck can be seen the planked road with logs on either side to guide the truck's wheels.
COURTESY OF THE SUNSHINE COAST MUSEUM AND ARCHIVES.
PHOTO #109. PHOTO BY HELEN MCCALL.

TRUCK LOGGING ON THE SUNSHINE COAST

While David Jeremiason and the Gustavson brothers were still logging with railroad shows in the late 1920s and early 1930s, other companies had begun to convert to truck logging. Railroads were more expensive to build but cheaper than trucks to operate; trucks could negotiate where the grade was too steep for locomotives. The first truck shows were a far cry from modern truck operations since the Leylands and Fageols and Macks they used were built with single rear axles that limited their load capacity, and they rode on hard rubber tires. Each truck camp also had to be equipped with a mill to cut lumber for the planked roads that had to be laid all the way from the cutting area to tidewater. Gullies and swampy areas were bridged with planked trestles, some of them a mile or more in length. In the Halfmoon Bay area two plank roads had been established by 1933, one of them a "west road" that followed Halfmoon Creek and the other an "east road" that followed Milne Creek and joined the main motor road (now Highway 101) at the north end of Trout Lake. Another network of plank roads radiated from Sargeant Bay, following Kenyon and Colville creeks.

Along the sides of the roads, timbers about a foot in diameter were laid to act as guiderails for the trucks, but they were not always successful in keeping the trucks on the road, especially when they were heavily loaded. Towboater Reg Paine recalled visiting Oscar Niemi's Halfmoon Bay Logging Company camp around 1927 and travelling in one of these hard-tired logging trucks over a planked road to the Trout Lake area where Niemi's crew was skylining with a diesel "duplex donkey." With eight drums and two engineers, this machine operated both the skyline operation and the loading of the trucks. Paine described the return trip to tidewater on a loaded truck as one of the most terrifying journeys of his life; even with the brakes fully engaged, the truck careened down the steep grade and only by some miracle halted short of the water. Two weeks later the same driver's truck went out of control before it got to the bottom; the driver was killed and the truck demolished.

Brown and Kirkland, better known as B & K Logging, were well-known logging operators on both Vancouver Island and the Sunshine Coast. Their camp at Sechelt Creek—known locally as "The Clear Cedar Camp"—was just across Salmon Inlet from the Gustavsons' railroad show in the early 1930s, but theirs was a truck-logging outfit with the logs yarded to the road by steam donkeys. In 1937 after all the enormous old cedars were logged out, B & K moved their trucks into the Roberts Creek area and logged there for nearly eight years, yarding with five steam donkeys and booming the logs at the mouth of Roberts Creek. Their camp, three miles inland from tidewater, and their timber lease were bought out by Burns and Jackson Logging in April 1943.

BURNS AND JACKSON LOGGING

L.S. "Al" Jackson was the moving force behind Burns and Jackson Logging. An Englishman, he had come to the Sunshine Coast in 1909 to work for the Robert McNair Shingle Company, but 10 years later, having married, he settled in Gibson's where he opened a butcher shop. It took him only a few years to discover that this was a mistake, and in 1923 he teamed up with his brother George and his brother-in-law Robert Burns to form Burns and Jackson

Logging with a camp on Gambier Island's West Bay. When the lease was logged out in 1925, Burns quit the company, but his name remained on the letterhead for another 25 years. The Jacksons moved their show to Bowen Island after that, but by 1933 they were at McNab Creek near Port Mellon, using gas donkeys for yarding and a caterpillar tractor for hauling to tidewater. They moved briefly back to Gambier Island, this time to Douglas Bay, and in 1936 set up camp at Wilson Creek. In 1943 the Jacksons bought out B & K's adjoining operation. During all this time, Jackson stayed with gas donkeys and high lead logging, using wooden spar trees. After he sold out to MacMillan Bloedel in 1950, L.S. Jackson retired; he died in October 1955.

L.S. Jackson's three sons, Phillip Scott "Pete" Jackson, Allen Jackson and Robert L. "Mike" Jackson, returned to the business as Jackson Brothers Logging in 1953, cat logging and high lead logging with wooden spar trees until 1960 when they invested in their first steel spar tree. When they sold their company in 1983 to Braiche Ltd., they were operating with three steel spars. Their company was later sold again to International Forest Products (Interfor).

KUCHINKA AND PETERSON

In 1932 the partnership of Frank Kuchinka and Jim Peterson set up a camp at the head of Narrows Inlet with one of the first caterpillar tractor operations on the Sunshine Coast. Here they hauled out fir and cedar with their cats at the rate of 25,000 board feet a day. Kuchinka, a short, stocky Austrian, had

Yarding logs with a caterpillar tractor at a Burns and Jackson logging dump at Roberts Creek, c.1937.
COURTESY OF THE SUNSHINE COAST MUSEUM AND ARCHIVES. PHOTO #3095.

set up his first camp at Killam Bay in Jervis Inlet in the 1920s with his first wife Emma working beside him as whistle punk. Sometime before 1928 he entered into a partnership with Peterson, a Norwegian, and they moved their camp to Jack Bay. According to Ted Girard who worked for them, Kuchinka was a "very, very good businessman and a good fellow to work for. They were both fair and honest men."[10] The partnership's next move was to the Narrows Inlet lease. After 1941 when they moved to St. Vincent Bay to the site of Phil Hiltz's turn-of-the-century camp, there were 40 to 50 men in the camp as well as wives and children. Kuchinka built a recreation hall there and kept the little community happy with regular dances and card parties. Their company and lease were bought out by H.R. MacMillan in 1952 and closed two years later. The buildings were burned in the early 1960s to prevent them being taken over by hippies.

OSBORNE LOGGING

E.F. "Ted" Osborne Sr., brought his Osborne Logging company to Halfmoon Bay from Mission, BC, in 1937. According to Osborne's foreman and high rigger on that site, Thomas Hugh Parish, this was a wooden spar, high-lead outfit that used gas-powered donkey engines to yard and trucks to take the logs to the water. When Osborne moved his company from Halfmoon Bay into eight-mile-long Narrows Inlet in 1944, its slopes had already been logged by Bert Whitaker, the Heaps company, and Kuchinka and Peterson, but Osborne was prepared to go far beyond the areas that they had cut. It proved to be an expensive operation. The two miles of road that he had to build to climb the first 1,700 feet of hardpan and heavily mineralized rock on his lease cost his company $25,000; three years later, he paid out another $14,000 to take the road an additional 3,000 feet higher up the mountainside. The road was no sooner built than it began to rain, then it snowed; as soon as the snow melted, the culverts overflowed and washed out the road, and construction began all over again.

The logs cut by Osborne's crew were taken out by Don Mackenzie Trucking Company, using one White and one Diamond truck, each leading a 25-ton Columbia trailer. On the steepest sections of the road, a donkey engine was used to snub the truck and trailer units up and down; each unit made six trips a day.

Osborne sold his company to MacKenzie Flavelle Ltd. in July 1945, but it was not the end of his logging career. Ten years later, with his son, E.E. "Ted" Osborne Jr., as his partner, he incorporated O & O Logging and opened a new camp at the head of Narrows Inlet. Twenty-three miles from Porpoise Bay, the camp was a model of the modern logging operation—separate houses for married staff, guest houses, offices, cookhouse, dining hall, garages and machine shops, all painted white with green trim. In May 1955 the first load of logs was dumped into the saltchuck; the Osbornes logged there for another 10 years then moved to Princess Royal Reach in Jervis Inlet.

LAMB LUMBER

The lower valley of Gray Creek was logged by its first pre-emptors, Arthur Bouillon and David Stewart Gray, but the rugged slopes of the canyon defeated the horse loggers and donkey engine outfits that came after them, so the virgin timber of the upper valley was still waiting to be cut when Lamb Lumber moved in a high lead outfit in 1941. It was about this time that Norman Burley of the BC Fir Company of Vancouver received an order from the federal government for a large quantity of 44-foot-long logs, and he came to Sechelt to offer a bonus to any company that could cut these very unusual, outsized timbers. Lamb Lumber's camp, situated in the midst of prime fir, undertook the job; unfortunately, when it came time to bring the logs down the mountain, they were so awkward to move that one of Lamb's more enterprising workers solved the problem by cutting them all in half. The bonus was forfeited.

Lamb Lumber was another of the family companies that operated in this area. Founded in Vancouver in 1910 by brothers Thomas A. and John B. Lamb, it was financed by the pile of gold nuggets they had dug from their mine near Dawson City. Thomas ran the family sawmill on False Creek while John became

Lamb Lumber's steam-powered tug Master *in Trail Bay about 1941.*
It is preserved at the Vancouver Maritime Museum.
COURTESY OF VANCOUVER MARITIME MUSEUM

the company's logging superintendent at Menzies Bay on Vancouver Island. The second generation of the family joined the company during the 1930s, so that by the time they moved into the Gray Creek valley, Thomas' elder son, Thomas II, had become the firm's accountant, his second son, Alexander, was the log buyer, and John's son, R. Bruce Lamb, had taken over from his father as camp superintendent.

Lamb Lumber had the distinction of operating one of the last steam tugs on the coast, the *Master*, a wooden-hulled vessel constructed at Moscrop's Shipyard on False Creek at the end of World War I. The ship is now preserved at the Vancouver Maritime Museum.

Thomas A. Lamb I, of the Lamb Lumber Company, which logged the Gray Creek valley between 1941 and 1959.
COURTESY OF THOMAS LAMB III.

In the fall of 1948, R. Bruce Lamb was killed in a loading accident at the camp, and his superintendent's job was filled by Alexander. John Lamb died in the 1930s, but Thomas A. Lamb survived until September 1960; the company was sold later that year to Fleetwood Logging. The third Thomas Lamb and his brother David came with their parents to live on the Sunshine Coast in 1959, and both have been involved in the industry.

JOHN BOSCH LOGGING LTD.

While many loggers went into the bush hoping only for not too many layoffs and a cheque that did not bounce when the camp closed down, others aspired to an outfit of their own. When John Bosch began logging on the Sunshine Coast in the early 1930s, the outfits he worked for included the Gustavsons at Deserted River, Jeremiason at Vancouver Bay, Burns and Jackson, "old Gus Crucil," and B & K Logging's Roberts Creek operation. He rigged spar trees for the Osbornes in Princess Royal Reach and earned his "Donkey Special" ticket to operate a steam donkey engine while working for the Newcombe family's logging show at Middle Point in Salmon Inlet.

Bosch finally got his chance to be independent in 1947 when the Newcombes decided to sell their camp; the price was $30,000 with "nothing down and so much a thousand. We took the kids out of school in Sechelt. We had two boats and we threw the furniture into one of them and my wife was standing on the dock ready to cast us off, when this wizenheimer came along. 'John,' he says, 'you'll be back but you'll be stone broke.' I told him, 'Mister, see my wife here and these two kids and that furniture there? That's all I got. Now you tell me how I'm gonna go broke.' We worked hard, day and night, Saturday and Sunday, and all I did from then on was make a good living."

The Newcombes' outfit, according to Bosch, was "mostly steam donkeys, yard and skyline and tightline. There was no rolling stock in most of those smaller gyppo logging outfits. Just high lead logging." The donkey was located about 900 feet above the beach with 1,200 feet of skyline; they yarded off the end of this setup. "The steam donkeys burned wood so you didn't have to buy any gas or diesel. Breakdowns were practically nil compared to what they are in logging today. Mind you, we didn't get much for logs neither."[11]

From the lease on Salmon Inlet, John Bosch moved his equipment to Narrows Inlet, two miles beyond Tzoonie Narrows, and just a few miles inland from the place where Kuchinka and Peterson had logged 15 years earlier. Bosch's company worked here for two and a half years, and when he moved out in 1950 to McMurray Bay in Jervis Inlet, he left his last steam donkey behind in the bush. Built in 1913 in Tacoma, Washington, with an 11-inch-diameter piston and a stroke of 13 inches, this sturdy old engine had been worked almost continuously for 37 years.

CHANGING TECHNOLOGY

A flight over the logging areas of this coast would probably reveal a number of steam donkeys like Bosch's old "1913 Tacoma" still sitting fully rigged in the bush waiting to go to work, but not all logging equipment had this extended lifespan. Trucks disappeared over precipices, rail cars were shunted into the saltchuck, and donkey engines collapsed from old age. A donkey engine that slipped over the cliff at Patrick Point and disappeared in 20 fathoms in the early years of the century was eventually recovered, but repairing the saltwater damage cost so much it would probably have been cheaper to buy a new one. Sometimes losses were simply the result of misuse of equipment, but most logging equipment that went onto the scrap pile was obsolete. However, if it was abandoned anywhere near the saltchuck, it was probably picked up by one of the entrepreneurs who made a living towing their barges into obscure bays to salvage scrapped equipment.

Loggers being generally an innovative breed, they were constantly bringing in new equipment that was better adapted to the terrain and the timber they were working or manufacturing what they needed right on the job. And since broken-down equipment meant irretrievably lost dollars, logging camp bosses relied on their machinery operators to make repairs on the spot. The need for such practical and inventive minds to keep these operations running naturally led to the development of a remarkable crop of mechanical wizards and rugged individualists.

Among them was George "Panicky" Bell who acquired his nickname because he was known to pick up his lunch bucket and head out of camp whenever things weren't going well, but since he was also an excellent machine operator and repairman, he was always welcomed back. At Rainy River in 1933 while Bell was taking a gasoline cat into the woods, he and the cat went right through the decking of an old bridge and landed on a huge rock below. As he had been warned not to use that bridge, he did not send back to camp for help, but instead planted blasting powder between the cat and the rock and blew the cat out of the ravine. When his foreman heard about the accident and came to investigate, Bell was continuing along the road as if nothing had happened. One bitterly cold and windy day Bell was on the way to the booming ground with foreman Lloyd Rodgers in an old steel-hulled boat that had no glass in the windows. When Bell got tired of freezing, he dumped a can of gasoline on the deck and threw a match after it. From the shore the boat looked as if it was being consumed by the flames, but it was just Bell's version of a heater.

By the mid-1930s logging technology had evolved to the point that when H.J. Hodgins prepared his 1933 forestry report for the provincial government, he could write that "practically all logging operations" in the Sechelt Forest District, except for a few handlogging shows, were using either high lead or skyline systems. However, there was more variety in log transportation; logs were still being sent down flumes into the water, although more and more were being transported by truck or on trailers behind caterpillar tractors. Railroads, which had provided at least half of the log transportation for nearly 25 years, were fast disappearing from the woods.

The most revolutionary innovations came, however, after World War II. Bill Bestwick's Misery Creek Logging Company, started in 1952, was typical. To log the area next to the Gustavsons' former timber lease, he brought in a Laturno Electric Arch. "I had the first electric, rubber-tired arch that pulled the trees to the tidewater," he later boasted. "The first one on the whole coast. I heard about it and I went down to Laturnos in Longview, Texas . . . Basically this was a machine they were building for other purposes, and they just added an arch onto it. It was kind of like a spar and a winch with a cable on it to pull the logs up and hold them. We dragged the trees into a landing with a gas donkey, then we made up a turn of maybe 10 trees, depending on their size, and dragged them down the road with this electric arch."[12]

Bill Bestwick's Laturno Electric Arch hauling logs
to tidewater at Misery Creek Logging site in 1952.
COURTESY OF BILL BESTWICK COLLECTION.

21ST CENTURY LOGGING VENTURES

While tracing early Sunshine Coast timber licences and their complicated chains of buyouts and bankruptcies is very difficult, present-day logging operations leave behind clearly marked, although equally complicated, trails of documents and even clearer anecdotal histories. For example, the Weldwood operation at the head of Salmon Inlet had two distinct histories, one of them following in a direct line from the pulp and paper industry. The other starts with Charles McDermid and Gunnar Wigard, who formed M & W Logging and began high-lead logging in December 1945 on the northern edge of the tiny settlement of Doriston just south of the Skookumchuck. In 1956 when the operation was employing about 50 men, Wigard sold his share to McDermid, and three years later McDermid sold out to Bob Malpass who wanted the company in order to build up his timber quota and thereby win the rights to the timber adjacent to Clowhom Lake. A year later McDermid and his son Bill began logging again, this time a mile south of Doriston with a six-man cat outfit; they were bought out again by Malpass in 1964 for the timber quota that came with their lease. Malpass then moved to the Thornhill Creek area of Salmon Inlet before finally securing rights to the Clowhom Lake timber.

Weldwood of Canada bought Bob Malpass out in 1971, brought in a 60-man crew and set up a permanent camp at the head of the inlet. In the years that followed, the company built approximately 225 km of roads and logged 3,113 hectares of timber in areas that include the Squamish and Red Tusk valleys, Nagy Mountain and the valleys of Bear, Fisher, Taqhaut, Dempster and Bennett creeks. In November 1994 Weldwood announced its intention to sell off all its coastal operations, including its logging camp at Clowhom, to Interfor, already the seventh largest logging company in BC. The provincial government reacted by setting up a panel to review the takeover under the provisions of the Forest Act to make sure that employment and community stability were maintained. The deal, which was completed the following year, made Interfor the dominant forest company on the Sunshine Coast.

In the new century Interfor also operates in Jervis Inlet (the Potato, Stakawus, Glacial and Perketts watersheds) and Narrows Inlet. The company logs up to one-third of its total annual harvest with helicopters in order to take timber from locations that would otherwise be economically or environmentally inaccessible. In 2007 they took approximately 20,000 cubic metres of wood by heli-logging in the Clowhom area. At that time all of the company's heli-logging was carried out by a subsidiary, Helifor Industries Limited, but in December 2006 the helicopter company was sold to Helifor Canada. Since that time all Interfor's helicopter harvesting has been contracted out as has its conventional logging projects.

Helicopter logging at Schelt Creek in 1981.
PHOTO COURTESY OF J.O. ALVAREZ.

Among the other forest companies operating on the Sunshine Coast in the 21st century is Terminal Forest Products, which heli-logged on the west side of Sechelt Inlet in 2006. The company also holds licences to log in Princess Royal Reach of Jervis Inlet and at Misery Creek in Salmon Inlet. Northwest Hardwoods, a division of Weyerhaeuser Company Ltd., is licensed to cut hardwoods—principally alder—in the vicinity of Kleindale. FAB Logging holds cutting rights around Snake Bay near the head of Sechelt Inlet.

The most significant new logging venture on the Sunshine Coast in the new century was initiated after the BC government passed Bill 34—Forest Statutes Amendment Act, 1998—in order to address forest management conflicts. The result was a new form of forest tenure called Community Forestry. In 2003 the District of Sechelt applied for and received a timber supply area for its newly constituted Sunshine Coast Community Forest; this tenure included the watersheds of Chapman and Gray creeks, which provide drinking water to Sechelt and environs, and an area around Trout Lake. It also provided for an annual cut of 20,000 cubic meters of timber, which is approximately 500 truckloads. By December 2006 its operating company, Sechelt Community Projects Inc., had received approval for its first Forest Stewardship Plan, and the Sechelt Community Forest completed its first full year of harvesting in November 2007, using local logging contractors. The majority of the hemlock harvested went to Howe Sound Pulp and Paper, while some of the cedar was used by West Coast Log Homes Ltd., located near Port Mellon; this company exports custom-built western red cedar home packages to the US, Europe, South America and Asia.

SAWMILLS

Throughout the Sunshine Coast's logging history, although many small sawmills have operated here—most of them attached to logging operations—most saw logs and shake bolts have gone to Lower Mainland mills for processing. However, a few good-sized mills have existed here to turn out finished products. One of these was established at Clowhom at the head of Salmon Inlet. Here the water from the Clowhom River once tumbled over a small drop, then forked around an island, forming two more falls on its eastern side before it cascaded into the Inlet. In 1901 Charles Ralston, a member of a logging family who had incorporated a company called Clowhom Falls Lumber, pre-empted L.2030 on the west side of the Clowhom River. Although the entire Clowhom valley had been devastated by fire around 1850, there was still plenty of red cedar available, and Ralston recognized the area's potential for a shingle mill. But before he could act on his idea, the Industrial Power Company secured a Crown grant to the adjacent lot, L.1901, and acquired the water rights on the Clowhom River with the intention of building a pulp mill there.

Ralston was forced to bide his time until 1906 when Industrial Power gave up on the idea. He was then able to purchase L.1901 and the Clowhom River water rights from them and thereby gained control of the falls. Financed by the family company, he built a log dam on the river to back the water up so that shingle bolts and logs could be floated down from the upper Clowhom Lake, and constructed a mill and auxiliary buildings on the west shore of the inlet. The Ralston mill, typical of those built for the shingle industry on this coast, was housed in a 40- by 50-foot single-storey building, sided and roofed with corrugated galvanized iron siding, with an attached two-storey section, 30 by 75 feet, roofed with corrugated aluminum. Wooden pipes reinforced by steel wire ran from the dam to the mill's water cannon, which fed a six-foot-diameter pelton wheel. Shafts attached to the pelton wheel turned the saws in the mill. Close to the mill was a blacksmith shop with a second pelton wheel that powered all the machinery in the shop. It was also connected to a seven and a half-kilowatt direct current generator that provided electricity for the entire camp, including a large "hotel" for the mill workers, timekeeper's cabin, manager's house and stables for horses. This second wheel remains at the mill site to the present day.

Charles Ralston obtained his Crown grant to L.2030 on January 24, 1908, and a month later transferred it to the Clowhom Falls Lumber Company, now headed by J.J. Grant, with two of the Ralston family—Peter Sr. and Peter Jr.—on the board of directors. The company already possessed $20,000 worth of timber rights in the territory surrounding the two Clowhom lakes and the Clowhom River. Later that year they brought in cement by scow from Vancouver to construct a concrete replacement for the original log dam. An inclined railway was built to transport the cement from the company wharf at the head of the inlet to the hilltop where it was transferred to horse carts for the trip to the dam site.

July 20, 1909, marked the beginning of 20 years of complicated financial manoeuvres in which the Clowhom mill changed hands again and again. On that date the directors of the Clowhom Company approved the sale of their company and all its assets for $50,000 to a company headed by Frank Llewellyn Buckley from Cass County, Iowa. Like many American lumbermen of his day, he found himself blocked by the stringent legislation in Washington state and saw BC's timber as the key to his future fortunes. Although educated as a teacher, he had gone into the lumber business as a bookkeeper and had worked at a mill in Enderby, BC. By 1910 he was the Vancouver president and general manager of the Iowa Lumber and Timber Company Limited, a holding company to which he transferred the title of the Clowhom shingle mill.

Buckley operated the mill for only seven years before he signed it over to English investors from whom he was raising money for his next venture. A year later, on June 30, 1917, the property was transferred to yet another new company, the BC–Iowa Lumber Company Limited, incorporated with Norman Whittall as president. Born in Turkey of British parents, he had come to BC in 1912 and quickly gained a reputation as a financial juggler because of his ability to rescue his investments from receivers by shifting assets from one company to another. Thus, it was no surprise that a month after acquiring the mill Whittall used it as collateral to secure a mortgage for $250,000 from the Montreal Trust Company to rescue one of his other companies.

All through these years, while ownership shifted between companies, the day-to-day business of producing shingles went on. The crews hired at Clowhom were made up of whites, Japanese and Chinese, but the Japanese and Chinese workers were always segregated from the white labourers. Chinese workers were given the more menial tasks—digging ditches, fetching water,

Clowhom shingle mill at the head of Salmon Inlet, 1933. On the hill above the mill is the "hotel" for the millworkers with the manager's house on the right. Frederick Leadbetter's 52-foot yacht Dorothy Vose *is on the extreme right.*
COURTESY OF AMBROSE CRONIN.

tending fires, taking care of the horses, laying skid roads and greasing them to make the logs slide freely. Japanese workers were generally employed to fell the trees and cut them into bolt-lengths. Their quarters were located behind the timekeeper's cabin and at sites such as Nagy Mountain, southwest of the lakes, where logging operations were in progress. Some of their liquor bottles, made out of clay from the local creeks, and opium bottles can still be found around these abandoned camps although they are now very difficult to locate as second-growth timber has covered the sites.

At first, Clowhom's cedar bolts were flumed down to the lakes from the cutting site and allowed to drift down the river, over the dam and then over the falls to the saltchuck where they were boomed and held until needed by the mill. Later, a railway was built from the cutting area with several small spurs that led to a landing above the mill; from there another short line ran down to the mill where the bolts were cut into shingles, strapped and packed onto barges to be towed to Vancouver.

After Europe's initial rebuilding period following World War I, lumber markets declined and production costs rose. The mill's owners responded by cutting the wages paid to their non-white labourers. In 1922, when BC–Iowa's financial position had not improved, another shuffling of the mill's owner-ship occurred, and both L.2030 and L.1901 were sold to the Brooks Lumber Company Limited, with the new company being given the name Brooks Iowa Timber Company. Whittall was also a director of this company with a man named Walter Thicke as secretary. The infusion of cash from Brooks permitted the mill to operate for another year, but the business continued to lose money. Then on July 25, 1923, Brooks Iowa went into receivership.

Whittall, the financial juggler, was unwilling to let Clowhom's rich timber rights go, and once again he performed a sleight-of-hand trick: he bought into B.W.B. Navigation, which was owned by Walter Thicke's brother Claude, assumed the company presidency and relegated Thicke to vice-president. The fol-lowing year B.W.B. purchased the idle shingle mill at Clowhom and a year later the company name was changed to the Blue Band Navigation Company. It was now a towing and milling operation with Thicke managing the towing side of the company while Whittall began producing shingles again at the 18-year-old mill.

For a time it looked as if Blue Band was going to succeed with the logging and milling side of the operation where BC–Iowa had failed, but in the late 1920s the company's officers began speculating on the stock market. To obtain investment funds, they mortgaged Thicke's tugboat fleet for one-tenth of its value. When the market crashed in October 1929, all Blue Band's assets were lost, and although Whittall had given his personal guarantee for $25,000 of the invested funds, he could no longer back it up. A meeting of creditors bought time but not enough to recoup the losses, and on September 11, 1931, Blue Band Navigation was adjudged bankrupt.

For Norman Whittall it was the end of 15 years' association with Clowhom Falls. For the Clowhom shingle mill, it was the end of the road. For the next 30 years, although a few small logging outfits would cut timber in the adjacent valleys, the old buildings and the trails criss-crossing L.2303 and L.1901 and winding around the Clowhom Lakes would only be used by sports fishermen in quest of cutthroat and rainbow trout.

THE PORPOISE BAY MILL

With most Sunshine Coast timber milled off-coast, the community welcomed the news in 1947 that the BC Fir Company of Vancouver had bought 19 waterfront lots on the east side of Porpoise Bay, just north of Indian Reserve #2, in order to build a sawmill. With an investment of $100,000, the company hired Herbert Blair Stockwell to build the mill, then installed a diesel-powered Swedish gang saw (built by Heaps Engineering in Vancouver) and a circular saw that were expected to turn out 40,000 board feet of rough lumber a day. The lumber was moved in the yard by a locomotive crane known as a "brown hoist" with a lifting capacity of 20 tons, and a dock was built out into the inlet for loading scows. A planer mill was to be installed later.

The sawmill was opened a year later, managed by Norman Burley, but in spite of its expensive equipment, it was not a success, and a year later Burley leased it to Vic Walters, newly arrived in Sechelt, who operated it for the next two years. It was then closed until 1954 when Burley took over once more, but it was badly damaged in a fire in 1957. It remained closed until it burned to the ground in 1987.

PULP AND PAPER MILLS

While the first half century of the Sunshine Coast logging industry's history is based on cutting saw logs and shakes, the emphasis in more recent times has been on cutting timber for pulp, but that story actually goes back to the establishment of the first pulp leases in BC. In 1904 the Industrial Power Company of BC, headed by G. Frank Beer, secured a Crown grant for L.1901 at Clowhom Falls at the head of Salmon Inlet, and a short time later won the water rights to the Clowhom River lying close to the eastern boundary of the lot. As the hydro-electric potential of this river was enough to run a pulp mill, the company began seeking a suitable timber lease from the BC government. At the same time, Herbert Carmichael, an Irishman who had come to British Columbia in 1889 to work as a mining inspector for the BC government, had gathered a number of partners and formed the Canadian Industrial Company. They chose the falls on the Powell River as the site for a mill and began looking for timber. "From my mining trips through the country," Carmichael wrote in a memoir, "I knew where the best timber was; but how to acquire it was the question as there was no legal machinery for taking it up. We jumped that hurdle by having the Legislature pass an Act to allow timber to be taken up for pulp purposes." When Carmichael learned that the rival Industrial Power Company needed timber as well, he suggested that they combine forces but keep their companies intact. Beer agreed.

The Pulp Act passed in 1901 offered leases of pulpwood forests for 21 years. "After this Act was passed," Carmichael explained, "the bright idea occurred to several gentlemen that they might horn in with profit to themselves, so at least four survey parties were sent out to select timber." While they were out in the field, Carmichael and Beer filed their applications with the Department of Lands, and when the other companies' surveyors returned, they found that the best of the mainland coast timber they had surveyed was already in the hands of Beer's Industrial Power Company and Carmichael's Canadian Industrial Company.

"Then these people stirred up the handloggers," Carmichael's story continued, "telling them they were going to lose their livelihood, and petitions began to come in to the government asking that the pulp applications be annulled. By government grapevine I heard of this in time to have other petitions arrive supporting the applications, and thus the one lot of petitions cancelled the other. The final result was that we had secured 400 square miles of timber from which we could survey 200 square miles. These were, of course, pooled."[13]

Unfortunately for Beer, no one was interested in financing the construction of a mill at Clowhom, and he sold his company and its holdings to Carmichael's company. In April 1912 the first paper left Carmichael's new mill at Powell River, and by February of the following year the first two paper units were running at capacity with a daily production of 102 tons.

HOWE SOUND PULP AND PAPER

Another pulp mill to benefit by the Pulp Act of 1901 was constructed at Port Mellon, but it had a much stormier history. It was initiated in 1907 when Captain Henry A. Mellon of Vancouver organized the British Canadian Wood Pulp & Paper Company and a year later purchased 85 acres of land at the mouth of the Rainy River. Mellon, a retired steamship captain, was 67 when he developed an interest in pulp milling after meeting Greely Koltz of Aberdeen, Washington, who was eager to start a soda pulp operation but was unable to find an adequate water supply in his home state. Mellon hired Koltz as fiscal agent and they began negotiating for the site at the mouth of the Rainy River, the southern half of L.1364, which by this time was owned by George Cates, who built the Seaside Hotel on the northern half.

Mellon's mill, a coal-fueled operation, was completed in 1909 with all its equipment—some of it new and some used—imported from the United States. It was christened "Pioneer Mills" and production began on October 14 of that year with paper made from some of the mill's own soda pulp mixed with bleached waste paper. Since this was not saleable, the mill switched to making a good grade of wrapping paper, which had a potential market in BC. A pulpwood supply was assured by the purchase of leases on northern Vancouver Island from the Western Canada Wood Pulp & Paper Company. However, the cost of coal and transportation were too high, and within four months the company's working capital was exhausted and the mill closed.

In 1912 both mill and timber leases were bought by American interests headed by Lester W. David of Seattle. The mill was renamed Colonial Lumber & Paper Mills, but it remained idle. About 1917 David sold the company's Vancouver Island pulpwood leases to the Whalen Pulp & Paper Company for the use of their Mill Creek sulphite pulp mill near Squamish. At the same time the Port Mellon mill passed into the hands of a new company called the Rainy River Pulp & Paper Company of Vancouver, under president Robert Sweeney, and it produced for almost two years before this company also went bankrupt. During this period it was converted from the soda pulp process to the kraft process and began using local second-growth logs that were hauled to the mill by horse teams or brought by water into a slough beside the river mouth. The mill was operated with 65 workers on two shifts: an 11-hour day shift and a 13-hour night shift with no spare workers; thus, if one operator was ill, his opposite number worked 24 hours without relief.

The next owner of the Port Mellon Mill was the Western Canada Pulp & Paper Company, financed by the Home Bank of Canada for about $750,000. When the bank failed in 1925, the company was forced into bankruptcy. Reincorporated by a court-appointed receiver as the Howe Sound Pulp & Paper Company Limited, the mill was left in the hands of a caretaker while awaiting its next buyer: Fred W. Leadbetter of Portland, Oregon, who paid $250,000 for it in March 1927.

According to Robert Noyes, who was his friend and employee for many years, Fred Leadbetter was "a true entrepreneur. He had a lot of ideas and was not afraid to put them into practice."[14] Born in 1868, Leadbetter had come into the lumber business at the age of 25 when he married the daughter of Henry L. Pittock, founder of *The Oregonian* newspaper and owner of the original Columbia River Paper Company at La Camas, Washington. Leadbetter worked briefly on Pittock's newspaper, but his real interest was in lumber and paper manufacturing, and by the turn of the century he had acquired control of the La Camas mill by purchasing its bonds for ten cents on the dollar. He also controlled several other lumber and paper companies.

After World War I, Leadbetter sold the La Camas Mill to Crown Zellerbach, but he took care to retain the water rights, without which the paper mill was worthless. The profit he made when he finally sold the rights, combined with his one-sixth share of Crown Zellerbach, made him a very wealthy man. Meanwhile, Leadbetter had moved on to his next venture, merging three of his major holdings in 1926 to form a new Columbia River Paper Company. A year later Columbia River purchased the Port Mellon mill. It was not the best deal the lumberman ever made. Its 20-year-old equipment was continually breaking down, and it soon became clear that he would have to modernize the plant if it were ever to make any money. As a first step toward renovation, Leadbetter induced Nils G. Teren of the Bates Valve Bag Company of Chicago to visit the plant and persuaded him to sign a contract to take the entire output of the mill after it was renovated. He then shut down the plant and began its reconstruction. It was to be a duplicate of the highly successful St. Helen's Pulp & Paper Company mill in Oregon, with identical machinery bought from the same German manufacturer. Work proceeded on a new booming ground, deep-sea dock, sawmill, planer mill, woodroom, and new recovery and digester buildings, as well as the installation of new machinery including a 1,500-kilowatt Westinghouse extraction-condensing turbine, four Krupp rotary digesters of 1,050 cubic feet capacity, four soapstone smelters, two rotary recovery units, and a seventh and eighth boiler. Unfortunately, a year later when construction of the new brick and steel buildings was still incomplete and the new digesters only partially installed, the price of pulp dropped from $60 to $30 per ton, and the Bates Company cancelled its contract. The Great Depression had arrived. Construction on the mill was halted, the workers were laid off and the property entrusted once more to a caretaker.

Leadbetter spent the Depression years struggling to keep his American mills operating. "He was a great improvisor," said Noyes. "He kept things together by sleight of hand. Doing things like announcing a holiday during the middle of the week—without pay."[15] He was also able to persuade his workers to accept 10 percent pay cuts on five different occasions. And when the shareholders of the Vancouver Kraft Company, to which Leadbetter had transferred title of the Port Mellon mill, grew anxious about their investment, Leadbetter gave his personal guarantee for their money.

Leadbetter's next move was to incorporate a new company called the Port Mellon Operating Company on September 7, 1935, to complete the mill renovations. The man in charge was Nils Teren, now Leadbetter's son-in-law. After the improvements were completed, the mill was reopened, supposedly to supply pulp to the Columbia River Paper mills in Washington and Oregon. However, some of the pulp that was produced was also sold to Japan and as a result, Teren hired Japanese workers. In fact, he had so many Japanese workers that the company had to hire a Japanese foreman in order to communicate with them—an act which created conflict with the white labourers. But there was no chance for it to grow more serious than a few grumblings because in 1937 Leadbetter paid a brief, unexpected visit to the mill during which he decided it could not be operated economically. Mill superintendent Tryg Iverson was given orders to shut Port Mellon down.

In 1939 the sawmill, steam plant and machine shop at Port Mellon were leased briefly to the Lake Logging Company; a year later Leadbetter reopened the pulp mill to provide kraft pulp for the Sorg Paper Company of Middletown, Ohio. In 1941 Sorg bought Leadbetter out for $2,500,000, ending the mill's longest ownership to that time. Sorg ran it at full capacity until the end of World War II, but demand slackened after 1946, and two years later poor market conditions forced the mill's closure yet again. When demand improved with the onset of the Korean War in June 1950, Sorg offered the mill for sale and accepted a bid from Canadian Forest Products Ltd. (Canfor), while still keeping a minority interest. Two years later, Sorg's interest was bought out by the majority shareholder, and the mill became officially known as the Howe Sound Pulp Division of Canadian Forest Products Ltd.

The latest chapter in the Port Mellon mill's history began in 1988 when it became Howe Sound Pulp and Paper Limited through an amalgamation of three companies: Canadian Forest Products Howe Sound Pulp Division, the sawmill and chipping plant of Westcoast Cellufibre Industries of Vancouver and the Oji Paper Company Ltd. of Japan. This signalled the start of a four-year, $1.3 billion modernization and expansion program. By 1991 the kraft pulp division had undergone a major upgrade, a newsprint division had been added, and over $100 million had been spent on environmental protection technology.

COUNTING THE TREES

The first loggers to come to the Sunshine Coast staked their timber leases so as to avoid the scrub forests along the shorelines, but they were even more careful to avoid the barren rock outcroppings and mountain peaks, swamps and lakes that cover a large part of this forest district. In fact, the 1933 Hodgins forest survey estimated that nearly three-quarters of this forest district could never be profitably logged. But the report concluded that although close to 36,000 acres had already been cut by that time, there were still approximately 200,000 acres of marketable timber left, with almost 78,000 acres of it both mature and accessible.

Soon after Hodgins' report was released, Canada's Ministry of Defence assigned the Royal Canadian Air Force the task of making aerial photographs of strategic areas of this country, and one of the areas they chose to photograph was the Sunshine Coast. Although primarily intended to teach aircrews the techniques of aerial reconnaissance and prepare them for the war that seemed to be inevitable, this assignment would also provide a check on earlier ground and marine surveys. Unfortunately, because World War II erupted soon after photography of the Sunshine Coast was completed, the photos became classified material and remained that way until after the war. However, by that time the air force had completed a new aerial survey, and the two sets of photos provided far more information in comparison than they could have provided separately. They were particularly valuable to the Forest Service as they showed reforestation of early clearcuts, changes in stream bed and runoff patterns, and major silting problems at the mouths of streams as the result of logging. They also showed a substantial decrease in available timber.

By 1950, the annual timber cut on the Sunshine Coast was 35 million board feet. Anticipating restrictions, the industry moved to educate the public. L.S. Jackson, then managing director of Burns and Jackson, was quoted in the *Coast News* as saying, "When people talk about this area being logged out, they are talking through their hats. This company . . . can operate, under present methods, 30 miles back from the main Sechelt highway. They are now back only nine and a half miles." And the industry predicted "hundreds of years of logging" ahead for the Sunshine Coast.[16]

A more detailed survey in 1953 still showed a total of 194,670 acres of mature timber in this forest district, even though another 50,000 acres had been logged since the 1933 report because new technology had enabled logging companies to get into areas that had been previously labeled inaccessible. However, because the annual cut had been steadily growing, of the 225,880 acres of immature timber documented in 1953, 48,080 acres of timber had only been growing since 1933, another 113,300 acres had been logged between 1893 and 1933, and 64,500 acres was land cleared before 1893. After allowance is made for the destruction of timber by forest fires, the figures showed that approximately 2,000 acres were being clear-cut in the Sechelt Forest District every year.

By the end of the 1970s the annual cut had increased even more, and mature, accessible timber had decreased to a degree that sounded the alarm bells in some forestry circles. Most of the mature timber on the Sunshine Coast has been allocated to logging companies through forest licences which require the companies to pay stumpage to the government, but in the 1990s there were still areas held under timber licences—the oldest tenures granted in the province, dating back to the early part of the century. The terms of these timber licences allowed the logging companies to cut in a specific area with no volume restriction placed on them—the next best thing to privately owned timber. On the Sunshine Coast they included several held by Canadian Forest Products near Chapman, Dakota, McNab, McNair and Sechelt creeks. MacMillan Bloedel owned timber licences near Roberts Creek, Chapman Creek, Dakota Bowl and the Skwakwa River. Interfor held a timber licence near Vancouver Bay. A third type of licence, the tree farm licence for small-scale forestry operators, was represented by four companies on the Sunshine Coast. They were Tideline Services, Gambier Forest Resources, Harper Logging and the oldest one,

Witherby Tree Farm, owned and operated by Bill Wright and his father, the former UBC forestry professor, Thomas G. Wright.

It is difficult to compare timber figures for the 1990s with earlier years since the Sechelt Forest District has been merged with the Powell Forest District, but the figures do show the relationship between timber cut on the various types of licences. In 1993, 26,102 cubic metres of timber was cut on timber licences, while 1,336,958 cubic metres was cut under forest licences and tree farm licences.

WAGES AND BENEFITS

In the first decade of the last century, wages for ordinary Sunshine Coast loggers were no more than 25 cents an hour although skilled men such as donkey engineers might make as much as 40 cents. They all worked a ten-hour day—from seven in the morning to six at night with an hour for lunch—six days a week. For accommodation and meals the men generally gave the company back 35 cents a day.

In P.B. Anderson's 1907–11 Flat Island camp the two bunkhouses, each accommodating approximately 20 men, were heated by cast iron stoves. The men slept in double-decker iron bunks on mattresses supplied by the company, which Dewey Anderson admitted, "wouldn't be considered fit for a pig today."[17] Some of the men cut cedar boughs to put under their mattresses to make them a little softer. The loggers brought their own blankets, and inevitably some of them were inhabited by bedbugs, lice and/or fleas so that, when the loggers left camp, *all* of their blankets were inhabited by vermin.

In an industry where the meals were often notoriously bad, those in Anderson's camps—at least according to his son—were hearty and wholesome although lacking variety. Supper was served at long, planked tables in the camp cookhouse; hot lunches were packed into pails and carried up to the men in the bush to be served in the lunch shack. The men who packed the lunches to the work site were generally Chinese who used shoulder poles with baskets balanced on either end.

However, the meals in the camp set up by Andrew Haslam in Vancouver Bay in 1905 earned the reputation of being the worst on the coast. When sides of beef became too gamey to be served as fresh meat, they were pickled for corned beef and served that way until the meat was so rotten that the men refused to eat it. On one occasion, a disgruntled logger made sure they would not be having it for dinner by dumping a tin of coal oil into it. Before they could eat that night, the camp boss had to send the men out to hunt deer.

Conflicts inevitably arose because of the working conditions and the long months of isolation. At Vancouver Bay during Jeremiason's day the first-aid man took a dislike to the bull cook and threatened him with a knife. Afterwards he hid in nearby bushes and from there attacked other loggers as they came in for dinner. When it grew dark, he returned to the first-aid shack, whereupon one of the offended loggers entered, baseball bat in hand. The first-aid man went out on a stretcher.

By 1921 the average wage paid to men working in BC's logging camps and mills had dropped to between 15 and 20 cents per hour. Workers—and even whole crews—were hired and fired at will, as evidenced by the telegram sent to Clowhom from the company's Vancouver office in October 1921: *Received your letter regarding Chinese wasting timber. Unless remedied in one week we will change crews.*[18]

When John Bosch began working in the woods in the early 1930s, a day's wages for a logger had risen into the three to five dollar range. And a three-man falling crew, working on contract, would aim to average 30,000 feet a day in good timber for which they were paid 40 cents a thousand. However, each man's board took about a dollar a day out of this sum, and so much of the rest went to the commissary for boots, shirts and rain gear that the loggers would be lucky to pick up a cheque for $25 at the end of two weeks.

Loggers were still required to carry their own bedding into camp until the late 1930s, and the work week was not reduced to five days a week until after the IWA strike of 1946. The union actually agreed at that time to a six-day week during the summer and a five-day week in winter, but when the five-day winter period was up, the men refused to go back to working six days.

Other aspects of camp life also began to improve in the 1930s and became standard after World War II. In 1926, David Jeremiason had been the first large company owner on the Sunshine Coast to allow wives and families to live in camp. By providing separate homes for families and a school for the children at his Vancouver Bay lease, he was guaranteed more productive loggers, and the practice caught on. In one- or two-man outfits, families always lived in camp, usually in floathouses, which simplified moving day when the timber in a lease was logged out.

By the 1950s, union pressure and economic realities compelled logging companies to improve living conditions in the camps with decent bunkhouses and comfortable beds as well as more varied menus in the dining hall. Gradually, even the remote camps where families had not been allowed lost their isolation as companies began bringing their men home by crewboat for weekends. By the mid-1980s even these weekday camps were mostly gone from the Sunshine Coast. Instead, loggers were living with their families in communities such as Sechelt or Pender Harbour, leaving marinas along the coast and within Sechelt Inlet between 5:00 and 6:30 a.m. (the time depending on the season) and coming home again in time for supper.

In the early days of British Columbia's timber industry, loggers were at higher risk of death or maiming on the job than in any other occupation, and injured loggers had little recourse to the law for compensation. Lost limbs, critical head injuries and death were accepted as the normal hazards of the job. But a revision of the Employers' Liability Act in 1910 allowed injured loggers to sue for damages, and a series of successful lawsuits began the move toward the slow upgrading of logging camp safety measures. In May 1912 Pender Harbour logger James Adams sued Dr. W.C. Acheson of Vancouver for improper treatment. It seems that Adams had been unconscious when brought to Vancouver to have his smashed leg set and put in a cast, but three weeks later it was discovered that the bones had never been set before the cast was applied. Acheson was forced to pay $2,500. In June 1912 Axel Gustafson sued and won $2,000 for leg and head injuries that he had sustained at Halfmoon Bay. P.B. Anderson was sued by loggers twice in 1914 while his outfit was working at Pender Harbour. One of them, a donkey fuel tender named Ivar Johansen, had been ordered by the foreman to cut a log while standing on the wrong side of it. Damages for his broken leg were $1,000. But the courts did not always side with the working man. A logger named Gabriel sued after a log attached to the donkey engine cable struck him when the engine failed to stop after the brakes were applied. Gabriel lost when the court decided the accident had been due to his own negligence.

Most of the injuries suffered by loggers on the Sunshine Coast during these early years were made worse because there was little medical help available, and that situation remained until 1930 when St. Mary's Hospital was built at Pender Harbour. Although the turnover of doctors there was high—most of them stayed two or three years at most—there was generally someone on duty to attend to the injured

But having a hospital did not improve safety in the bush. "Staying alive in one of those camps," commented John Bosch, who began logging in the early 1930s, "was a big, big issue, so we had to look after each other. If you weren't standing in the right place, you were asked to stand someplace else. Furthermore, in those days there were so many more people employed in the bush than there are today. When we rigged one of those big wooden spar trees and put on a boom—or what they called a hayride—there was always a donkey engineer, a loading engineer, generally two second loaders, a head loader and a chaser. And we all looked out for each other."[19]

Alan Douglas Wood was just 18 years old in 1939 when he was badly injured while working for Burns & Jackson above Wilson Creek. "I got hit with a loading line on the loading rack," he recalled in an interview in 2007. "The line hung up on a spike and then let go and I happened to be in the road . . . [I've] still got scars from it on my head . . . my back and my legs." The other loggers on the job simply detached the trailer from one of the logging trucks, threw him into the cab and took him down the hill to the main road where they transferred him to one of the Jacksons' cars and drove him to the hospital in Pender Harbour. There among his many injuries they discovered he had a fractured skull; he was unconscious for five days and off work for more than a year.[20]

On a single day in 1945, two Sunshine Coast loggers met with the same accident. Andrew Grifter, hooktender at Britain River for Oscar Niemi Logging, was struck across the back when a turn of logs was released, knocking down a nearby tree; he died two hours later. Jerry Sigurdson was loading logs at Halfmoon Bay that day for A.E. Ritchey Logging, when a log rolled and struck him across the back; he lived. At Glacial Creek in Jervis Inlet, Vincent Michael Sullivan, donkey operator, died in November 1947 when his engine toppled over on him. That same month, boom man Robert N. Kennedy drowned at Osborne

Logging's Narrows Arm camp. In April 1948, Lamb Lumber truck driver James McCallum was killed when an eight-ton log crushed his truck cab at Gray Creek. Six months later, Lamb's camp superintendent, R. Bruce Lamb, was crushed to death in an almost identical accident.

Deaths and injuries continued in the camps at the same steady rate well into the 1950s, even though the Workmen's Compensation Board had begun to impose safety regulations on the logging industry. Dr. Alan Swan, who came to work in Pender Harbour in 1954, recalled that "in those days there were so many more loggers and it was so dangerous. I've got a total lifelong respect for those men. They worked with danger every day of their lives . . . Hard hats had come in so a lot of men were saved by hard hats, but

Dr. Richard Alan Churchill Swan graduated from Queens University with his MD in May 1953 and came to Pender Harbour in November of the following year.
COURTESY OF ELEANOR SWAN, THE DR. ALAN SWAN COLLECTION.

the faller's pants hadn't so that was a common injury—a cut in the front of the leg. They now have battens that protect the men's legs." He estimated that during his 36 years of practice on the Sunshine Coast at least 70 loggers died on the job. "About a third of them were fallers. Some busted tree or limb would get them. It was staggering . . . About 20 drowned but not from falling off booms. They all drowned in boats . . . [because] most of them were not good seamen in spite of the fact that they were on the water so much."[21]

The worst drowning accident occurred on Wednesday, April 13, 1960, when six loggers lost their lives while returning to Sechelt from their small logging camp just south of the Skookumchuck. A storm was already raging when they set out in a 15-foot, open aluminum boat powered by an outboard engine. Winds quickly reached 60 miles per hour, and although home was only 15 miles away, they never arrived. The boat was spotted at four the next morning, swamped and empty.

Dr. Swan and Dr. Eric Paetkau, who arrived five years after him, also made regular visits to the larger camps in the Jervis Inlet area, but they certainly didn't get rich doing it. "The logging camps often had MSA or some other insurance policy," Dr. Swan recalled, "which was a godsend to us, but I remember one December—probably December 1960—that Eric [Paetkau] and I worked constantly and lost $500. We had to pay rent and staff and telephone and medical supplies and we took in $500 less than we spent."[22] It was only gradually, as safety equipment was invented and procedures were put into place and enforced, that the awful toll in the woods diminished.

SUNSHINE COAST FOREST FIRES

Lightning-caused fires have ravaged Sunshine Coast forests ever since they began forming after the last ice age, clearing patches of old-growth and making room for new stands. One such fire around 1850 swept the valleys of most of the tributary streams leading into Clowhom Lake, leaving only isolated stands of timber, mainly hemlock and very old cedar. Although the cedar still provided the shake bolts that were milled at the head of Salmon Inlet between 1906 and 1931, it was more than a hundred years after the fire before a new crop of timber was ready for cutting on this site.

Other fires that occurred in pre-contact times were deliberately set by the Native peoples. Evidence gathered in University of Washington forestry and botany research has proved conclusively that the Native people of the Pacific Northwest made a habit of setting fires when the forests encroached too closely on their settlements, crowding out the coastal meadows that furnished them with roots and berries and provided browse for deer. By burning off sections of forest, they returned balance to their environment.

The cause of many later forest fires was land clearing by settlers. A 1906 clearing fire that began at the north end of what is now Leek Road between Gibsons and Roberts Creek and spread eastward toward Howe Sound burned five square miles of old- and new-growth timber. Some fires in the Sechelt Forest District were deliberately set for gain. Pioneers of the Pender Harbour and Egmont areas tell of the mysterious fires in the Depression years that would break out in the scrub timber on the local mountainsides, fires that seemed to be marvellously synchronized with the periods of greatest economic need in these communities, and that always hit approximately the same areas of scrub timber. At such times the Forest Service would recruit the local men, provide them with a few dollars a day and chits to buy groceries, and send them off to fight the fires.

Other fires were the result of sparks from logging equipment, especially before logging locomotives were equipped with spark arresters. Wood-fired donkey engines were such a frequent cause of fires that a 1921 Forestry report suggested that it would be possible to draw up a chart of this province's logging operations by charting the forest fires.

British Columbia's fire losses in the hot, dry summer of 1919 totalled almost $1,000,000 in equipment and timber, nearly half of this the result of two Jervis Inlet blazes. In July of that year when a company logging southwest of Patrick Point ignored the Forest Service's order to burn their slash, forest wardens set fire to it themselves. Unfortunately, a strong northeast wind came up shortly after they got the slash burning, and within hours it was out of control. It roared through eight miles of cedar and fir on the north side of Princess Royal Reach, jumped Britain River, then burned its way south along Prince of Wales Reach nearly to Dacres Point. At the same time, a lightning fire that had been smouldering for several weeks on the south side of the inlet at Glacial Creek was blown into fresh activity and spread southeast across the timber on Marlborough Heights.

Lightning fires are very common in Jervis Inlet because there is a recognized "lightning belt" stretching from the Deserted River area in the east, roughly following Princess Royal Reach west through the Britain River watershed and out to the coast at Powell River. Almost all the lightning fires in the inlet have occurred in this belt, including the most disastrous of all, the fire of 1951. It began when lightning struck a snag high above the inlet east of Osgood or Boulder Creek. The Forest Service recruited a half dozen men from a nearby logging camp to make the dangerous climb up the cliffs to investigate. After most of a day spent climbing, they reported that the fire was completely inaccessible and nothing could be done to extinguish it. In any case, it was not making much progress as there was little wind, and since it was on the edge of the 1919 burn, they thought it would probably burn itself out. But the next day a northeasterly blew up and the fire was soon out of control. This time Britain River was not spared, and although the camp and the equipment being operated there were evacuated, all the timber was burned. The fire continued west past the head of Hotham Sound as well as forking south as the 1919 fire had done.

The effects of fire on terrain of this kind are catastrophic. While the Forest Service expects land that has been clear-cut and replanted to provide a new crop of trees ready for harvesting in approximately 100 years, burned-over forestland is expected to take twice that long because of soil damage and erosion. In the case of the Jervis Inlet fires, however, foresters estimate that a minimum of 500 years will elapse before a timber crop can be harvested, because there was such a thin layer of soil supporting tree growth there in the first place. The fires of 1919 and 1951 burned this soil away, right down to the bare rock. Until new soil can form, only scrub trees and brush can be expected to grow in the rock crevices. At the same time, the area is liable to more fires because it is in the lightning belt, and because the exposed rock formations retain heat in summer, drying out the meagre vegetation that has taken root and making it all the more vulnerable to fire.

Modern firefighting techniques have limited forest fire destruction in these inlets in recent years, but along Sechelt, Salmon, Narrows and Jervis inlets, the leafless spires that rise above the green of immature forests speak of the days when mountainside fires were virtually uncontrollable. Such is the amazing durability of cedar, however, that Harold Swanson, climbing in the Glacial Creek area around 1970, found trees that had been killed in the 1919 fire that could still have provided marketable shingle bolts.

DEEP WATER, SMALL BOATS AND BIG FISH

The Sunshine Coast is renowned for its sunny skies, but it is almost equally as well known for the temperamental behaviour of its waters. In fair weather they provide a means of transportation, a source of food, hydro power, drinking water and even sport and entertainment; in foul weather they are a means of destruction.

When Captain Vancouver complained that the shores of "this dreary country" were "composed principally of rocks rising perpendicularly from an unfathomable sea,"[1] it was not simply the remark of a man who failed to appreciate the scenery. He understood that it was the sheer cliffs bordering the inlets and the deep water beneath his boats that were making his voyage so difficult.

During winter, the masses of arctic air from BC's interior plateau that are forced down the Cheakamus and Squamish valleys become the "Squamish" winds that funnel between the steep slopes of Howe Sound. At times they reach gale force, gusting from 50 to 70 miles an hour, churning the water and battering ships. But the Squamish have their vagaries. Depending on whether the wind is driving from a little west or a little east of north, the water can be boiling onto the beach at Port Mellon while it is fairly calm in the main channel, or there may be a nasty sea running off Hood Point and a slight chop in Horseshoe Bay. Summer reverses the winds. When the interior plateau is hot, stiff westerlies develop from the cool air blowing inland off the sea. But both summer and winter winds can drive ships out of Howe Sound or onto the rocks.

The high winds blowing from the interior down Jervis Inlet are intensified by the narrowness of the inlet, and frequently make travel dangerous for small boats. "In summer-time," M. Wylie Blanchet wrote in her 1930s memoir *The Curve of Time,* "the wind blows up the inlet in the morning, down the inlet from five o'clock on." Local handloggers and fishermen told her that in winter the wind blew down the inlet all the time, bringing "such heavy williwaws that no boat can make against it."[2] Crosswinds blow out of the deep valley of Britain River, down Prince of Wales Reach and up the valley of Vancouver River. More winds whistle out of the valleys of the Deserted River and its tributaries, howling down Princess Royal Reach. Queen's Reach, however, is generally reported to be somewhat calmer than the lower reaches.

The inland sea—the finger-like Sechelt, Salmon and Narrows inlets—has conflicting winds, some blowing north or south over the isthmus at the town of Sechelt, others blowing down Narrows and Salmon inlets from the east, bringing the cold air from the plateau and creating dangerously rough waters.

Only a thousand feet separate Sechelt Inlet's shores at the point where it joins Jervis Inlet, and the waters are studded with rocky islets. This is the Skookumchuck or Sechelt Rapids. As the bottom at this point is no more than 30 feet down, the rapids become a bottleneck for the deep waters of the inland sea, so that before the tides have time to reach maximum rise and fall inside, the tides outside have already changed and are rushing in the opposite direction. This results in an average slack tide of only nine minutes and at high water slack a water velocity of 10 to 12 knots, creating roaring turbulence and gigantic whirlpools. During spring tides when the water outside the rapids may be rising and falling 15 feet or more, there is a wall of water and foam in the Skookumchuck and a constant, deafening roar.

The indigenous Sechelt and Squamish people whom Vancouver found on the Sunshine Coast had been watching the moods of these waters throughout the centuries, had developed boat designs that suited their needs and had become skilled in manoeuvring the boats they built from cedar logs. Manned by 10 or 12 paddlers, these canoes were used for fishing and sea lion hunting expeditions as well as for general transportation between villages. Not being governed by time, the Natives accepted the fact that it was sometimes prudent to stay on shore.

Captain Vancouver and the rest of the explorers and surveyors who were the vanguard of the European invasion were on time-limited expeditions and were forced to sail onward no matter what the weather. They came in boats that had been designed for seaworthiness but not necessarily for manoeuvrability in narrow waterways like those of the Sunshine Coast, and their logs show that they found navigating the inlets far more difficult than sailing the open sea. Even in the summer months their boats were buffeted by sudden vicious storms, and the steep-sided, deep waterways provided few safe anchorages where they could rest out of the wind. The Europeans who came after them to log and fish and carry passengers in these waters were governed by sawmill deadlines, fishing ground closures, and shipping schedules, but since they had come to stay, in time they adapted ship designs to suit the waters and invented new navigational skills to keep their craft afloat even in bad weather.

PASSENGER SHIPS

The Sunshine Coast's island-like isolation has always meant that those who choose to live here have been dependent on watercraft for their transportation and communication with the rest of BC's southern coast, and before the advent of a system of roads, boats were the easiest and often the only means of travelling from one point on the coast to another. Ship services were irregular at first. Around 1880, a man known to history only as "Navvy Jack" sailed his sloop between Vancouver and Howe Sound on an on-demand basis, but by the time 20-year-old William A. Grafton came on the scene in 1888 with his four-ton sloop, there was no one providing passenger or freight service between Vancouver and the Sunshine Coast. Grafton's "ferry" had "no engines, just sails, no name."[3] He docked it at Andy Linton's boathouse wharf at the foot of Carrall Street in Vancouver and ran it up to Howe Sound and Sechelt once a week, providing both passenger and freight service to handloggers and ox-team loggers along the shore. But as the Sunshine Coast population began to grow, it was inevitable that scheduled shipline services would have to be developed to meet local needs.

THE SECHELT STEAMSHIP COMPANY

Herbert Whitaker launched the Sechelt Steamship Company in 1903 to ensure regular service for his Sechelt Hotel and his logging camps, and his first ship was the 52.5-foot-long converted steam tug *New Era*. Hiring Captain Sam Mortimer as master, Whitaker put the little ship on a passenger run between Vancouver and Sechelt. Although built just two years earlier in Vancouver, the *New Era* had already established a reputation as a waterfront workhorse, but it had never been intended for work outside the harbour. It had only a 13.5-foot beam and a draft of 5.6 feet and was reputed to have so little steam that, whenever its whistle was blown, it lost power and nearly came to a standstill. It had a permanent starboard list, which had to be remedied every time it encountered rough water. One passenger recalled how on one particularly rough crossing he had been handed a scoop shovel and told to help trim the ship by shifting the coal supply.

The *New Era*'s shortcomings notwithstanding, however, in 1906 when its crew was witness to the collision of the Canadian Pacific Steamship *Princess Victoria* and the Union Steamship tug *Chehalis,* they were able to manoeuvre their ship close enough to the wreck to launch a rescue boat in the rough seas. They were responsible for saving the lives of four of the *Chehalis'* crew by putting them aboard the *Victoria* before the *Chehalis* sank.

Whitaker expanded his operations in 1906 by buying the small, shelter-deck screw steamer *Hattie Hansen*—a 73-foot-long coal-burner—that had begun its career on Lake Washington 13 years earlier. Whitaker renamed it the *Sechelt.* Like the *New Era,* it had been built for sheltered waters; it was very narrow for its length—only 15.2 feet wide—and very high-sided. A small lounge on the top deck provided accommodation for passengers. In rough weather, the large, recessed side doors that were used to load cargo and livestock also allowed the sea to flood the main deck and pour down into the engine room.

The 91-foot-long *Tartar* was added to the fleet in late 1908. It had been built as a steam tug in Scotland in 1906 and sailed to Vancouver via Cape Horn under the command of Captain Charles Polkinghorne. It was nearly lost during a gale in the Bay of Biscay when its deckload of coal was washed overboard and some of the large lumps jammed the rudder. When it slid into the trough of the sea, water poured into the engine room and put out the boiler fires. But the crew worked valiantly to make repairs and succeeded in getting it underway again. Crossing the Atlantic they were delayed by head seas, so off the coast of South America the crew had to row ashore to cut enough firewood to get to the next coaling station. Having survived these initial trials, the *Tartar* then proved its worth in its first two years on the BC coast by towing booms from northern logging camps.

Whitaker bought it for his Vancouver–Pender Harbour service and sent it to Hind Brothers' boatworks at the foot of Gore Avenue in Vancouver to be converted into a passenger ship. The conversion added an upper deck and wheelhouse, but with the ship's narrow beam and all this extra topside weight, it became "a bit cranky and tender,"[4] especially when fully loaded. Its first trip with passengers was on May 7, 1909, from Vancouver to Sechelt, but it was so unstable that, before its next trip, pig iron and cement had to be put into its bilges. In spite of this, it continued to be difficult to handle in rough seas.

After its initial run, the *Tartar* was skippered by a man named Sparrow who had captained deep-sea vessels. Accustomed to having his ships docked by pilots, he had a great deal of difficulty bringing the *Tartar* alongside the

Sechelt Steamship Company's 91-foot Tartar *after its conversion from a tugboat to a passenger ship in 1908. The addition of a full upper deck made it "a bit cranky and tender," especially when loaded to capacity.*
COURTESY OF THE SUNSHINE COAST MUSEUM AND ARCHIVES. PHOTO #1216.

Sunshine Coast's wharves, and on one particular dead-calm summer day, he made several attempts to dock the *Tartar* at the Sechelt wharf before running it right up onto the beach. Fortunately, the ship was undamaged, and when it floated free on the incoming tide, a crew member took over the wheel and docked it safely.

Once the *Tartar* was put into service, Whitaker transferred the *New Era* to Porpoise Bay to service the logging camps in the inland sea. There the ship shared the Porpoise Bay wharf with the *Babine,* a wood-burning passenger steamer owned by Whitaker's younger brother Cecil. The *Babine's* career was very brief; it burned and sank in 1911 in Sechelt Inlet. (Cecil Whitaker died of tuberculosis not long afterwards; the family blamed it on the fact that he had often taken the *Babine* out at night, sticking his head out of the window to watch for floating debris.)

Herbert Whitaker's fourth ship was the steam ferry *Belcarra,* bought in January 1910 from the Terminal Steamship Company, which had been running it between the Fraser River and Howe Sound. The *Belcarra* was a 172-ton wooden-hulled vessel, and Whitaker sent it to Pender Harbour to establish a run that would service the logging camps of Jervis Inlet.

Until 1910 the *Sechelt* and the *Tartar* operated from Ward's Wharf at the foot of Abbott Street in Vancouver, ending their runs at Donley's Wharf in Pender Harbour after making regular stops at Bowen and Keats islands, Hopkins', Grantham's and Gibson's landings, Roberts Creek and Whitaker's wharf at Sechelt. Where no wharves existed, the settlers rowed out to pick up or deliver passengers. At a few places, such as Roberts Creek, a float where the steamer could dock briefly was anchored offshore. Horses and cows consigned to these settlements were simply urged overboard and forced to swim for the shore.

The years 1909 and 1910 were to prove disastrous for Whitaker's Sechelt Steamship Company. During a wild storm on April 13, 1909, his 35-foot pleasure craft, the converted tug *Kootenay,* was battered on the rocks at English Bay. It had been anchored in the bay after an engine refit in the city and was waiting for the *New Era* to tow it home when it dragged anchor. Damage to its port side was extensive.

Six months later the *New Era's* engines broke down near Canoe Reef while the ship was on a charter to the Cowichan Gap. While disabled it hit a rock and was heavily pounded by rough seas before drifting onto the beach at high tide. Rescue was delayed until the shallow draft tug *We Too* could approach close enough to pull it off and tow it into Nanaimo for repairs. Whitaker sold the *New Era* shortly afterwards to a Vancouver firm; a few years later it was purchased by a Captain W.T. Cotsford and disappeared from the shipping registry.

In a heavy fog on September 17, 1910, the *Belcarra* left Pender Harbour under command of Captain John Edgar Fulton, bound for Jervis Inlet with 17 passengers. His first stop was to be Dempsey's logging camp in Agamemnon Channel, but when the ship arrived there around three in the morning, the customary light was not burning on the float; Fulton mistook another light some 200 yards onshore for his marker and went hard aground on the rocks. With the *Belcarra* badly holed in the bow, Fulton ordered the crew and passengers ashore. A cable was then fastened to the ship and anchored to rocks but shortly afterwards it started to go down stern first, snapping the cable as it plunged into 65 fathoms. Although numerous attempts have been made by members of the BC Underwater Archaeology Society to locate the wreck of the *Belcarra,* no trace of it has ever been found.

Sechelt Steamship Company's 172-ton wooden-hulled Belcarra. *It went to the bottom in fog in Agamemnon Channel on September 17, 1910, after the captain mistook an onshore light for the customary light on the Dempsey logging camp's float.*
COURTESY OF THE SUNSHINE COAST MUSEUM AND ARCHIVES. PHOTO #991.

An inquiry a month after the mishap established that the sinking was primarily due to the misplaced float. However, the inquiry also heard that during the ship's recent annual inspection, its compass had been found unreliable. Since Whitaker had not replaced it, Fulton had been navigating by echoes from his steam whistle. He had compounded his problems by sailing through the narrow passage in the heavy fog at the ship's full speed of seven knots.

As if Whitaker's losses were not heavy enough, on August 7, 1910, the *Sechelt* stranded on Prospect Point in Stanley Park and had to wait there until high tide to be refloated. On November 6 it grounded again, this time at Cowan Point on Bowen Island where it waited three days for a tide high enough to refloat it.

With the sinking of the *Belcarra* and strengthening competition from other day-steamer lines, Whitaker decided to liquidate his shipping business. He sold the *Sechelt* in January 1911 to the British Columbia Steamship Company and it was put on the Juan de Fuca run between Victoria and Sooke. Two months later it was caught in a storm and went down with all hands. When he could not find a buyer for the *Tartar*, he tied it up at his dock in Porpoise Bay.

THE ALL RED LINE

One of the new steamship companies to start up after Whitaker sold his ships was the All Red Line, incorporated in January 1911 with captains Sam Mortimer and Charles Polkinghorne as two of its principals. Their company began business with the purchase of the steam yacht *Santa Cecilia*, which Polkinghorne delivered to Vancouver from England. It had been built in 1881 by John Elder & Company of Glasgow to accommodate the lavish parties of the "mad" Marquess of Anglesey. Clipper-bowed and luxuriously appointed, it was 144 feet long and capable of doing 13 knots. After purchase by the All Red Line it was renamed the *Selma*, and with Captain Polkinghorne at the helm began running three times a week from Vancouver to Powell River, stopping at all the landings and harbours in between. In 1914, a sister ship, the 154-foot *Santa Maria*, was purchased, allowing the line to expand to a daily schedule. Each

The Glasgow-built steamship Santa Maria *at Donley's Landing in Pender Harbour in 1918. Formerly a private yacht, it was put on the Vancouver–Powell River run by the All Red Line in 1914. After purchase by Union Steamships, it became the* Chilco.
COURTESY OF THE SUNSHINE COAST MUSEUM AND ARCHIVES. PHOTO #966.

morning at 9:30, one ship left Vancouver while the other left Powell River, so that they met at Sechelt, sometimes tying up there at the same time.

Around 1914 the All Red Line also acquired seven acres of land just south of Sechelt. They named it Selma Park, constructed a wharf off the point of land locally known as Holy Joe's Rock and laid out a picnic park on the flatland above it. By 1917 it appeared that the All Red Line was ready to expand again, but instead in October of that year they sold out to Union Steamships. The *Selma* was renamed the *Chasina* and the *Santa Maria* became the *Chilco*.

UNION STEAMSHIPS

The first Vancouver-based shipping company, Union Steamships, was founded in 1889 and entered the coastal service as a towing firm after purchasing the assets of the Burrard Inlet Towing Company. These assets included the three steam tugs *Skidegate, Leonora* and *Senator* and eight scows.

Union Steamships' first passenger vessel was the 184-foot *Cutch,* built as a pleasure cruiser for the Maharaja of Cutch. It arrived at the Union wharf at the foot of Carrall Street in Vancouver on June 3, 1890. Although designated for the regular run between Nanaimo and Vancouver, it also made excursion trips, among them the first recorded Union excursion to Pender Harbour on July 18, 1891, carrying 250 passengers. After a lunch served on Henry Point, the holidayers walked to Hotel Lake where they fished and bathed. Returning to the ship, they left Pender Harbour at 7:00 p.m. for the four-and-three-quarter-hour trip back to Vancouver.

The first Union ship to visit the Sunshine Coast on a regular run was the *Comox*. This 101-foot steamship was constructed in Vancouver, although its hull sections had been prefabricated in Glasgow and shipped to Vancouver aboard the steamer *Granholm*. The keel of the *Comox* was laid down at a makeshift shipyard in Coal Harbour on August 26, 1891, and the ship entered service for Union on December 19 of that year. On May 2 of the following year it sailed with Captain Charles Moody as master on its first logging camp run, leaving Vancouver on that Monday morning with passengers and freight destined for more than 40 points on a 500-mile trip that would take it as far as Port Neville on the mainland side of Johnstone Strait. Both Sechelt and Gibson's Landing were fixed stops on this schedule, but whenever there was a demand, waypoints in between and up Jervis Inlet were added. A typical cargo included groceries, crates of poultry and pigs, sides of beef, perishable goods, drums of oil for donkey engines, sacks of feed and bales of hay for the horse teams used in the camps, tinned tobacco, barrels of beer and the household effects of loggers who were bringing in their families. Union also received a federal subsidy for the *Comox* carrying the mail. It began twice-weekly runs in

1894, alternating ports of call in order to service all the logging camps on the route. It was sold in 1919 for scrap but instead was rebuilt as the *Alejandro* and put into service in the Mexican coastal trade.

The *Chasina* and the *Chilco* (later renamed the *Lady Pam)*, both acquired from the All Red Line, continued on their scheduled runs to the Sunshine Coast during these years. Meanwhile, Union Steamships made extensive improvements to the former All Red Line Selma Park property, and then, to service their expanded facility, the company launched the *Capilano II,* a wooden-hulled, 135-foot day-steamer licensed to carry 350 excursionists. On June 16, 1920, it began sailing three times a week to Selma Park and waypoints, extending these trips once a week as far as Halfmoon Bay and Thormanby Island.

Among the other Union ships to visit the Sunshine Coast during the early post-World War I years were the "Lady ships"—*Evelyn, Alexandra, Cecilia,* and *Cynthia.* The *Lady Evelyn* was the first of Union's ladies. Purchased in October 1923 from the Howe Sound Navigation Company, it was already 22 years old and had plied the St. Lawrence for most of its years as the *Deerhound.* At 189 feet long, it could carry 480 day-passengers, and Union initially put it into service on the Pender Harbour run under Captain Billy Yates. However, when they discovered how much fuel it used, it was restricted to the West Howe Sound run.

The *Lady Alexandra,* with her three spacious decks featuring a luxury dining room and a hardwood dance floor, had a 1,400 day-passenger capacity that

Union Steamships' Comox *embarking passengers at Irvine's Landing float about 1911.*
COURTESY OF THE SUNSHINE COAST MUSEUM AND ARCHIVES. PHOTO #766.

made it the largest excursion liner north of San Francisco. The *"Alex"* as it was affectionately known, was built for Union at Montrose, Scotland, and launched in February 1924. It was 225 feet long, 40 feet wide and had a maximum speed of 14 knots. Although its most famous run was the regular cruise to Bowen Island, it was well known for its excursion trips to Gibson's and other West Howe Sound landings.

The *Lady Cecilia* and the *Lady Cynthia* had been the British navy mine-sweepers *Barnstaple* and *Swindon,* converted to excursion vessels in Scotland. They were 235 feet long and 29 feet wide and licensed to carry 900 day-passengers and 75 tons of freight. The *Lady Cecilia* arrived in Vancouver in April 1925 and was placed on the daily Howe Sound run to Squamish under Captain Neil Gray; both ship and master remained on this run until 1937. The *Lady Cynthia* arrived four months after its sister ship and was put into service on the Powell River run with Captain John Boden as master. The two ships became the best known of the Sunshine Coast's "Daddy Boats," carrying thousands of families to camp or cottage there every summer and bringing husbands and fathers to join them on the weekends. The fare to Sechelt was regularly two dollars, but with a family book of camper's tickets, it worked out to 90 cents each way.

On the night of December 27, 1925, a thick fog lay off Roberts Creek as the *Lady Cecilia* headed north from Vancouver with a full load of 500 mill workers returning to Powell River from their Christmas excursion to Vancouver. Fifteen minutes behind her came the *Lady Cynthia* carrying another 75 passengers, the overload from the *Cecilia.* Meanwhile, Captain Bob Wilson on Union's *Cowichan,* a 157-foot vessel that serviced the logging camps north of Powell River, was working his vessel south through the fog, sounding his whistle con-stantly. Right on time, he heard the *Lady Cecilia* pass him safely. What he was not expecting was the *Lady Cynthia's* whistle a few minutes later, and there was no time to change the *Cowichan's* course to avoid a collision with the oncoming ship. While the bow of the *Cynthia* remained firmly rammed into the midship of the *Cowichan,* all the latter's passengers and crew were safely transferred, but as soon as the ships drifted apart, the *Cowichan* sank in deep water. It was all over in 11 minutes from the moment of impact.

Nearly 70 years later a fisherman snagged a piece of the *Cowichan's* deck railing, and that event inspired a search for the wreck by a group that included members of the RCMP, the Underwater Archeological Society of BC and the Vancouver Maritime Museum. Their search began in 1996 using the RCMP patrol vessel *Lindsay* dragging a metre-long torpedo-shaped sonar scanner in a precise grid pattern over the water south of the White Islets. After nearly a year of searching, they were on their last pass of the day in May 1997 when the shadowy image of a bow and mast appeared on the on-board monitor. The deepest ship-wreck ever found in BC waters, the *Cowichan* lies 60 fathoms down—too deep for recreational divers to view. The hull is intact and the mast upright.

Twenty-five years after the sinking of the *Cowichan*, on October 10, 1950, the *Cynthia* was involved in another sinking when it cut in two the wooden-hulled BC Forest Service cruiser *A.L. Bryant* in Howe Sound. Although three of the log scalers on board were drowned in the accident, four were pulled to safety by the crew of the *Cynthia*. An inquiry found both ships' masters to blame.

The *Lady Cecilia's* career was much less eventful, but it did go aground in 1930 on the gravel spit off the mouth of Chapman Creek; fortunately it was not damaged and was pulled off by tugs at high tide. Then on December 23, 1947, it suffered damage that nearly ended its career. On a special Christmas trip from Vancouver to Powell River, the ship went hard aground on Tattenham Ledge off Buccaneer Bay, tearing open 75 feet of its bowplates. The passengers were taken off safely, but the ship remained stranded for three days before three Straits tugs pulled it free and beached it in a nearby sandy bay. With temporary patches applied and bilge pumps working furiously, it was towed to Vancouver for restoration.

Union's 25-passenger gas-boat *Comox II* was built in 1924 and began its career as a ferry on the Whytecliff service, but because it also ran the occasional trip on the logging camp circuit, it soon became well known to people on the Sunshine Coast. It went aground on Captain Island off the eastern tip of Nelson Island shortly before midnight on Tuesday, May 26, 1925, during a furious

Union Steamships' Lady Cecilia *aground on the gravel spit off the mouth of Chapman Creek, 1930. The spit was created after the creek's other mouth was sealed off about 1921. The ship was not damaged and was pulled off by tugs at high tide.*
COURTESY OF THE SUNSHINE COAST MUSEUM AND ARCHIVES. PHOTO #624.

rain squall coupled with an exceptionally strong tide. As the tide went out, the bow was left high and dry while the stern was in 15 feet of water. The crew and passengers stepped ashore on the uninhabited island just before the vessel rolled onto its side and filled with water. However, when it was discovered that the *Comox* had sustained no hull damage, the Union Steamships' salvage barge *Skookum #2* pumped it out and refloated it a week later.

Five years later the *Comox* was refitted to take excursionists on some of the first day-cruises to "the wonder fjord of the world," as Jervis Inlet was advertised. Then in 1931 the ship was moved to Sechelt Inlet to run day-trips from the wharf at Porpoise Bay to Clowhom Falls in Salmon Inlet then back down the inlet and out through the Skookumchuck and back to Sechelt via Pender Harbour. Meanwhile, the Jervis Inlet run was taken over by the *Lady Cecilia,* which carried as many as 900 sightseers at a time up Prince of Wales Reach to Vancouver Bay.

Competition between Union's Selma Park and Bert Whitaker's Sechelt resort ended when the latter's company was bankrupted in 1926; his hotel, general store, post office, and all his lands were held in receivership for nearly two years before being bought up by Union Steamships. This acquisition gave the company a new base of operations for its Sechelt–Salmon–Narrows inlets routes. Union Steamships successfully weathered the Depression years by cutting back on its runs, and during the war years when many of its men had joined the forces, the company made do with its aging vessels and reduced crews. But the post-World War II years brought fresh competition and new anxieties.

UNION'S COMPETITION

In May 1946 Gulf Lines, owned by Davidson Marine Limited, began a fast passenger and express service with two converted minesweepers, the *Gulf Wing* and the *Jervis Express,* from Vancouver to Powell River and up Jervis Inlet with stops at Sechelt and Pender Harbour. This route coincided with the *Lady Cecilia's* run, but Gulf's service lasted only until April 1951.

On the route between East and West Howe Sound, competition for Union Steamships came initially from Howe Sound Transport, a company incorporated by former airline pilot C. Gordon Ballentine and naval officer George Frith in 1944. Since Union's single trip per day schedule made it impossible for Sunshine Coast people to travel to Vancouver and back in one day, the new company planned to initiate a regular ferry schedule of two round trips per day from West Vancouver's Fisherman's Cove to Gibson's Landing.

But Ballentine and Frith had stiff competition in the bid for the franchise. When they applied to the Public Utilities Commission in 1944, they were opposed by both Union Steamships, which proposed a motor launch service on the route, and North Shore Navigation, which was offering a car ferry service with three trips a day between Horseshoe Bay and Gibson's Landing. It was January 1945 before Howe Sound Transport was awarded the franchise, and the decision was immediately appealed by North Shore Navigation, although they dropped the appeal three months later.

For the new service Ballentine and Frith leased the *Commuter* from Union Steamships, a new, twin-screw gas-boat built by Coates Watercraft of Sea Island. At 30.1 feet and 4.97 tons it was just under the limit for services operating without fully licensed crews. It made its first crossing in one hour and ten minutes on November 1, 1945, from Fisherman's Cove—where a waiting room, restaurant and bus stop already existed—to Gibsons's Landing. A bus met the ferries at each terminus.

In June of the following year the company's name was changed to Sea Bus Lines Ltd., and that fall the partners bought the 30.6-foot, 4.94-ton *Sea Bus I*, a sister ship to the *Commuter,* although with its curved deckhead and raked after-bulkhead, it was far more streamlined in appearance than its box-like sister. The 3.13-ton *Sundance,* built by the Canadian Powerboat Company, was acquired in May 1947 to serve as a backup. By the time the *Sundance* was purchased, Sea Bus Lines was making at least two round trips per day, taking up to 30 passengers per trip in two ferries. One person operated each vessel, docking it stern first and holding it against the dock by running the engines in reverse. Unfortunately for the passengers, in all three vessels the engines were located in the main cabin area so that the noise and working of the vessel against the seas could not be ignored. There were no toilet facilities on any of them, and the passengers routinely suffered from seasickness in rough weather.

By 1948 Ballentine and Frith realized that Sea Bus Lines required capital expansion, but rather than sell shares to the public and lose control of the company, they elected to sell out to Gibson Brothers of Victoria. In April of that year the new owners moved their West Vancouver terminus to Horseshoe Bay and began making two returntrips per day to Gibson's Landing with the 140-passenger converted Fairmile cruiser *Machigonne.* Its master was Captain John Bunyan of Gibson's Landing, who had also been senior skipper for Ballentine and Frith. Within the year the *Machigonne* was making a third trip each day on a regular basis and as many as five trips a day in summer.

However, pressure for a regular car ferry service was mounting, and both Gulf Lines and Sea Bus Lines were edged out of business by the summer of 1951 when the American company, Black Ball Ferries, began service in West Howe Sound. The *Sundance* was sold to Freemac Amphibious Taxis operating out of Horseshoe Bay; it was torn from its moorings during a fierce gale on January 26, 1951, driven onto the beach and smashed beyond repair. The

Sea Bus was sold to Continental Logging and burned at the company dock on Porpoise Bay in 1952. The *Commuter* was returned to Union Steamships then sold to a logging company and ended its days on Harrison Lake.

Service by Gulf Lines had lasted only six years, and that of Sea Bus Lines and its successor only five, but their competition had existed long enough to seriously undermine Union Steamships' position in the Sunshine Coast service. Union's local passenger service was cut back in the fall of 1949, and the company withdrew entirely from both the Pender Harbour–Jervis Inlet route and the West Howe Sound route in November 1950.

BLACK BALL FERRIES

On August 12, 1951, there were approximately 3,000 people living on the Sunshine Coast with not more than 50 automobiles among the lot of them when the car ferry MV *Quillayute* first carried Black Ball Ferry's house flag—a black circle on a red field—from Horseshoe Bay to Gibson's Landing. This 35-car, 600-passenger ferry had been launched in April 1927 on Bainbridge Island in Puget Sound for the Sound Ferry Line, which was later absorbed into the Puget Sound Navigation Company, owned since 1820 by the Peabody family of New York. When Puget Sound created its Black Ball Ferries subsidiary, *Quillayute's* ownership was transferred to that company, and when Black Ball moved into BC waters, *Quillayute* began service with five sailings per day from Horseshoe Bay to the Sunshine Coast, with the versatile skipper John Bunyan at the helm.

The Black Ball Ferry Quillayute began plying the waters between Horseshoe Bay and Gibson's Landing five times a day in 1951.
COURTESY OF THE SUNSHINE COAST MUSEUM AND ARCHIVES. PHOTO #22.

The *Quillayute's* sister ship, MV *Bainbridge,* joined it on this run about a year later. For backup, Black Ball brought in the SS *Smokwa,* the only steam ferry on the coast. Originally named the *Scotian,* it had been built at Pictou, Nova Scotia, in 1946 and had spent its first five years as a Halifax harbour ferry. Although considerably smaller than the other ships on the West Howe Sound run, it could take 48 cars to their 35, but it could only carry 470 passengers.

In 1952 the company also began service on the Earls Cove–Saltery Bay run. The road improvements that followed this extension encouraged more tourist ferry traffic, and within five years after it was established, Black Ball's Sunshine Coast route had become extremely lucrative. Thus, when the company's troubles began, they were not the result of lack of business. In fact, Black Ball's problems were the result of a strike on May 17, 1958, by employees of Canadian Pacific Steamship Lines (CP). As CP operated all the major ferry services on the West Coast, the strike had an immediate effect on commerce, but since the company had a federal charter, the provincial government was powerless to interfere. The BC cabinet did have the power, however, to intervene if there was trouble with the remaining service between Vancouver Island and the mainland, a service that happened to be operated by Black Ball Ferries under provincial jurisdiction. As a result, when Black Ball's employees gave 72 hours' strike notice on June 21, it took the BC cabinet only 48 hours to invoke the Civil Defence Act, which authorized the government to take possession of the company. Black Ball's employees were thereby denied the right to strike, but they went on strike anyway on July 18. Premier W.A.C. Bennett promptly responded by announcing that his government intended to establish its own ferry fleet by the following summer. In fact, the first ship of the new fleet was in operation by October 1959, and the government purchased Black Ball's entire operation—including its ships, docking facilities and Horseshoe Bay terminal—in late 1961.

In 1963 the former Black Ball motor vessel *Kahloke,* which had been on the Nanaimo run, was renamed the *Langdale Queen* and moved to the Langdale–Horseshoe Bay run. It had been built in Philadelphia in 1903 as a steam-driven ferry and, as the *Asbury Park,* had served as a New York excursion boat. After that, as the *City of Sacramento* it had ferried passengers across San Francisco Bay, but construction of the Golden Gate Bridge had put it out of work, and it had been sold to Black Ball for service in Puget Sound. It had been rebuilt at Yarrows in Esquimalt in 1953 before being put on the Nanaimo run.

The new BC Ferries sent the *Bainbridge* to work on the Earls Cove–Saltery Bay run. *Quillayute* was sold to Nelson Brothers who rechristened it *Samson IV* and converted it into a floating fish camp. *Smokwa* suffered a similar fate, becoming a fish camp for J.H. Todd and Sons in Rivers Inlet.

TOWBOATING

The first towing operations in Sunshine Coast waters were those of the hand-loggers. Confined by law to human-powered boats, they generally used small lapstraked rowboats, often no more than 12 feet long, to marshal logs five and six feet across at the butt and more than 200 feet long. Like the Native people, they soon learned to time their operations to take advantage of favourable winds and tides, although they were still vulnerable in the sudden fierce storms that sweep the inlet waters.

Steam power was introduced with the paddlewheeled towboats that pulled the log booms of the Sunshine Coast to the mills in Burrard Inlet. Most of them had been designed as passenger or cargo craft and converted for towing. Economically, they were not an outstanding success, for although the flat booms they towed varied in volume according to the size and power of the boat's engines, the average paddlewheeler could manage a mere six to eight sections of logs per tow. They were extremely dangerous to operate in rough weather because their towlines had to be anchored high on the wheelhouse to avoid interfering with the paddlewheel, an arrangement that meant that in heavy seas with a log tow underway, they were in danger of going to the bottom stern first. As a result, it became standard practice during storms for paddlewheel towboat crews to cut their towlines in order to save their boats and to return later to pick up their tows. In prolonged storms these loose tows frequently broke up on the rocks before they could be rescued, becoming hazards for other shipping coming down the inlets.

Even in calm seas, the paddlewheelers were at risk in the inlets because the tows could easily be caught in the riptides that exist around all the major points, and when towing booms out of Salmon, Narrows and Sechelt inlets, they faced the added danger of the Skookumchuck. The towboat masters learned to time their trips carefully, bucking into the tide so that they would hit the middle of the rapids at slack, and be more or less pushed out the other side. Sometimes, however, a whirlpool or riptide would wrap the boom around one of the islands, and days would then be spent rounding up the logs.

After paddlewheelers were retired from the log-towing business, they continued to ply the inlets as supply boats for the logging camps. The side-wheeler *Mermaid* was one of the oldest of them. Launched at Hastings mill on May 22, 1886, it towed booms and barges from the Sunshine Coast for two or three years, then was sold in 1892 and sentenced to pull coal barges for a Nanaimo company. Its troubles began two years later when it struck a rock in a storm off Port Valdez, Alaska; after several anxious days, it was eased off the rock and towed into port for repairs. In 1902 it struck a rock off Newcastle Island and sank in shallow water. This time B.A. Wardle of Nanaimo bought the ship, raised and refitted it to run passengers and freight to the logging camps of Jervis Inlet. It was now valued at $22,000.

The *Mermaid*'s final tryst with a rock came off Moorsam Bluff in Jervis Inlet during a fierce storm on Friday, March 25, 1904. Returning to Vancouver from Deserted Bay with three loggers as passengers and a crew of five, the ship was hugging the shoreline as it ran down Princess Royal Reach. At five in the morning it struck a rock and was badly holed. The *Mermaid*'s master, Captain Walters, headed the ship across the inlet toward the shelter of Britain River and had managed to coax it close to the river mouth before it started to founder. The passengers and crew climbed into the ship's boat and abandoned it before it sank in 65 fathoms. All aboard made it safely to the logging camp just inside the river mouth and were picked up the following day by Union Steamships' *Comox I* on its regular inlet run.

BLUE BAND NAVIGATION

One of the earliest independent towing companies to do business in Sunshine Coast waters was Claude Thicke's Blue Band Navigation. Thicke, an inventive man, started towing in 1909 with the 71-foot steam tug *Coutli*, which had been built in 1904 at McAlpine's ways in False Creek for Union Steamships. It was one of the few early tugs that had been designed specifically for towing, but Union sold it because it burned too much fuel. Thicke bored holes into the firebox door to improve combustion and turned the ship into an asset for his fledgling company. It became a regular sight off the Sechelt Peninsula as it towed barge-loads of sawmill waste from Vancouver to be used for fuel in the Powell River Company's pulp mill. Thicke went overseas with the Royal Navy in World War I, but after his return in 1920 he bought the four tugs of the Progressive Steamboat Company and with them launched B.W.B. Navigation Company Limited, putting all his boats to work towing log booms from Jervis Inlet.

When financier Norman Whittall bought into B.W.B. in 1923, the company's name was changed to Blue Band Navigation. After purchasing the Clowhom mill and its timber rights, the company expanded from towing into logging, with Thicke's tugs making regular trips with log booms from Clowhom, out through the Skookumchuck to mills in Vancouver. However, when Whittall's financial manipulations caused the whole company to collapse in 1931, Thicke lost his entire fleet.

THE HOPKINS FAMILY

In 1912, when Bert Whitaker was unable to find a buyer for his steamship *Tartar*, he moored it in Porpoise Bay where it waited two years before being bought by the Vancouver engineering contractors, Sir John Jackson and Company, who converted it back into a tug. The company used it to tow barge-loads of granite from Nelson and Hardy islands to build the Victoria breakwater. Then in the summer of 1927 the Hopkins brothers—Gordon, Philip and Eustace—of Hopkins' Landing bought the ship, brought it back to the Sunshine Coast as the *Hawser* and put it to work towing logs and barges.

The Tartar *after 1927 when it was owned by the Hopkins brothers of Hopkins' Landing and had been renamed the* Hawser. *Built on the Clyde as a steam tug in 1906, it had served as a passenger vessel for Bert Whitaker and been reconverted into a towboat in 1914. It was sold for scrap in 1937.*
COURTESY OF THE SUNSHINE COAST MUSEUM AND ARCHIVES. PHOTO #1668.

In November 1928 the *Hawser* answered an SOS from the freighter MV *Arran Firth,* which was on the rocks off the south end of Texada Island. The crew had escaped to the shore, but when the *Hawser* arrived at half tide, the hatches of the ship were awash, and the stern was in deep water. A salvage crew arrived late that night and by daybreak the ship was afloat and under tow by the *Hawser* with a salvage barge alongside to keep it pumped out. They anchored it safely in English Bay later that day. Sadly, it was an accident on board the *Hawser* in March 1930 while it was taking on bunker coal at Union Bay that caused the death of Eustace Hopkins. His brothers sold the *Hawser* for scrap in 1937.

The Hopkins brothers' most famous boat was the steam tug *Hopkins* designed for Captain Gordon Hopkins by Arthur Moscrop. A wooden-hulled vessel, it was built right on the beach at Hopkins' Landing in 1910–11, and is one of the few early West Coast vessels to have been photographed at various stages throughout the building process. The *Hopkins* remained with its builders until 1925 when it was bought by Island Tug & Barge and renamed the *Island Rover.*

Early in the 20th century steam-powered, screw-driven tugs like the *Tartar* had replaced the paddlewheeled towboats in the log-towing business, and these steam-powered boats were replaced in turn by gas- and diesel-powered ones. By the 1930s the average tow assembled on the Sunshine Coast and destined for mills on the Lower Mainland was 40 to 50 sections, with the largest tugs, such as the old *Dauntless*, pulling tows of 80 to 100 sections containing as much as 3.5 million board feet of lumber.

While navigating the inlets with tows was hazardous, negotiating the outside waters of Malaspina and Georgia straits was just as perilous. Tug masters had to be prepared for storms as bad as any they experienced in the inlets, especially in winter when, without warning, southeast winds can whip Malaspina Strait into a seething mass of swell and foam. Shelter for boom-towing tugs along the western shore of the Sunshine Coast is limited to a half dozen bays. They include Blind Bay between Nelson and Hardy islands, and Pender Harbour, Secret Cove and Halfmoon Bay on the Sechelt Peninsula. Quarry Bay on Nelson Island has been used in dire emergencies but it provides only token shelter for a large boom. The Trail Islands were dreaded by the early towboaters because a tow sheltering there had to be moved every time the winds shifted. Along the stretch of coast from the Trail Islands to Howe Sound there is no shelter at all from storms, and capricious tides could slow the early tugs' progress to a standstill. In winter they had to deal as well with Howe Sound's Squamish winds.

Some storms have lasted for weeks. Fierce winds and waves pounded this coast all through the final week of November and the first two weeks of December 1914, forcing more than 30 tugs with booms in tow to find shelter. None of the tugs were lost but logs were scattered from one end of the Strait of Georgia to the other. Freezing winds in January 1954 broke up log booms that were part of a tow waiting out a storm within Gambier Island's Long Bay. Days later when the winds finally died, it took 12 tugs to herd the logs against Keats Island, then push them back into Long Bay to be boomed again.

Tug masters have no love for the currents off Gower Point even in quiet seas, but in the high winds of mid-July 1955, seven tugs with their cumber-some booms ran into trouble as they tried to round Gower Point from Trail Bay, heading for Port Mellon. Two of them had almost reached the safety of Howe Sound where the winds were calmer when they were forced back, with one boom breaking up in the high seas. The five remaining tugs held their tows in the bay between Gower and Byng points, but their booms were blown ashore in spite of the arrival of extra tugs called out to help. One boom lost about a quarter of its logs while tugs pulled and pushed, trying to keep it on course.

The booms that partially grounded fared better, and after the seas flattened out and the tide rose in late afternoon the following day, they were successfully towed into Port Mellon. But throughout the night and most of the next day, beachcombers were busy salvaging logs, and the search by sea and air for missing timber was still going on three days later.

LOG SALVAGE

During the 1870s, if log booms were scattered as they were being towed from Sewell Moody's Gower Point lease to the Moodyville Sawmill Company, the boom men seldom went after them because it was cheaper to cut more trees. But sometimes after a storm the Sechelt Native people would collect the logs and tow them to Moodyville where they would sell them back to the mill for a few dollars. After this had happened several times, Moody encouraged Chief Schelle to get his people to collect more of the company's strays since this was an economical way to reclaim his lost logs—as well as a few that had been lost by other logging outfits. And this was how log salvage or "beachcombing" came to the Sunshine Coast.

The first non-Natives to beachcomb worked in pairs in open wooden dories that they stood up to row or in very small steamboats. At that time, the law of the sea did not cover log salvage, and it was a case of first come, first served. Many of these early beachcombers were not above tampering with booms left untended in secluded bays, uncoupling boom chains so that they would release as soon as the boom hit the first swell or sawing almost through the tailstick so that it would break and allow the logs to scatter. This could be especially disastrous for the tug skipper in the inland sea if he moved his tow out during the night in order to hit the Skookumchuck at slack tide and did not check his raft until after daylight.

To put a brake on the worst excesses of beachcombing zeal, in the 1930s new laws were introduced that required owners to brand all of their logs with their timber mark and made it a criminal offence to mill unmarked logs. Booming practices were also improved with watchmen riding each end of the raft. However, some beachcombers still went outside the law when they were rounding up a spill, collecting for themselves all the badly marked logs or deliberately smearing the marks on the biggest and best logs with the point of a Gilchrist jack. They took some risk in selling such logs and sometimes sneaked them into the millpond under the cover of night. A few beachcombers · continued to give the business a bad name by carrying off valuables from untenanted summer cottages and other buildings along the shore. Some even robbed the log booms of their chains to sell or exchange for gas. However, this type of chicanery disappeared after log-towing insurance was introduced, and with the advent of gas-boats and diesel tugs, beachcombing became so much more efficient in rounding up strays that it was recognized as a legitimate business and assumed a new name: log salvage.

Subsequent provincial legislation placed log salvaging in the hands of the Gulf Log Salvage Co-op Association and the BC Log Spill Recovery Co-op, and restrictions on log salvaging gradually cut the number of men and women willing to risk their lives in this dangerous but very necessary West Coast occupation. In 1995 there were approximately 30 full- and part-time log salvors working from bases on the Sunshine Coast, and at that time they joined with other BC log salvors to form the Western Association of Salvors and Handloggers (WASH) to address some of the long-existing problems in the industry.

Perhaps the most famous salvage boats on this coast were those owned by Harry Smith, proprietor of Smitty's Marina in Gibsons. Best known was the squat, black *John Henry*, which as the *Persephone* was piloted from 1972 until April 1992 by Bruno Gerussi in the television series *The Beachcombers*. Smith also owned the jet salvage boat skippered by Robert Clothier on the show, as well as the *Silver Gale* which was used as the series' police cruiser. After the show's cancellation, all three boats were returned to their working roles, salvaging logs and hauling scows and freight. In 2003 the Town of Gibsons, which had acquired the *John Henry/Persephone* as a gift from the Smith family, donated it to the Sunshine Coast Museum and Archives. After volunteers put in hundreds of hours restoring it to its original glory, it was returned to the town in 2008 and placed on display in the heart of the Landing.

Harry Smith's salvage boat John Henry *was known to fans of* The Beachcombers *television series as the* Persephone. *It was put on display in the heart of Gibson's Landing in 2008.*
COURTESY OF
ROSELLA LESLIE.

BOOMING GROUNDS

During the 1950s good boom men found work at Andy's Bay on Gambier Island where Coastal Towing Ltd. had established a booming ground to break up the Davis rafts that had been towed from the Queen Charlottes. Andy's Bay is 300 feet deep and has three miles of shoreline, ideal for accommodating these 3 million-board-foot units with their 40 feet or more of submerged timber. Fed by several streams, the bay also has a high freshwater content, which kept the teredos away from the logs for the three weeks that it took a 24-man crew to break and sort one of these rafts into 20 or 30 flat booms and send them on their way to the mills on the Fraser River. Davis rafts were still being sorted here as late as 1956 under camp superintendent Walter Morrison.

However, they were not the only means of transporting logs down the coast. As early as the 1920s some logging companies had begun to convert old sailing ships into barges by enlarging the deck hatches and removing the bulkheads in order to tow them south loaded with logs. The big breakthrough in this technology came after World War II when Straits Towing converted four steel-hulled military landing craft to carry logs. Then in 1957 MacMillan Bloedel built two 104-metre, self-dumping log barges. These were so successful that by the early 1960s log barges had replaced Davis rafts completely and were carrying one-third of the West Coast's log output. As a result, Andy's Bay became even more important as a sorting ground and remains so to this day.

THE CONTINUING TOLL

The Sunshine Coast's outside waters have been a treacherous place for more than towboats and their log booms. Dozens of ships ranging from pleasure craft to freighters have gone to the bottom or been driven onto the shore during storms, especially in the waters between the Trail Islands and Gower Point.

On August 7, 1907, the 8-ton cargo steamer *Prince Rupert* foundered within a mile of the Trail Bay shore, but no help was available and its crew of three drowned. In 1911 the 10-ton *Pastime* went to the bottom in the bay close to Selma Park, but that crew was rescued. The 474-ton barge *KN#2* capsized and sank in Trail Bay on December 5, 1920, after it was cut loose in a storm.

The *B and M,* a 48-foot gasoline-powered tug owned by M.R. Cliff Towing, left Vancouver on December 11, 1928, bound for Jervis Inlet with a load of stumping powder and logging chains on board. That evening, when a screaming easterly caught the tug off Sechelt, the cargo shifted and a fire broke out in the hold. The captain of the tug *Hawser,* sheltering a boom of logs behind the Trail Islands, saw the fire and went to the rescue, but all that the *Hawser's* searchlight could pick out in that black night was an oarless, damaged lifeboat half full of water. To it clung the engineer, Harry Webster. After rescuing him, the *Hawser* cruised for an hour but failed to find Captain J. Gillen and he was presumed to have died in the fire. The hull of the *B and M* was found on the shore the next day; it had burned to the waterline.

More powerful engines have made it possible for modern boats to ride out storms that would have sunk earlier ones, but there are still exceptional circumstances in these waters for which no skipper can prepare. The 289-ton barge *Coast Quarries Jr.* went to the bottom off Sechelt on June 2, 1945, when it collided in heavy fog with the old tug *Sea Lion*. In April 1948 the 52-foot tug *Tyee 7*, owned by the Horie-Latimer Construction Company, ran aground and sank off Merry Island in a southeasterly gale. Fortunately, its crew of six was rescued and the tug raised weeks later. The tug *C.P. York* ran aground on a reef off Thormanby Island in December 1953 when the barge it was towing overran it during a storm. The wheelhouse was crushed and the crew thrown into the sea; the captain was picked up by another tug and the chief engineer, Bill Macdonald, was found alive but injured on the beach of Nelson Island by Yolanda and Lee Roberts, children of Harry Roberts. Macdonald had floated 10 miles on the hull of an overturned lifeboat. Five other crewmen were drowned. This catastrophe became the catalyst for changes in the towboat industry. After April 1954 the radios in all tugboat wheelhouses were to be tuned to the distress frequency, and a centralized system was developed to respond to distress calls. In time this led to the establishment of a Search and Rescue system on the West Coast.

One July night in 1960 the fishboat *Unimak* hit a scow off Gower Point and rolled over. When rescuers arrived, they heard someone banging from inside the wooden hull, but they knew that, if they cut into the hull to rescue him, the boat would immediately sink. As the water was extremely rough, the CPR ferry *Princess of Vancouver* was diverted from its Nanaimo to Vancouver route to make a breakwater while towlines from two tugs were strung under the *Unimak* so it could be towed to shore. However, before this could be successfully accomplished, the fishboat righted itself briefly and then sank. Its crew, two men and a woman, drowned. The boat was raised a week later and beached at Davis Bay where the bodies were removed and temporary repairs made. The *Unimak* was eventually returned to service but went down for good when it was hit by a tanker off Prince Rupert.

And on January 11, 1967, Rivtow Marine's 66-foot *Gulf Master*, valued at $250,000, disappeared in heavy seas a mile and a half off Sechelt. The three-year-old vessel had been returning to its Vancouver base after delivering a tow when it hit the storm. It apparently capsized so suddenly that there was no time to send out an SOS. A single, four-foot-square life raft was located some hours later with deckhand Rodney Seymour aboard; he was rescued by helicopter but died in hospital without regaining consciousness. Lost were the tug's master Forrest Anderson, engineer Richard McPhail, and two deckhands.

MARINE SALVAGE

For 25 years, beginning in 1929, marine salvage operations on the Sunshine Coast were most frequently carried out by Captain William Higgs' Nanaimo Towing Company, partly because of the strategic mid-gulf location of his Vancouver Island headquarters and partly because he had the only heavy equipment suitable for these jobs. His boats included a pair of former rum-runners, the *Yucatrival* and the *Revuocnav* (Vancouver spelled backwards). Higgs had strong ties to Pender Harbour because he had married Ida Donley of that pioneer family, and in 1941 their son, Captain Leonard Higgs, started a subsidiary company, Sechelt–Jervis Inlet Towing, headquartered at Donley's Landing. The Higgs family was the first on this coast to recognize the potential of wartime landing craft for salvage work, and their *Tractor-Transport*, skippered by Herbert Spalding, was in business by the end of the war salvaging logging equipment up and down the coast. It was more or less routine for the two Higgs companies to raise sunken fishboats and pleasure craft, but they were also capable of more complicated jobs like raising a barge-load of granite blocks that had sunk beside the Vancouver Granite Company's Kelly Island dock. The Higgs family sold out to Straits Towing in December 1951 but kept the Sechelt–Jervis Inlet company name, and this company was reactivated by Leonard Higgs in 1960 with headquarters in Sechelt. It ceased business in 1985.

DIVING FOR TREASURE

Many of the ships wrecked along this coast have gone down in waters too deep for salvagers to raise them, but the remains of a number of them have been located by the Underwater Archaeology Society. One of these was the steam-powered fish packer *Aliford*, discovered in the early 1970s by John Seabrook of Egmont. The *Aliford* had left "old" Egmont in the fog one day in 1917 and was scarcely underway when it went aground in Agnew Passage off the eastern tip of Nelson Island. The crew managed to get to the beach, but as the tide went out, the boat shifted and a kerosene lantern on board tipped over. While the crew watched helplessly, the vessel burned to the waterline and sank.

Recreational diving in the inlets of the Sunshine Coast received an important media boost in 1992 when the Artificial Reef Society chose a site just off Kunechin Point Marine Park in Sechelt Inlet for the sinking of the 367-foot Canadian destroyer *Chaudiere*. The old destroyer's fittings were removed, holes cut in its sides for divers' access, and explosive charges laid that were designed to blow holes in the port end of the boiler room so that the ship would sink stern first. Over determined protests by local environmentalists and an attempt by the Sechelt Indian government to obtain an injunction to prevent the sinking, the ship was towed into place and sunk on December 5, 1992. Contrary to plans, it went down listing to port; its stern now rests at a depth of 50 feet and its bow at 90 feet, deeper than the society had anticipated, which changed the wreck from a beginner's dive to an intermediate dive with advanced features. Diving clubs from as far away as Korea have been attracted to the site.

There are other artifacts beneath the surface besides wrecks. In the fall of 1990, diving master Patrick Patterson of Vancouver found a jade Indian hammer in Porpoise Bay; it has yet to be checked for age and source. Amidst the debris off logging camps and resorts, divers have discovered old bottles and other articles of a bygone era. Most diving enthusiasts, however, take part in the sport to view the wealth of undersea life in the inlet waters, especially in areas such as the Skookumchuck where oxygen levels are high and plants and animals flourish.

TRADITIONAL NATIVE FISHERIES

For thousands of years before Europeans came to this coast, salmon was the most significant food source for the Sechelt and Squamish Native people. Camping at the mouths of streams, entire communities waited for the sockeye, chinook or spring, pink or humpback, coho and chum salmon to return, then used nets, traps and weirs to capture the fish needed for their winter consumption.

Evidence of the ingenuity they used to harvest fish has been found in recent times along the Sunshine Coast. In two small bays at Smuggler Cove, rocks remain where they were piled to form the walls of fish traps; the gaps between the rocks were blocked with woven branches that allowed the sea-water to leave as the tide receded but prevented the escape of the fish. At the head of Porpoise Bay where a small stream enters from the Sechelt marsh, the Sechelts constructed a trap that ran from below the low tide level up the creek for several hundred yards. It was composed of hundreds of thin pilings interwoven and set close together in two rows that converged at the beach end. The remains of this trap were discovered in the late 1960s when the beach area was being dredged.

While the young Sechelt men were engaged in fishing, using these traps as well as basket-nets and spears, the women and elderly men gutted the salmon, then dried them on racks in the sun. When the salmon fishing season was over, the Sechelts moved to the clam beds on the little beaches of Sechelt Inlet, and to places like Granville Bay on Hotham Sound, and Clam Cove near Killam Bay, or back to the beds of Native or Olympic oysters in Pender Harbour. They also fished for herring, cod, perch and halibut in the inlets, and trout in the lakes. And at a creek mouth just south of Nine Mile Point on Sechelt Inlet they gathered herring roe by setting boughs just below the low tide level for the herring to spawn on.

THE WEST COAST CANNERY ERA

After the first West Coast cannery was built in 1870, a huge international market for Pacific salmon developed, and fishermen began moving into waters that had been the exclusive fishing grounds of the Native people. A small colony of Scottish fishermen settled on the island in Pender Harbour known as Fishermen's or "Bolshevikie" Island. Markets for their catch were the fish-buying station and store that had been established on the south side of the Harbour by Bert Whitaker in 1898, a floating cannery that was brought into Jervis Inlet around 1904, and a cannery built in Bargain Bay in 1906 by the P.H. Alder Company. But after 1907 the fishermen were left with only Whitaker's station because the floating cannery had been moved farther up the coast and Alder's cannery closed for the season and never reopened. The fishermen then began travelling north to Knight Inlet for the summer fishing season in order to sell to the canneries established there. The trip was extremely dangerous as their boats were only one-man gillnetters with small inboard Easthope engines, so before they went away, many of the fishermen "banked" their money and valuables with Robert Donley who lived at that time on Edgecombe Island in Bargain Bay. In the fall they returned to Pender Harbour and fished locally during the winter.

This was the pattern of their lives until 1912 when Whitaker closed his station as he was unable to compete with the floating cannery that the Jervis Inlet Canning Company had stationed near Saltery Bay. When that cannery was taken out of the inlet again after only two seasons, Robert Donley took advantage of the void to build a store and a fish-buying station on the site of Whitaker's old station. As agent for the Crown Fish Company of Vancouver, he bought up all the sockeye that the Scottish fishermen took from the Sakinaw River and other local salmon runs. He also bought excess fish from the settlers who got in on the spring "blueback" run by handlining off Texada and Lasqueti. Donley lost his monopoly in 1917 when the C & L Packing Company built a cannery at Green Bay on Nelson Island to fulfill a government contract to provide canned salmon for the army. Although the contract ended and the Green Bay cannery closed when the war ended, within two years Donley had competition again when a man named Pope set up a fish-buying station at a landing just west of him. The fishermen took advantage of this proliferation of markets to improve the price, playing off the buyers and the cannery against each other.

There were Japanese fishermen in Pender Harbour at this time as well, although the names of just three families who actually lived in the vicinity of the Harbour have been recorded: Ikeda, Kawasaki and Kaihara. (In 1942 when the federal government ordered the "evacuation" of all Japanese from coastal communities, there were 10 members of these three families still living in Pender Harbour.) The other Japanese fishermen who fished out of Pender Harbour were headquartered in Steveston and financed by overseas money. They arrived in the Harbour in 40-foot boats constructed with a forward cabin for steering and a stern cabin for living quarters. Under a canopy stretched between the two cabins were large tanks of seawater to hold their catch. In those days Pender Harbour was visited by enormous schools of herring, and the Japanese women would jig for bait herring using barbless hooks and coloured silk thread lures tied on a long line. The herring would be stowed live in the onboard tanks. Later, these same tanks would hold the catch of live ling cod. Back in Pender Harbour, the fishermen would unload their cod on the wharf in order to kill and pack them for sale in Vancouver. During World War I these Japanese fishermen also did a big business in herring, salting them down and exporting them to Japan in 100-pound boxes. Donley bought both ling cod and herring from the Japanese to supply the Crown Fish Company and also kippered some of the herring for sale in Vancouver.

In Egmont many of the earliest settlers were handtrollers, fishing for ling cod in the inlets and selling them to the Japanese fish buyers established at "old" Egmont on the northeastern shore of Sechelt Inlet, just north of the Skookumchuck. In order to keep their bait and their catches alive, these fishermen followed the Japanese technique of equipping their boats with watertight bulkheads, then drilling holes in their hulls to let the seawater run through.

The fish-buying stations that belonged to George Hatashita and the partnership of Takai and Maeda included floats large enough for a number of boats to dock at the same time, and many of the fishermen who lived aboard their boats tied up there for the winter to be close to the stores. Secured to the inside of the station's floats were large live tanks made of wooden slats that allowed the water to pass through. Some contained live herring that were sold as bait for salmon and cod; others held the live ling cod until it was time to take them to town. Although herring was the favourite bait, perch was used at certain seasons of the year as bait for cod, and when neither were available, spoons and flashers were substituted.

Until 1950 when Jervis Inlet was closed to net-fishing, the Egmont fishermen used gillnets there to catch the big runs of humpback and dog salmon and the occasional run of sockeye. Salmon was sold to the local fish buyers already dressed then kept on ice in their fish houses. In the winter, the fishermen dug clams for extra pocket money and sometimes of necessity. Octopi, which made fine halibut bait and were also eaten by the Japanese, were delivered in gunny-sacks to the ice house. Occasionally, one of these monsters would escape from its sack and there would be great excitement as it started to climb with great rapidity up and around the walls.

The fish buyers made regular trips to Vancouver in their packers with loads of cod and salmon, returning with ice and supplies for the stores. Often they took passengers who were in a hurry or short of cash. Hatashita's first packer was the *Matsu* and later he acquired the *Matsu II;* Takai and Maeda operated the *Kiku,* and later the *Kiku II.* When these Japanese families were interned in March 1942, the role of fish buyer in Egmont went to Ernie Silvey.

By the 1930s about 20 boats, most of them constructed within the community, were based in Egmont, mainly fishing the local waters, although some were trollers large enough for salmon fishing off Vancouver Island. John West and his wife Mary were typical of Egmont's fishermen, starting out in the early 1930s with a homebuilt, 14-foot gas-boat to fish for cod in the inlets and graduating by stages to a 43-foot, diesel-powered troller that allowed them to join the salmon fleet and even to fish for tuna a hundred miles off the west coast. Although the population of Egmont grew as the years passed and the community was eventually linked to the rest of the peninsula by road, the family names of the early fishermen—Vaughn, Phillips, Griffiths, Silvey and West—are reflected in the names of those still living in the community.

The fishing fleet anchored in Gibsons Harbour waiting for the area salmon opening c.1932. A Union Steamship vessel is tied up at the wharf. The old LePage Glue Factory building is at centre on the shoreline. The picture is taken from the Bluff.
COURTESY OF THE SUNSHINE COAST MUSEUM AND ARCHIVES.
PHOTO #3451. PHOTO BY HELEN MCCALL.

At the other end of the Sunshine Coast, from the turn of the century until the 1940s a number of Gibsons settlers—among them Axel Anderson, Emil Peterson, Phil Fletcher and John Husby—trolled for salmon, especially during the annual dog salmon run off Port Mellon. J.J. Corlett joined the Gibsons fishing fleet in 1920 when he purchased a Japanese troller, but most Gibsons fishboats were locally built and propelled by oars or inboards. Dougal Harris' gillnetter *Gimlet* was built on his North Road property around 1913 and hauled by horse and sled to Gibson's Bay; while it was anchored there, Harris and Axel Anderson built the cabin and installed the gear. (Harris was drowned in March 1922 when he fell overboard in Pender Harbour where he had gone to fish for herring.) Sometimes fish buyers from Vancouver collected from the Gibsons-based fishermen, but until the 1940s when the Howe Sound dog salmon run petered out, local fish buyer Murdo Stewart generally bought all of that species.

Many Gibsons people supplemented their family food supply by hand-lining for spring salmon on calm winter nights, and in time the process became almost a ritual. The fishermen left Gibsons in their one-man rowboats in mid-afternoon, heading for the north end of Pasley Island or Harry White's Bay on Keats Island. They wore heavy woollen clothes and thick mitts and sat on a sack of straw. L.S. Jackson, who handlined there before World War I, recalled that "the first peeking stars were considered the precise time to be at the right place." The gear that was used was very light, so if the fish that struck was heavy, the fisherman fastened his line to a large block of cedar and heaved the block overboard, leaving the fish to wear itself out, at which point he collected the block and brought the fish on board. The average catch before it became "black night" would be three or four 14-pound springs, but the going price for reds in the early years when Jackson was fishing was 25 cents a pound and ten cents for whites. By the 1930s when Roberts Creek novelist Hubert Evans, author of *Mist on the River* (1954) and *O Time in Your Flight* (1979), was hand-lining off Salmon Rock, the price had fallen to four cents a pound. Sometimes when returning home, the fishermen had to buck a strong westerly or a Squamish and might even have to row around the south end of Keats Island but, remembered Jackson, "there was beauty in it, either the moon and stars looking at you from sky and sea, or wondrous patterns of phosphorescence in the swirl of the oar wake."[5]

THE LEPAGE GLUE FACTORY

Fishing provided Gibsons with an unusual industry for a brief time at the end of the 19th century when the LePage family of glue-making fame purchased a section of George Gibson Sr.'s waterfront property to build a factory that would make glue from dogfish livers. Constructed partly on pilings over the water, it was joined to the new government wharf by a catwalk. All the glue-making machinery was installed by 1898, and the company sent instructions to Bert Whitaker, who had just opened his fish-buying station at Pender Harbour, that they would take all the dogfish he could get them. However, the first glue was not even marketed before litigation began on patent rights because the LePage family had recently sold their glue recipe as well as the LePage name and trademark. The plant was closed and sat idle until 1910 when it was converted into an apartment building. It was torn down in 1958.

FISH SALTERIES

At Deserted Bay in Jervis Inlet a saltery was established around 1904 to take advantage of an unexpected market for dry-salted salmon in Japan; the source of the fish that had been traditionally used for this product had been cut off by the outbreak of war with Russia earlier that year. A man named Tanaka was either the owner or the manager of the original Deserted Bay Saltery, and it seems likely that all the plant workers were Japanese because the Japanese salting method was used there. Chum salmon, gutted and gilled, then filled with salt, were placed in rows on matting and covered with more salt. Other rows were placed on top of them until the pile was nine or ten feet high, and the whole pile was covered with matting. After a week the fish were relaid and again covered with salt. Finally, each fish was packed into a matting bundle for shipment to Japan where most of them were used for New Year's gifts.

Unfortunately for the Deserted Bay Saltery, when the Russo–Japanese War ended in 1905, Japan regained access to its salmon fishing grounds, and the Japanese government slapped an enormous duty on imported salt fish to speed the recovery of its own industry. The Deserted Bay Saltery was closed in 1907 for lack of a market, although it produced again briefly during World War I. In 1924, when Japan's needs finally exceeded its domestic production, the plant was purchased and reopened by C.D. Vincent then resold two years later to R.G. MacLeod who operated it for the next 10 years. Production levels during this time varied from 800,000 pounds in 1932 to one-quarter that amount in 1935, partly in response to the size of the salmon run and partly because the quality of the product MacLeod was exporting was not always acceptable in Japan.

Although the federal government had begun a policy in 1923 of reducing the number of fishing licences issued to Japanese and Japanese Canadians in order to force them out of BC's fishing industry, in 1935 the Department of Fisheries suddenly began encouraging MacLeod to sell his saltery to two Japanese Canadians, H. Tsuchiya and J. Asahina. The sale seems to have been motivated by the realization that only salters of Japanese descent had the necessary expertise in this traditional industry, and that if Canadian salters continued to export inferior products to Japan, BC's chum fishery would lose a valuable market. Tsuchiya and Asahina operated the saltery until the beginning of the war with Japan when they were interned and the plant was closed. Nothing now remains of the building.

Two other salteries are known to have existed in this area. According to Fisheries records, William Beck of Vancouver operated a saltery at an unspecified location in Jervis Inlet prior to 1926. It was not licensed after 1926, an indication that it was probably a floating enterprise that was towed to a new site. Henry Silvey also operated a small saltery at Egmont before World War II.

ORCAS

Although whaling fleets operated in the Strait of Georgia in the last century and a flensing station was set up on Pasley Island, there is no history of whaling on the Sunshine Coast. Instead, there is a collection of tales of killer whales or orcas existing alongside man, sometimes in harmony, sometimes in antagonism.

Native legends suggest that in earlier times, orcas were frequent visitors to Sunshine Coast inlets, and even for the fishermen of Egmont it was not unusual to see a pod of them outside the Skookumchuck, waiting for the right tide in the rapids. Others remembered watching them "play" in the fresh waters at the head of Narrows Inlet where it is believed they went to get rid of the barnacles and other pests clinging to their hides. Pioneers also told of whales congregating in Andy's Bay on Gambier Island and the noise of their battles with "thrashers" echoing from shore to shore.

Two men hunting blue grouse on Bowen Island's Cowan Point watched with interest one day at the beginning of the 20th century as a man rowed toward the point. A large orca cavorted around his boat, which was piled high with groceries. The man was George Glassford of Gibson's Landing and it seems that the whale had joined him away back in Vancouver Harbour's first narrows. The hunters yelled at Glassford to come ashore and have lunch with them and give the whale time to find something else to capture its interest. Glassford joined them on the point, enjoyed a lunch of blue grouse cooked over an open fire, and in mid-afternoon returned to his boat. A half mile from shore the whale awaited him and accompanied him all the way home.

In 1968 and 1969 some northern resident groups of orcas ventured into Pender Harbour where a number were captured for aquariums. Hyak, who died in 1991 at the Vancouver Aquarium, was one of these animals. No whales have been taken since the late 1970s when new government regulations prohibited captures without a special permit. Public sentiment has also acted as a deterrent.

Today such visits by orca pods are rare, and when they do occur, they attract widespread attention. On April 26, 1991, a pod of 18 entered Sechelt Inlet and remained there for 11 days. Although under normal conditions the members of a pod constantly "vocalize," during the early days of their stay in the inlet, these orcas stopped vocalizing and began "pacing" constantly back and forth in a confined area on the western side of Porpoise Bay. Later, after moving into Salmon Inlet, they became calmer and proceeded to vocalize again and feed normally. Toward midnight on May 6 the whole pod approached the Skookumchuck Rapids and hesitated there, then about 45 minutes before low slack tide, they rushed through. When they reached the other side, they took off at high speed.

This group of animals, according to Graeme Ellis of the Pacific Biological Station in Nanaimo where they have been studied since the early 1970s, is known as J-Pod, a fish-eating resident group. It was the first time they had been known to enter Sechelt Inlet although they had been sighted on other occasions in Jervis Inlet. Several of the animals in this pod were even then very old. A male known as J-1, distinguished by his "crinkly fin," was at least 40 years old and had a life expectancy of another 10 to 20 years. Female orcas, however, live to 80 or 90 years; one of the females in J-Pod was believed to have been born in 1908.

Recreational fishermen have reported seeing individual orcas in the inland sea since the visit of J-Pod in 1991, but as most of the sightings have been reported after the fact, they have caused only mild interest. However, in March 2007 a group of 100 to 200 Pacific white-sided dolphins was seen entering Sechelt Inlet through the Skookumchuck after an absence of a quarter century. They remained in the inlet all summer, breaking up into smaller groups to feed. Some of them ventured into Salmon Inlet as far as Newcombe Point while other groups worked their way south toward Porpoise Bay. According to the BC Cetacean Sightings Network at the Vancouver Aquarium, the last reported sighting was on August 23 near Snake Bay. The dolphins did not return in 2008.

DWINDLING SALMON STOCKS

Until the 1930s Sunshine Coast fishermen believed that the massive runs of salmon that surged along the coast at spawning time would continue forever. Pender Harbour novelist Bertrand "Bill" Sinclair, who later became a fisherman himself, wrote of purse seiners fishing off Lasqueti Island where "a thousand salmon at a haul is nothing. Three thousand is common. Even five thousand is far below the record."[6] Ida (Donley) Higgs recalled fishing with her cousin in Pender Harbour around 1922 and coming back with a rowboat full of salmon before breakfast. "We sold them for 25 cents a piece and that was good money. It was so easy to catch them in those days right out here in the harbour."[7]

Forty years later, it was impossible for fishermen of the Sunshine Coast to ignore the fact that whole salmon runs were vanishing—the chum and spring runs in Jervis Inlet and the dog salmon run in Howe Sound—and that other stocks were dwindling. Ironically, the federal fisheries department had recognized the danger as early as 1903, but a royal commission at that time laid all the blame on American fishermen who used trap nets along the shoreline to catch salmon hatched in BC streams. The commission recommended lengthening the BC fishing season and building hatcheries, and by 1922 there were 12 government hatcheries, costing $140,000 a year to operate, which distributed 100 million salmon fry annually along the BC coast. None of these hatcheries were on the Sunshine Coast, and a new royal commission that year recommended that no more hatcheries should be built while the effectiveness of the existing ones was studied.

Overfishing, however, was only one part of the Sunshine Coast's declining fish problem. Pollution was the other. Industrial and household wastes had been allowed to pour untreated into streams and inlets for nearly a hundred years, and waterways that had once provided rich spawning beds had become lifeless. Streams like Payne (Chaster) Creek that had been a heaving mass of dog and coho salmon every fall during pioneer days had no fish after the Pratt brothers finished logging there. Other bodies of water began producing fish and shellfish that were contaminated. But it took decades of lobbying by environmentalists before Howe Sound was closed indefinitely to shellfish harvesters in April 1990. The closure notice cited pollutants from the pulp mills at Woodfibre and Port Mellon and acid runoff from the slag piles at the Britannia copper mine.

The first privately owned fish hatchery on the Sunshine Coast was constructed on Chapman Creek in 1986 by Cockburn Bay Seafarms, a salmon farming company based on Nelson Island. It had an initial capacity of 4 million smolts, and Cockburn Bay announced their intention of using it to raise Atlantic salmon smolts for the farmed fish industry. However, Cockburn Bay sold out to Royal Pacific Seafarms later that same year, and when Royal Pacific went into receivership in 1990, the hatchery was taken over by Scanmar Seafoods Ltd. Two years later the Sunshine Coast Salmonid Enhancement Society, which was formed in 1977, bought it, financing the purchase entirely by community donations. The society, which works to rebuild local salmon and trout stocks to their historic levels, partnered with Howe Sound Pulp and Paper in 1998 when the mill built an incubation facility that utilizes excess warm water to incubate 150,000 chinook eggs for the society. In 2002 the society also began raising trout to stock five local lakes. By 2008 hatchery manager Robert Anstead could declare the hatchery a successful operation with an allocation of 1.5 million salmon per year. The hatchery, he said, was "important to the well-being of the Sunshine Coast, both economically and ecologically. It is community support that keeps the hatchery operating and keeps salmon in our streams."[8] The Department of Fisheries pays approximately 10 percent of the hatchery's annual $125,000 budget; the rest is acquired through donations, memberships and fundraisers.

Chapman Creek Hatchery under reconstruction in March 1986. The hatchery was built for Cockburn Bay/Royal Pacific Sea Farms Ltd. but became a locally operated salmon enhancement facility in 1992.
COURTESY OF JON VAN ARSDELL.

The Sechelt Indian Band hatchery at McLean Bay on Sechelt Inlet, which operated on contract with the federal fisheries department's Salmonid Enhancement Program, was constructed in 1979. This hatchery, with water supplied from Shannon Creek, concentrated on increasing chinook and coho stocks, and the return rate of mature salmon at spawning time suggests it was extremely successful. In addition, four years' work with pink salmon paid off in 1991 when approximately 10,000 returned to spawn. These programs had the added benefit of reintroducing a sports fishery to Sechelt Inlet. However, in the early years of the new century the hatchery began to have problems, first with low water levels in Shannon Creek and then with sand being washed into the creek as the result of a series of torrential rains and activity related to a proposed residential development on the former Pacific Rim Aggregates gravel pit site. The hatchery then switched to collecting eggs from broodstock in McLean Bay, incubating and rearing them at the Chapman Creek hatchery, then returning the young fish to McLean Bay in the spring for several weeks of imprinting before they are released into the wild. They return to the inland sea in one to three years, providing a recreational fishery. Five other enhancement projects were initiated under the umbrella of the Sunshine Coast Salmonid Enhancement Society, founded in 1986. Most of them are on creeks small enough to be stepped over because it is these creeks that give young salmon their greatest chance of survival. The society also organized several small hatcheries operated by volunteer groups, but these are extremely vulnerable to natural disasters. A clogged culvert that diverted a stream leading to the Pender Harbour Wildlife Society's salmon hatchery in February 1991 destroyed a year of that club's work. The culvert, which lies under a logging road between two clearcut blocks, became plugged in heavy rains and the diverted water cut a new, 10-foot-deep channel that exposed the bedrock. All the silt, sand and gravel that was gouged out went into the creek and from there into the hatchery's water intake. The mishap killed 100,000 chum alevins—two-week-old salmon still carrying their egg-sacs—and 51,000 coho eggs. Grants from two sports fishing foundations allowed the society to rebuild and improve the hatchery and enlarge its work on Anderson, Klein and Myers creeks and Sakinaw, Mixall and Waugh lakes.

OYSTER FARMING

As fish stocks declined, the people of the Sunshine Coast turned to aquaculture. Native or Olympic oysters *(Ostrea lurida)* had been an important food source for the Sechelt Natives of Pender Harbour, but they have never been commercially cultivated here because they are no larger than a dollar coin and very sensitive to temperature changes. After Japanese loggers planted Pacific oysters on the beaches of Pender Harbour around 1914, it became apparent that this species would thrive, and in 1923 commercial farming was initiated—rather reluctantly—by Ian McKechnie after his Vancouver doctor-father set him up in business in Pender Harbour's Oyster Bay. Dr. McKechnie imported the seed from Japan and the set arrived on lengths of rope coiled in small wooden barrels. But his son was more interested in baking pies for the local pub than in tending his oyster beds, and a few years after they were established, the oysters spawned spontaneously. As a result, by 1932 naturally set Pacific oysters could be found all over Pender Harbour and as far away as Hotham Sound. This result was unexpected because, for oysters to spawn and the resulting larvae to survive, there must be a critical balance of water temperature, salinity, oxygen and nutrients. McKechnie, having lost interest in his oyster beds, hired his neighbour Bill Klein to look after them, paying him with oyster seed. Klein established his oyster beds across the bay from McKechnie, right next to his mother's homestead, and within 10 years his oyster farm had flourished while McKechnie's beds had ceased to produce.

Tom and Mirabelle Forrester's Garden Bay oyster lease, just across the bay from the Kleins, was also started with seed from Ian McKechnie: six cases of seed in exchange for repairing an engine. The lease that they were granted by the provincial government's Lands Branch around 1930 cost one dollar per acre and an annual rent of $25. They managed their beds successfully for more than 30 years, abandoning them in 1959 when they retired.

By the early 1930s oyster seed was arriving from Japan in wooden boxes of approximately four-cubic-foot capacity, each holding from 10,000 to 15,000 larvae attached to "cultch" or pieces of broken shell. On the journey to BC, which took from 14 to 19 days, the boxes were stored as deck cargo, covered with rice matting and periodically watered to prevent them from drying out. A series of 1970s experiments, however, successfully transferred "eyed" oyster larvae from a hatchery in California to be set in other areas. This technique, known as the remote setting of larvae, eliminated the cost of bringing them all the way from Japan and provided a reliable new source of seed for local growers.

Readying fish for market at Moccasin Valley Marifarms near Earls Cove about 1975. Larry Meneely is on the left of the homebuilt trough, biologist Jon van Arsdell on the right.
COURTESY OF JON VAN ARSDELL.

Sunshine Coast oyster farmers practised bottom culture in the early years, a system requiring a firm beach of fine gravel or sand on which to place their seed oysters. They were therefore limited to a few areas in Pender Harbour and Sechelt Inlet, since most of the remaining sheltered shoreline is steep rocky cliffs. New sites were pioneered, however, after Dr. Dan Quayle of Nanaimo successfully experimented during the 1950s with off-bottom culture—suspending oysters from rafts or floats. This system continues to be used by the numerous oyster farmers of Sechelt Inlet to the present time.

SALMON FARMING

The first aquaculture licence ever issued in British Columbia by the federal Department of Fisheries and Oceans went to Allan C. Meneely on June 6, 1972. Moccasin Valley Marifarms, located close to Earls Cove on Agamemnon Channel, was based on Meneely's privately owned 29-acre parcel of land. The province granted him a licence to draw water for a hatchery from the creek that flowed from North Lake through his property and a foreshore lease on the adjacent salt water where he would anchor his netpens. His goal was to raise pan-sized salmon that would be suitable for the supermarket and restaurant trade.

Meneely and his two sons, Vince and Larry, developed their farm by adapting information gleaned from books and pamphlets. Although sophisticated netpen technology had existed in Europe and Asia for years, they relied on their own engineering skills for the construction of equipment, so it took Larry Meneely almost three years to design an effective salt water enclosure to hold Moccasin Valley's fish. In the meantime, the farm was going from disaster to disaster, including the failure of a 24-foot-diameter fibreglass tank that burst, spewing fish fry all over the ground.

By far the most serious problem the Meneely family faced was procuring eggs for their hatchery. Since it was against federal law to import eggs except under permit or even to release fish from a privately owned hatchery into the wild in order to recapture them when they returned to the hatchery stream to spawn, Meneely had to rely on eggs from government hatcheries. On August 25, 1972, he was assured by the provincial Ministry of Recreation and Conservation that he could purchase 150,000 coho eggs through the Commercial Fisheries Branch. By mid-September he was told that only half this quantity would be available since so much stock was required for salmon enhancement programs. When Meneely applied for a permit to import the balance, the federal fisheries department vetoed it on the grounds of the possible importation of diseases.

By 1975 the Moccasin Valley operation consisted of living quarters, a hatchery with aluminum spawning beds and plastic tanks, a laboratory, salt-water netpens and a complicated water system with pipes running from a dam on North Lake down to the hatchery. But by this time Meneely was being investigated by federal tax inspectors on the grounds that his venture was really a hobby farm, not a legitimate commercial enterprise; three audits in two years failed to turn up any proof of this allegation, but the government did impose a "gift tax" on his wife's share of the property. Production was slowed by Meneely's continuing conflict over eggs with the Department of Fisheries and Oceans. Without a steady supply of chinook eggs, Meneely could not guarantee delivery to his customers on a year-round basis, and in July 1976 Moccasin Valley farms ceased operations.

In spite of the failure of Meneely's farm, the concept of farming salmon on the Sunshine Coast did not die. Within two years of the closure of Moccasin Valley farms, John Slind of Vancouver obtained Aquaculture Licence #4 for a hatchery and salmon farm on the east side of Sechelt Inlet between Tuwanek Point and Nine Mile Point. Water for the operation was supplied via a gravity system from a creek close by.

Slind's first 50,000 coho eggs were obtained from the Department of Fisheries and Oceans' Capilano Hatchery, and by the time they had reached the smolt stage and were ready to enter salt water, he had built four 20- by 20-foot seapens. He took his first pan-sized coho to market in the fall of 1979. That same year he started a second site on the west side of Sechelt Inlet with another hatchery and grow-out pens.

Meanwhile, two young couples—Brad and June Hope from Winnipeg and Tom and Linda May from Seattle—were starting salmon farms on Nelson Island. In 1978 the Hopes bought property at Hidden Basin. Once a hideout for rum-runners during prohibition, the site provided 80 acres of upland property, access to fresh water, and a calm, clean harbour with a good exchange of salt water with every tide. They had little knowledge of fish farming but it was their intention to become self-sufficient, and they began building up their Tidal Rush Farm and researching mariculture.

With the advice of the scientists at the Pacific Biological Station, the Capilano fish hatchery and the Vancouver Public Aquarium, the Hopes built a dam to create a freshwater reservoir, and a log cabin hatchery containing gravel boxes for the salmon eggs and fibreglass troughs for the newly hatched salmon. Their initial problems involved the system of pipes that supplied fresh water to the hatchery as the eggs could be destroyed within minutes if airlocks in the system deprived them of water. The Hopes installed an alarm mechanism to warn of malfunctions but still got up seven or eight times a night to check the system.

After seapens were constructed, the first smolts were successfully transferred to salt water, but during a spell of hot weather, hydrogen sulphide gas, which is caused by the natural processes of decay, seeped out of the mud beneath the seapens and destroyed most of the first crop. The Hopes marketed only enough fish to cover their expenses and go on to the next harvest.

At Cockburn Bay, just around the corner from the Hopes' farm, Tom and Linda May were also experimenting with a salmon hatchery, but Tom May had the advantage of a degree in marine biology. The 150 acres purchased by the Mays had been homesteaded in 1929 by Lorne and Carole Maynard; it included the log cabin in which the Maynards had raised their family as well as numerous garden buildings, a garage and a generator shed complete with a working generator.

The Mays' first seapen was made from netting attached to an aluminum frame and supported by tire floats, and they stocked it with 10,000 chum salmon purchased from the Hopes. They lost all but 27 of that first crop to blue herons that perched on the foot-high fence surrounding the pens to pick off the smolts. With their next sea crop they tried outsmarting the birds with sound devices, electric fences and netpen covers. Finally, they discovered that raising the fences to just over two feet and running an electric wire around the top was enough to discourage them.

Cockburn Bay Seafarms initial smolt-rearing set-up. 1985.
COURTESY JON VAN ARSDELL.

In May 1981 the Sunshine Coast Regional District passed a bylaw to establish the Sunshine Coast Economic Development Commission, a body that was mandated to create jobs and encourage capital investment on the Sunshine Coast. One of their earliest achievements was to focus public attention on the aquaculture industry—attention that triggered a rush of entrepreneurs who saw salmon farming as the road to instant wealth.

Although at this time there were only six salmon farms on the Sunshine Coast and they employed a total of 30 people, the local aquaculturists formed the Sunshine Coast Aquaculture Association, and in September 1984, in conjunction with the Economic Development Commission, they held their first International Aquaculture Conference. Tidal Rush was one of the companies represented at the conference that was held at the Bella Beach Motel in Davis Bay. With a second site in Hotham Sound managed by the Hopes' son Ken, the company now had 1 million fish in the water. But the Hopes had expanded Tidal Rush as far as they could on their own, and in September 1984 they merged their operations with two other BC companies to form Pacific Aqua Foods (PAF). On April 19, 1985, it was listed on the Vancouver Stock Exchange at $1.50 per share; within six months the price had gone up to six dollars.

At the Mays' Cockburn Bay hatchery, sales for 1985 were $414,000, and toward the end of that year they began the construction of a modern hatchery on Chapman Creek. In December the Mays joined forces with the well-known Sunshine Coast building contractor Norb Kraft and his wife Yvonne, co-owners of Kraft Marifarms Ltd., which operated two farms in Hotham Sound. The Mays and the Krafts incorporated Aquarius Seafarms Ltd. and began filing applications to construct 11 farms on the inland sea at an estimated cost of $1 million each.

In March 1986, however, the Mays decided to end their marriage and sold their Cockburn Bay holdings to Dr. Sergio Kumar, the owner of a Vancouver-based company called Pacific Crystal Sea Farms Ltd. A few weeks later Kumar incorporated a new company, Royal Pacific Sea Farms Ltd. (RoyPac), with both Mays holding shares in it. In the meantime, Aquarius had entered into a credit agreement with Aqua Technology & Investments A/S (ATI), a large Norwegian financial group and purchased the waterfront property that the Mays had owned at Gray Creek. Its value lay in the fact that Tom May had already applied to the SCRD for rezoning of the property to permit construction of a hatchery and in July approval was granted. The Mays, facing a potential conflict of interest with their Royal Pacific holdings, resigned as directors of Aquarius.

Encouraged by the lack of restrictions on the industry here, Norwegians began to invest heavily in Sunshine Coast salmon farming. Not only could they develop larger farms here with less interference by the government, but they could use their Canadian investments to reduce their taxes in Norway. Among the investors was Jamek A.S., one of Norway's largest aquaculture equipment manufacturers and a leader in developing that country's fish farming technology. With three local residents, Carsten Hagen, Clarke Hamilton and Bernt Rindt, Jamek formed an aquaculture support company called Scantech Resources Ltd. Besides a wide range of other services to the industry, Scantech provided turnkey operations. For a fee they set up complete fish farms, selecting sites, acquiring all permits and licences, and procuring and installing the necessary equipment and supplies.

One of Scantech's turnkey operations, Wood Bay Salmon Farms Ltd., near Middle Point, was to become one of the most controversial farms on the coast.

Wood Bay's major shareholder, Roger Engeset, was a recent immigrant to Canada from Norway, and he arrived here in the midst of a battle between Scantech and the residents of the properties adjoining the new farm. Scantech had ordered 175,000 smolts to be delivered to the farm from the Cockburn Bay hatchery, but in July 1985 when the smolts were ready, it was discovered that the company had neglected to apply to the provincial Ministry of Lands, Parks and Housing for the required foreshore licence of occupation. Meanwhile, extraordinarily warm summer weather had increased water temperatures at the hatchery, and if the young smolts were to survive, they had to be moved to salt water quickly.

Scantech appealed to Deputy Minister Tom Lee, who responded to the emergency by directing the department's Burnaby office to grant Wood Bay a temporary permit, bypassing the usual process of advertising the foreshore application in newspapers and discussing the licence with the Sunshine Coast Regional District directors. Netpens were installed at Wood Bay four days later and the smolts were safely delivered from the hatchery.

For Scantech, the crisis was over. For others it was only beginning. Wood Bay homeowner Mac Richardson led the fight against the noise and pollution caused by the farm, but since the industry did comply with the zoning regulations set down for the Wood Bay area, there was nothing he or the regional district could do. Wood Bay Salmon Farms were there to stay.

Skookumchuck Salmon Farms owned by Hans Kuck
and Paul Herberman. November 1985.
COURTESY OF JON VAN ARSDELL.

The aquaculture gold rush was well underway. By October 1985 there were 20 salmon farms and more than 130 people employed in the local industry. Aided by a provincial grant of $50,000, an Aquaculture Resource Centre was opened at Capilano College.

But while this was happening, Sunshine Coast residents were becoming deeply concerned about salmon farming. The controversy surrounding Wood Bay Salmon Farms, which had received a permanent lease in spite of SCRD objections, the magnitude of Aquarius Seafarms' plans, and the increase in foreshore applications for other farms, all pointed to an industry that was growing too fast for the amount of information available on its environmental impact. Public hearings for zoning changes became commonplace as homeowners feared the devaluation of their property. Commercial fishermen were worried that the farms would spread disease to wild stock and that hatchery eggs intended to build up the wild resources were being used to stock salmon farms. However, in early July 1986, while the public's attention was directed to these controversies, Sunshine Coast fish farmers were coping with a major harmful algal bloom. An estimated 150,000 fish were lost to a plankton called *Heterosigma,* which causes fish to produce mucus that plugs their gills. Those not killed by suffocation often died from stress within days or weeks of the bloom.

The mountains of dead fish or "morts" accumulated during the bloom sparked a fresh controversy. A number of farms, including Wood Bay, were given approval by the Coast Garibaldi Health Unit to dispose of the morts in large pits. Residents protested that the pits would attract bears and that groundwater surrounding them would be contaminated. Other salmon farmers illegally towed barge-loads of morts out to sea and dumped them or deposited them on uninhabited islands.

But there was more trouble brewing for the industry. In the summer of 1984 Pacific Aqua Foods had gained permission from the Department of Fisheries and Oceans to import Atlantic salmon eggs to their farm sites. It took two years for opposition to these imports to really gel, but by then the public had become very vocal in its concern that the introduction of Atlantics would endanger the health and genetic composition of wild fish stocks. Government officials discounted the risks.

In November 1987 a regular inventory of Pacific Aqua's holdings revealed that the actual number of fish in the Hopes' Hidden Basin and Hotham Sound seapens was far lower than estimated, with the result that the company registered a $4 million loss for the six-month period ending November 30, 1986. Although Pacific Aqua survived to rebuild its holdings in other areas, the Hopes were dismissed from its board, the farms at Hidden Basin and Hotham Sound were closed down and the netpens dismantled.

Meanwhile, Royal Pacific Sea Farms had become the largest and most diversified salmon farming corporation in North America. The company was listed on the Vancouver Stock Exchange in 1987 and the following year on the Toronto Stock Exchange. Although its growth was not as spectacular as Royal Pacific's, Aquarius had also been expanding and by the end of 1988 owned 12 farms, a processing plant and warehouse in Egmont and the hatchery on Gray Creek.

By the end of 1988, for the first time in six years, Crown land referrals for salmon farm leases began dropping off, but by then there were 48 salmon farms, four processing plants, and at least seven private hatcheries on the Sunshine Coast. Aquaculture spokesmen expressed the belief that the industry had never been stronger. Then suddenly everything changed.

On January 31, 1989, a fierce storm, nicknamed the Alaskan Express, struck Jervis Inlet. Winds of up to 100 miles an hour and 10-foot waves smashed salmon farms; boats were destroyed and seapens sank as ice built up along their fences. Other pen systems broke away from their anchors while terrified farm employees rode out the storm trapped in their floating bunkhouses. Hardest hit was Osgood Creek Salmon Farms located on the north side of Princess Royal Reach: all of Osgood's harvestable fish escaped from the pens, as did unknown numbers of smolts. Aquarius' farms in Hotham Sound were also damaged and a large number of fish lost.

An aerial view of Sechelt Salmon Farms Ltd. at Big Bear Bay in Sechelt Inlet c.1987.
COURTESY OF BJORN SKEI.

Throughout 1989 world production levels for farmed salmon increased, and that same year BC's wild harvest was one of the best in decades. The result was a glut of salmon on the world market and a drop of 40 percent in the price of farmed salmon. By mid-1989 it was costing farmers three dollars a pound to raise fish that they could not sell for more than $1.60 a pound. At the same time, the Norwegian economy was experiencing a downturn and Norwegian investors were unable to supply Sunshine Coast companies with further financing.

And just when things appeared to be as bad as they could possibly get, a new series of *Heterosigma* blooms hit Sunshine Coast waters. There had been algal blooms during 1987 and 1988, neither of them as devastating to the industry as the one in 1986, but no one was prepared for this new series which covered a much wider area and lasted from August until mid-October. More than 15 farms were severely affected by the bloom, some of them, like Saga Seafarms in Agamemnon Channel, losing up to 50 tonnes of fish. Others, such as Hardy Seafarms and Aquarius, resorted to towing their pen systems away from the blooms; aircraft flying over Jervis Inlet reported an armada of tugs towing strings of netpens in an attempt to avoid the bloom. But this was an extremely expensive rescue mission and throughout the summer and fall of 1989 one Sunshine Coast salmon farming company after another went into receivership. In October it was the turn of Royal Pacific Sea Farms; although the company had sold 3,000 tonnes of salmon in 1989—more than in any other year of operation—they closed with a $15 million debt. Aquarius followed RoyPac into receivership six months later, leaving Sunshine Coast merchants with $260,000 in unpaid bills.

By 1992 only one salmon farming company remained on the Sunshine Coast, Target Marine, which had taken over the fish processing plant built by Scantech in Egmont and also operated a number of salmon farms in Jervis Inlet and the inland sea. All of the other farms that survived receivership moved their pens north to colder waters where algal blooms are less frequent. Some farmers blamed the failure of the industry on lack of support from local governments and opposition from residents. Steve Marsh, former manager of the Aquaculture Resource Centre at Capilano College, contended that when research was completed on chinook salmon and more became known about algal blooms, solutions to the problems encountered here would be found. It was his opinion that chinook salmon could replace Atlantics as the species of choice, and that salmon farms could return to Jervis Inlet and the inland sea.

But it turned out that chinook were not the answer to farming salmon on the Sunshine Coast. Target Marine, which had been raising coho in Jervis Inlet, became very successful with this species, and by January 2007 when the company sold its processing plant and farm sites to the Norwegian-based

Grieg Seafood BC Ltd., it had become the largest producer of farmed coho salmon in North America. Target kept the Gray Creek hatchery in order to concentrate on a sturgeon-rearing project at that site.

FRESH WATER AND HYDRO POWER

While historically the saltchuck has provided the Sunshine Coast with its major means of transportation and its food resources, it is fresh water that provides this area's power. The initial move to exploit this resource came in 1908 when the Port Mellon mill harnessed the waters of the Rainy River to generate power to operate the mill's turbines, but it was not until 1937 that a public power system was established on the Sunshine Coast. In that year the Columbia Power Company built a powerhouse on Sechelt Indian Band land beside Chapman Creek and installed a large pelton wheel, backing it up with a diesel generator for times when the creek was low or choked with debris. The water to turn the wheel came downhill by pipe from a large tank on the sidehill, which was filled from a penstock to the creek. Bert Sim, whose father, Albert, was one of the engineers operating the plant, recalled that when his father was "on call" he would take home an alarm device that was activated whenever the power went off. Sim would then bicycle down via local trails from his home in Selma Park;

The interior of the Columbia Power Company's first electric plant, built in 1937 on Sechelt band land beside Chapman Creek. Plant operator Albert Arthur Sim stands beside the Pelton wheel. By 1947 the plant was supplying 337 customers with power.
COURTESY OF THE ALBERT "BERT" GEORGE SIM COLLECTION.

one night he rode right into a tree that had been felled across the path by a neighbour who objected to people shortcutting across his property.

By 1947 the plant was supplying 337 customers with electric power, but the following year it was operating at almost full capacity, and the BC Power Commission began to look for a source of additional electricity for the communities of the Sunshine Coast. At this point, someone remembered that a survey of Clowhom Falls at the head of Salmon Inlet had been completed in 1922 and that the provincial Water Rights Branch had recommended it as the best location on the Sunshine Coast for a hydroelectric facility. The Power Commission already owned Clowhom's water rights because Columbia Steamships had allowed its rights to lapse in the late 1930s, and in May 1951 the commission purchased portions of the three lots still owned by Columbia Steamships in order to build a powerhouse.

By September 1950 Dawson, Wade & Company had begun construction of an 18-foot concrete gravity dam above the falls. Because there are no roads to Clowhom, all materials and equipment for the construction had to be barged up Salmon Inlet. And in order to bring Clowhom's power to Sechelt, a 22.5-mile transmission line had to be constructed along the south side of the inlet to Black Bear Bluff, cutting inland from there along Gray Creek and thence south to the Sechelt substation. As the route is steep and access difficult, workers often faced a full day's climb before they even reached the construction site. Every piece of equipment had to be transported first by water to the shoreline then hauled up the mountainside using compressors and winches mounted on rafts.

Although the project was slowed by forest closures during the summer of 1951, the job was complete by May 13 of the following year, and power flowed along the 66,000-volt line, providing more than 1,300 customers with electricity. But as impressive as this construction appeared to be, it was in operation for only four years when demands for more power called for an even larger dam.

In the meantime, the BC Electric Power Company had acquired a contract to run a transmission line from Squamish along the Sunshine Coast as far as Powell River. To facilitate this project, they bought the Clowhom development from the Power Commission in 1955 with the proviso that the Electric Company would supply power to Pender Harbour. Besides a new concrete dam, the BC Electric's Clowhom project included a new penstock and switchyard and a powerhouse containing a 30-megawatt Westinghouse generator. The transmission line was upgraded to 138,000 volts and the whole system joined to the Dunsmuir Line which linked Powell River, the Sunshine Coast and Squamish. The development was officially opened on November 26, 1957, by the Honourable Ray Williston, Minister of Lands and Forests.

When the BC Electric Company was expropriated by the Social Credit

BC Hydro dam and generating station at Clowhom Falls. In the left foreground is Clowhom Lodge and in the middle the spillway. At the bottom of the picture at right is the 1952 BC Power Commission 4,000-hp powerhouse. At far right is its replacement, a 40,000-hp power station opened by the BC Electric in 1957. In the background is the 10-mile-long Clowhom Reservoir. The concrete gravity dam is 402 metres long at the crest and 21 metres high. The station has a capacity of 33 mw and an average energy production of 12 gwt.
COURTESY OF BC HYDRO.

government in 1961, the BC Hydro and Power Authority took on the job of providing power to most of the province, and the Clowhom plant became part of the provincial power grid. Thirty years later, electric power to the Sunshine Coast's 12,000 customers was still being supplied through the line coming from Clowhom Falls, with excess power transferred to, and emergency power drawn from, a total grid that extends as far north as the Peace River.

The Sunshine Coast's power picture changed again in the mid-1990s when Regional Power Inc. of Toronto, a subsidiary of Manulife Financial, was granted the right to install a 16-megawatt run-of-the-river hydroelectricity project on Sechelt Creek, which empties into Salmon Inlet, and connect it to BC Hydro's grid via the existing transmission line to Black Bear Bluff and over the mountains to Sechelt. The project involved building a weir and penstock intake at the confluence of Sechelt and Jackson creeks at the 360-metre level of the mountainside, diverting the creek water through a 4.2-km penstock buried under an unused logging road that follows the creek downhill and constructing a powerhouse close to the creek's mouth. The project was completed in 1997 and Regional Power began selling power to BC Hydro on a long-term contract.

More changes came after 2001 when the provincial government made dramatic modifications to BC Hydro's mandate. One-third of the company's internal operations were contracted out to Bermuda-based Accenture Inc., and the remainder of the utility was split into two corporations: a new entity, BC Transmission Corporation, would take care of the transmission of electricity, while BC Hydro would continue to look after power generation. At the same time, Hydro was "relieved of the necessity of generating any new sources of power"; instead, all new energy was to be generated by private sector providers, otherwise known as independent power producers (IPPs), which would be granted 20- and 30-year contracts to supply electricity. The announcement of this change created a frenzied scramble by companies determined to cash in on the bonanza and within two years nearly 500 rivers and streams in the province had been "staked" for power projects.

The Sunshine Coast was one of the areas that was especially targeted because of the abundance of streams flowing down its precipitous mountain-sides and its proximity to existing transmission lines. The government approved the first wave of these projects in 2003, and by November 2004 a company called the Renewable Power Corporation (RPC) was operating a 9.8-megawatt capacity generating plant on McNair Creek near Port Mellon on the site of a former gravel pit. RPC's next project was approved in 2007 for Tyler Creek, which flows in a northwesterly direction into the upper reaches of the Tzoonie River, emptying at last into the head of Narrows Inlet. But RPC was not alone in staking that watershed. Among the 12 power project applications that the Hawkeye Energy Corporation submitted was one for the upper Tzoonie River as well as for Seshal and Osgood creeks, both flowing into Jervis Inlet. Hydralto Renewable Energy applied for an IPP on an unnamed creek that flows into Narrows Inlet just above the narrows, and the Stlixwim Hydro Corporation applied for permits to build two generating stations on Ramona Creek on the east side of upper Narrows Inlet and four more on creeks flowing into the Tzoonie River, for a total capacity of 62 megawatts. Meanwhile, Regional Power Inc., which built the Sechelt Creek plant, had a project in mind for Misery Creek on Salmon Inlet while other companies were lined up to build IPPs on every other creek on the inland sea and Jervis Inlet.

WATER EXPORT

The fresh waters of the Sunshine Coast have also attracted entrepreneurs intent on selling tanker-loads of water south of the border. In 1984 Colin Beach, president of a West Vancouver company called Aquasource, asked the Sunshine Coast Regional District to approve the export of fresh water from Freil Lake, east of Hotham Sound, a project that would have required damming the lake in order to raise its level by seven and a half feet, and shutting off the spectacular 800-foot Freil Falls for eight months every year. During the remaining four months, a small amount of water would be allowed to flow over the falls "for aesthetic reasons," a concession to ferry users who can see the falls while they are travelling between Earls Cove and Saltery Bay. Sunshine Coast regional directors refused a permit on the grounds that export would interrupt the natural flow of the falls and because the water from this lake is part of an ecosystem that sustains the balance necessary for local mariculture.

In August 1990 Beach made a second application, this time to export 5,000 acre feet of water a year from Freil Lake to the city of Santa Barbara. The request was again denied, although by the time it was processed, Santa Barbara had decided to build a seawater desalinization plant instead of importing water. In March of the following year, Beach approached provincial Municipal Affairs Minister Lyall Hansen to ask for the designation of a resort township site on Hotham Sound to allow construction of a "major recreational resort development" to be called "Harmony." He was turned down on the grounds that his proposal was a private development and his application should have been directed to the regional district. In answer to that body's concern that Beach would reactivate his water export scheme if allowed a resort licence, Beach assured directors his earlier proposal was still very much alive and that it was entirely compatible with his resort plans.

Beach was not alone in his determination to export water from this coast. ICE Water of Canada Limited, represented by Thurber Consultants Limited, applied to the SCRD on June 14, 1990, to remove 100,000 gallons of fresh water a month from Crabapple Creek on Queen's Reach of Jervis Inlet. The water would be bottled in North Vancouver and marketed in the United States. Teri Dawe, spokesman for the Ocean Resource Conservation Alliance (ORCA), condemned the proposal and pointed out to the SCRD that no studies have been made of the long-term effects of interrupting the flow of fresh water into saltwater inlets. "Inlets are not just cracks in the ground," Dawe explained. "The water levels don't mix. There are fresh layers and salt layers and each has its own forms of life . . . Water is a finite resource that must be protected. I think the whole attitude toward water has to change. We have to see it's not an unending resource that's free for the taking."[9]

PART SEVEN

QUARRIES, MINES AND ETERNAL OPTIMISM

Financial hardship was routine for the first Sunshine Coast settlers, and while they struggled to establish farms or businesses, many supported themselves by fishing or logging. Some, however, took their "cash crop" right out of the ground.

CLAY AND BRICKS

When Frederick L. Keeling beached his rowboat in the little bay near Irby Point on the southern tip of Anvil Island in 1884, he knew he had found the perfect farmsite, and he set about clearing his L.845 and planting an orchard. It did not take him long to discover that nearly 90 acres of his pre-emption was solid clay—yellow-blue and blue-grey clay that was very uniform in texture and practically free of stones. It had been deposited there by receding glaciers approximately 12,000 years ago.

By 1897 Keeling had sold the site to the Columbia Clay Company Limited, which set up a brick factory, scooping the clay out of the slopes on which his orchard still grew. Although it was a primitive operation, within eight years it had become the largest brick factory in the province. Workmen shovelled the clay into hand cars that ran on a small railway downhill to a "soft mud" brick machine set up close to the water. After the bricks were formed and air-dried, they were burned in a continuous kiln from which they were loaded directly onto barges to be towed to market, mainly in Vancouver. Columbia Clay turned out 30,000 bricks per day until 1913 when all the premium quality clay at the site ran out.

Beginning in 1910, another brickworks, the Anvil Island Brick Company, operated in another section of Keeling's clay beds, using the dry press method, which eliminated the air-drying stage of production. This company went out of business in 1917, but by then many of Vancouver's finest buildings had been constructed with bricks stamped "Anvil Island." For a short while in 1922, barge-loads of Anvil Island clay were sent to Granville Island in Vancouver to be made into bricks by Ceramics Industries Limited, but by the end of that year the company had turned to other sources.

A company called Sechelt Brick & Tile, with Vancouver entrepreneur Walter Hepburn as president, began operating a small brickworks at Storm Bay at the mouth of Narrows Inlet in late 1907. Two years later it closed, the Storm Bay clay having proved too soft and crumbly for high quality bricks. The abandoned plant was discovered by William Winn and Robert Donley a few years later, and they loaded the remaining bricks aboard Donley's boat and took them to Pender Harbour to form the foundation of his kipper smokehouse.

After World War I, the federal government bankrolled a major brickworks on this same site as a "returned men's project," shipping firebricks from a Vancouver kiln to build extensive underground furnaces and a large smokestack. Unfortunately, Storm Bay's clay was no more suitable for bricks in 1921 than it had been in 1907, and soon after the plant was built, the project was cancelled. Once again, the bricks were put to good use by settlers, like the Gilmour family who sailed over from their pre-emption at Doriston in the mid-1930s and carried off enough bricks to build the fireplace for their new home.

The Anvil Island Brick Company's works near Irby Point, March 1910. Above the open face of the clay deposit are the orchard and house of pioneer F. L. Keeling. The clay was dug by hand and wheelbarrowed down planks laid on the ground to the brick-making machines.
COURTESY OF THE SUNSHINE COAST MUSEUM AND ARCHIVES. PHOTO #24.

A 1932 BC government report on clay and shale deposits noted that there had also been bricks made "at one time" in Pender Harbour, but the operation they referred to had actually been at High Creek in Jervis Inlet's Vancouver Bay. It was set up by the legendary Joe Gregson—Boer War veteran, logger, farmer and brickmaker—who arrived on the Pacific coast around 1904. He began handlogging the High Creek area the following year in preparation for farming the land and apparently set up his brick kiln about the same time. But his brick making was intermittent and came to an end before World War I when Joe went homesteading on Cortes Island instead.

Crude saki bottles found at the sites of early Japanese shake cutting operations on the Sunshine Coast show that their makers had found the clay they used to make them along local creeks. The bottles were fired in rough, raku-style kilns to a grey-black finish similar to that on the earthenware that is made from the clay found at the heads of Gambier Island's long bays.

SAND AND GRAVEL QUARRIES

George Glassford and George Soames, who pioneered on waterfront properties east of Gibson's Landing at the end of the last century, were not lucky enough to find clay deposits on their land, but they did find gravel, and it provided the cash they needed to support their families. Beginning in 1899 the two men shovelled the gravel off their beaches onto barges, selling it in Vancouver as road base. Four years later, Glassford moved the operation northeast to the beach that would become known as Hopkins' Landing and took on a new partner, Clare Chamberlin. When George Hopkins bought the 160-acre parcel of land above this half mile of beach in 1907, he found an encampment of Japanese loading barges with beach gravel for Champion and White Limited of Vancouver. The barges were beached at high tide, gangways were set up, and the Japanese workers used them to run their wheelbarrows loaded with gravel onto the barges. Hopkins took advantage of this labour pool close at hand by hiring them to clear land for him in the intervals between the departure of one barge and the arrival of the next.

In Sechelt, when Herbert Whitaker's empire was beginning to fail in 1919, he also raised capital by selling the fine gravel off the beach in front of his cottages and hotel, even though the beach was one of the main attractions for tourists. They watched while gangs of Chinese labourers stripped it and loaded the gravel onto barges to be sold in the city. These denuded beaches became Sechelt village's heritage.

After all the high-quality beach gravel had been exploited, entrepreneurs began looking for sand and gravel deposits farther inland. They found them generally within a few hundred yards of the water since these deposits had been left on the Georgia Lowland by the departing glaciers; only a hundred yards farther inland was bare granite bedrock. The pits developed in the early years of the century were usually short-term projects—most of them operating on a small scale for no more than a dozen years—since the layers of marine and river sand and gravel suitable for building materials were often shallow, and they overlay hard-packed glacial till. However, they were excellent business opportunities for penniless entrepreneurs since there was little financial outlay involved in taking the product out.

After the small deposits were worked out, big business moved in on the more extensive deposits of sand and gravel on the alluvial fans that had formed at the mouths of rivers and streams. Champion and White operated gravel pits at a number of Howe Sound sites from the turn of the century until the 1950s when the company was bought by Ocean Construction Supplies, an amalgamation of a number of old BC sand, gravel and cement companies. Another Ocean subsidiary, Hillside Sand & Gravel, began excavating near Port Mellon in 1942; this operation was taken over in 1974 by Construction Aggregates Limited, which had become an Ocean subsidiary in 1969. It was this gravel pit that provided more than 750,000 tonnes of granular fill to reclaim the 159-acre Expo 86 site.

The Hillside Sand & Gravel operation near Port Mellon
showing the conveyor system and scows being loaded c.1950.
COURTESY THE SUNSHINE COAST MUSEUM AND ARCHIVES.
PHOTO #3018. PHOTO BY HELEN MCCALL

Several of the largest gravel deposits were not discovered until after clear-cut logging operations had laid the sand and gravel bare. At Treat or Beaver Creek on Jervis Inlet, the pit site had been logged by Bob Campbell's outfit in the mid-1930s and when he went broke, John Klein had taken over, followed by the Olson brothers. Only when all the accessible mature trees had been removed and the thin layer of topsoil scraped away was the high-quality gravel underneath it exposed. In 1966 Jack Cewe Limited of Coquitlam moved a crushing plant to the site and began shipping washed and crushed aggregates out by barges with capacities up to 14,000 tonnes. The pit's output has varied between 3 million and 1.2 millions tons a year since then. However, as the water depth at the loading facilities was only 20 feet, the company made plans in 2008 to extend the dock into deeper water, a project estimated to cost $6 million.

On the east side of Sechelt Inlet at Earl Creek, just north of the Skookumchuck Rapids, Argus Aggregates, a division of Fraser River Pile Driving, established a gravel operation in the 1950s on a site that had been logged off by Pacific Logging, a company owned by the Canadian Pacific Railway. Argus began barging out aggregates suitable for roadwork and for making asphalt, then installed a wash plant in the early 1970s to produce washed rock. In the fall of 1975 Argus was bought out by Lafarge Concrete, later known as Lafarge Canada Inc. In 2008 Lafarge installed a new crusher capable of reducing rocks five feet in diameter to gravel.

The most dramatic example of an alluvial fan of high-quality sand and gravel was discovered adjacent to Chapman Creek. Although this creek's single mouth now empties into the Strait of Georgia at Mission Point just southeast of Davis Bay, during the immediate post-glacial period it had two widely separated mouths, one emptying into Sechelt Inlet opposite Poise Island and the other into Trail Bay. As the sea level dropped, the creek beds shifted back and forth over the whole area from Porpoise Bay Park to Wilson Creek, depositing silt, sand and gravel from the 200-metre level right down to the shore.

In the winter of 1970-71, Sechelt Sand and Gravel Ltd. developed a pit on the edge of this alluvial fan at McLean Bay, just north of the mouth of Angus Creek on Sechelt Inlet. Partners in the company were Vic Walters of Sechelt, Al Shrieves of Nelson and the Vancouver company Rivtow owned by

Employees of Champion and White line up in front of one of the company's four hard-rubber tire trucks c. 1936. Man at far right is plant superintendent Jack Campbell. The gravel crusher was powered by electricity generated by the nearby Dakota and McNair creeks.
COURTESY OF THE SUNSHINE COAST MUSEUM AND ARCHIVES. PHOTO #1211.

the Cosulich family. The pit produced seven different products for the asphalt and concrete aggregate market and these were shipped by barge through the Skookumchuck to markets as far away as Alaska. In 1973 Rivtow bought out its two partners and renamed the company Pacific Rim Aggregates. BA Blacktop, owned by Bill Elphinstone, Rick Genovese and Rudy Ernst, joined Pacific Rim on this site in 1979 in order to produce asphalt. According to company reports, massive reserves of gravel were still waiting to be exploited when Pacific Rim Aggregates ceased operation in November 1989.

Snow camouflages the Construction Aggregates gravel operation adjacent to Sechelt in the winter of 2005. At centre right is the town of Sechelt, at centre left is Porpoise Bay, and upper left are the Trail Islands. In the foreground are poplars that are part of the company's reforestation program.
COURTESY OF ROSELLA LESLIE.

In 1989 Construction Aggregates was given a lease on Crown land just east of the town of Sechelt in exchange for giving up the company's Howe Sound site, which the Sunshine Coast Regional District wanted for an industrial park. The company's new operation takes sand and gravel from the hillside overlooking Sechelt's St. Mary's Hospital to funnel it via a conveyor belt through the Sechelt Indian Band's Reserve #2 to a loading dock that dominates the Trail Bay waterfront. In 1993 Heidelberg Cement, through its subsidiary, Lehigh Canada, acquired Construction Aggregates, and in 2000 the loading dock was extended far enough into the bay to accommodate ocean-going ships. By 2008 the company was shipping five million tonnes of sand and gravel annually, with four 5,000-tonne capacity barges loaded each day to supply the Lower

Mainland (including a sister company, Ocean Concrete) and one or two 50,000- to 60,000-tonne ships a month carrying product as far south as San Francisco and as far north as Alaska. The site is recognized as the largest open pit sand and gravel operation in North America.

EXPLOITING THE BEDROCK

The Sunshine Coast's grey granite bedrock was probably quarried as early as 1885, but the first record of its use for a large scale project was in 1894 when the United States Bureau of Yards and Docks chose Nelson Island granite for a new, 800-foot-long dry dock at Port Orchard, Washington. According to a story published in the Victoria *Colonist*, this rock was chosen because of its extraordinary weight. At 184 pounds per cubic foot, it outweighed most other North American granites by at least 150 pounds. The quarry that produced this remarkable granite was on a 350-acre site at Quarry Bay on the southwest corner of Nelson Island. It was registered to a man named J.C. Prevost of Victoria, but at that early date he seems to have operated it only when he had a contract. To provide the rock needed for the Port Orchard dry dock, contractor R.I. Fox of Seattle came to Nelson Island to work the quarry himself, but he hired his crew from BC because they were considered the most skilled in the trade.

The following year Quarry Bay granite was chosen for the base of the legislative buildings and the sea wall of Victoria's inner harbour. This time the quarry workers were hired in Victoria and they set out for Nelson Island on March 22, 1895, on a barge towed by the tug *Velos*, even though a violent southeaster was pounding Vancouver Island's southern coast. When the weather worsened, Captain Anderson of the *Velos* attempted to turn the tug about and head for Cadboro Bay but it was swamped and smashed on a reef. The barge drifted with the half-submerged *Velos* as an anchor until it was swept into a small bay on Trial Island, from which the workers were rescued next morning by the steamer *Maud*. Four of the tug's crew and the quarry superintendent, Frederick Adams, were drowned, but two weeks later a fresh crew arrived safely at Quarry Bay to begin producing the stone for the legislative buildings.

A few years later the Quarry Bay site was bought by the Vancouver Granite Company, but in 1903 the new owners closed it down and moved the operation to little Granite or Kelly Island, which is north of Billings Bay off the northwest corner of Nelson Island. Kelly was more attractive because the vertical fractures of its solid grey granite made quarrying easier than on Nelson Island. The new quarry was established on the south end of the island where deepwater vessels could be loaded from an inclined tramway. The actual quarrying was contracted out to "Messrs. Kelly and Murray of Vancouver," and for the next five years they supervised an operation that was performed entirely by hand on a 160-foot-long working face about 90 feet above the sea.

Vancouver Granite reopened its Quarry Bay site in 1908 in order to lease it to the Ellis Granite Company of Seattle to fill contracts for that city. By this time new quarrying techniques had been developed that involved drilling holes the depth of the block to be extracted, then using small dynamite charges to begin a fracture line that could be enlarged with blasts of compressed air.

When Ellis Granite's lease expired, Vancouver Granite resumed management of the quarry, contracting out the final cutting and finishing to independent operators who set up mills right on the site. With this system, the company supplied stone for the Vancouver courthouse as well as the foundations for dozens of the city's commercial buildings, such as the Hudson's Bay Company store at Granville and Georgia, the Bank of Commerce at Main and Pender, and the Credit Foncier Building on Hastings Street. The quarry's output in 1923 was 96,000 cubic feet of stone, most of it sold to the federal government for a dry dock at Esquimalt and to the University of BC for the construction of the new campus buildings at Point Grey. By 1926 the quarry had been excavated to a depth of 250 feet and so much rock had been removed that the working face was now 60 feet high and 500 feet wide. Each year 500 scow-loads of rock left the dock; 15 men were employed for 10 months of the year to quarry and load it.

The only Sunshine Coast competition for Vancouver Granite during those years was a small quarry located just north of Sechelt at the foot of Norwest Bay Road. Sechelt Granite Quarries was launched in 1912 by Thomas R. Nickson, whose parents, John Reginald and Jane Nickson, had earlier that year pre-empted L.1384 on the Sechelt waterfront east of the quarry site. Nickson's quarry tramway, built on a rockwork cribbing, allowed the dollies loaded with granite blocks to run downhill to the beach where they were transferred to scows. As Nickson had no on-site mill, the barge-loads of rock were towed to a mill on the Fraser River where they were cut and finished then shipped to Vancouver to be laid down between the streetcar tracks.

One day shortly after the quarry began operations, a man with three blonde lady companions disembarked from the Union Steamships' boat and hiked along the beach to T.J. Cook's property. Just west of his home, they pitched a tent beside a very large rock with a flat surface on its eastern side, a rock that happened to be close to the trail running from the quarry past Cook's home to the Sechelt Hotel and the wharf. When Cook demanded to know what they were doing on his property, the man said that he had brought his lady barbers there to combine a seaside holiday with work cutting the quarrymen's hair. However, when night fell, it became obvious to Cook what the ladies had really come for, and he ordered them off his property and onto the next boat out of town. The rock became known as "The Bawdy Stone."

In 1913 Nickson won a contract to provide rock for a breakwater in Victoria, but this contract seems to have been the end of his quarry's working life. The equipment was removed within two or three years, but some of the tramway's rock cribbing and a number of blocks of unfinished granite that were discarded on the beach identified the site until recent years.

The demand for stone began to slump around 1930 as Canada skidded into the Depression and steel and concrete construction technology improved. In the face of these setbacks, the Vancouver Granite Company converted to "dimension-stone" quarrying on Nelson Island, only hiring a crew to cut stone when orders were received. Business picked up again in the war years, and by 1944 ten quarrymen were filling orders. The records also show that in 1947 nine workmen were still supplying stone and rubble for construction in Vancouver, but the company closed the site two years later. It was only reopened for a year in 1961 by the BC Slate Company, which marketed quarry rubble for split-faced granite building veneer.

Darker grey granite, which was in demand for monuments and statues, was discovered a half mile southwest of Billings Bay on Nelson Island around 1915. For a decade it was worked intermittently by a company founded by Alexander MacLennon and James Craig to supply tombstones as well as blocks of granite destined to become World War I monuments.

However, it was black granite, more highly prized than dark grey granite for monuments and architectural facing stone, that prospectors were looking for when they began following a suture in the granite bedrock of the Sechelt Peninsula, and between 1907 and 1911 almost three dozen claims were staked along a line that stretched from Snake Bay on Sechelt Inlet to Lyon Lake in the Caren Range. In the late 1930s an attempt was made to open a black granite quarry above Snake Bay, but the project was abandoned after it was discovered that the deposit was seriously fractured and the white streaks in it made it uncompetitive on the world market. Most of the other claims were forfeited within a few years, although a number of the prospectors—believing that markets and a means of access to their claims would be developed in the future—persevered with their annual assessment work and converted their claims to Crown grants in 1911. They held them until the 1930s when they were reclaimed by the government for delinquent taxes.

No further claims were staked in this area for nearly 35 years. Then in 1969 Rudolph Riepe, the owner of a small quarry specializing in decorative stone, began re-exploring this area in search of the white marble that his customers were demanding. "That's when I ran into an old prospector-turned-machinery salesman," Riepe explained, "and he said 'I know where there's some white marble, Rudy. All you have to do is go there and get it!' We looked all over that country for three or four weeks late in the fall, and finally on the last day when we were ready to quit, we found an outcrop of white marble. Right then it started snowing and we had to wait a week before we could come back and map the outcrops and get a feel for the size of the deposit."[1] Riepe staked the entire suture area from Lyon Lake to Carlson Lake; he named his claims Candol.

A year later he discovered that his marble deposit was accompanied by a huge amount of dolomite. Both are limestones, the main difference being that the marble has been repeatedly crystallized by pressure exerted on it from the granite walls on either side. Dolomite, which has a higher magnesium content, is used for fertilizer and also as a source of magnesium metal, but most of it is used as refractory or insulating material for high temperature applications.

Riepe continued to explore the suture line southward and rediscovered the black granite that had been staked in 1907. In addition, just three kilometres from the head of Mason Road, he found another black granite deposit, which he claimed was neither fractured nor streaked with white. More durable and less susceptible to acid-rain damage than marble, black granite is in demand for architectural facings, floors and monuments, especially in Southeast Asia. Riepe sold his claims to Tri-Sil Minerals Inc. of which he is a director, and the company began developing the site, bringing a quarry master from Italy in October 1989.

A bonus for Tri-Sil was the discovery of deposits of wollastonite and garnet associated with the granite. In a feasibility test of a mining project here, nearly 300,000 tons of wollastonite were drilled out and shipped to Tilbury Cement of Delta where it was ground up and added to cement as a source of silica. Similar to asbestos in structure, it is non-carcinogenic and is gradually replacing asbestos for insulation and many other uses. According to the company's estimates, there were 50 million tons of wollastonite available on their property.

In November 1993 Tri-Sil became a wholly owned subsidiary of Tri Northern Resources which operates in BC and Alberta. A year later Tri Northern announced plans to start construction on an open-pit mine above Snake Bay that would take out 30,000 to 40,000 tonnes of industrial minerals a year and employ up to 30 local people. Two years later all plans were put on hold again after financing problems arose.

However, in April 2005 Pan Pacific Aggregates plc (PPA) acquired majority control of Tri-Sil, which was by then back in the hands of Rudy Riepe; then, using the BC government's new online staking system, the company secured the mining rights to 540,000 hectares of the Caren Range. Next, PPA announced a "large-scale mining operation" covering a 215-hectare area at the head of the Carlson Creek watershed; mine production capacity would be 6 million tonnes per year for 25 years. A processing plant would deliver product to Snake Bay where barges would be loaded to export it to coastal markets. By August 2005 the company announced it had completed mineral explorations and infrastructure development and was ready to submit an application to begin the environmental assessment process. About the same time it also announced that rather than barge from Snake Bay, the company would be constructing a 10-km-long conveyor system to carry the ore to a marine barge load-out facility at Wood Bay near Secret Cove. Local opposition, already strong, became extremely vocal.

Meanwhile, in 2004 Canadian Forest Products had sold a 15-hectare site near Chapman Creek to AJB Investments Ltd., which planned to log the property and develop a gravel mine there; two years later AJB was bought out by Columbia National Investments Ltd. (CNI), controlled by brothers Herb and Steve Dunton, and in February 2007 they acquired a mining permit allowing them to extract 240,000 tonnes from this property, an amount just low enough to avoid an environmental assessment. Opposition to this kind of activity within the watershed mounted. Then suddenly in June 2008 CNI began operating as a subsidiary of Pan Pacific Aggregates. A PPA news release in September of that year advised that "the company's operational focus" would centre on their aggregate business in the Fraser Valley as well as "utilizing our small producer permit at Sechelt (Caren Range)." No subsequent action occurred at either the Carlson Creek site or the CNI site adjacent to Chapman Creek.

While black granite deposits appear to be confined to one small area of the peninsula, limestone has been found in many other parts of the Sunshine Coast. The deposits most familiar to the general public are the limestone caves of Homesite Creek Park just off the Sechelt–Pender Harbour Highway. There are other known deposits, but most of them are inaccessible. One of them was staked in the early 1940s by Ken Whitaker, the son of the man who built Sechelt's first hotel. His claim was located in the rugged country on the north side of Salmon Inlet, but he forfeited it when he was unable to keep up his assessment work. On a return trip in 1947 with his friend Robert Hackett to look the claim over again, the two men met a pair of prospectors on the mountainside who were searching for the forfeited deposit with the intention of staking it themselves. When Whitaker denied any knowledge of it, the would-be stakers moved off in another direction and Whitaker and Hackett turned back rather than betray the site. But Whitaker never restaked it and neither has anyone else.

Both limestone and marble appear as outcrops in the Thornhill Creek canyon on the south side of Salmon Inlet, but although this area has been staked repeatedly, the steepness of the canyon walls has prevented development of a quarry. In 1990 the Thornhill Creek area was designated a marine recreation area and further staking was prohibited.

Early in the century the slate deposits at Deserted Bay from which the Sechelt people had fashioned arrowheads were discovered by white men, and around 1910 a company moved in to begin quarrying tiles. Camp buildings were constructed, a wharf built and a boiler plant set up to operate the cutting equipment. When the camp closed, probably around 1916, the face of the quarry was 30 feet high and more than 100 feet long. All that remained of the camp by 1924 were the ruins of the boiler-house and the bunkhouses. A nearby waste-dump of broken slate was pillaged by every passing boater who wanted to embellish his home or garden.

From 1947 to the early 1950s a quarry was operated at McNab Creek by G. W. Richmond to exploit a vein of dark grey to black slate. The product was shipped to Vancouver where it was prepared for asphalt roofing.

GOLD MINING

The Sunshine Coast has never been very productive territory for placer mining, but in 1900 free gold was discovered on "Canyon Creek" which—despite the deliberately confusing descriptions of its location on the miners' claim forms—appears to have been an early name for one of the branches of the Skwakwa River at the head of Queen's Reach in Jervis Inlet. This was not the first time that interest had been shown in this area; more than a dozen pre-emptions had been filed there in 1891, presumably by prospectors rather than farmers, but all had been abandoned in short order. But on February 11, 1900, six discovery claims, laid out side by side along the course of the streambed, were staked by a six-man company that was incorporated as the Canyon Creek Mining Company Ltd. On that same day the Thulin brothers, Charles and Frederick, staked the ground adjoining the discovery claims, then all of the miners caught the steamer for Vancouver to register their claims. Since this happened to be the high point of the Klondike gold rush, Canyon Creek sparked little excitement in the mining community, and only four more prospectors filed claims on the creek between 1900 and 1902. Apparently all of these claims were worked and enough profit earned during these years to encourage the miners because they renewed their claims registrations annually and the Canyon Creek Mining Company obtained Crown grants to its claims.

There was no fresh activity here until 1906 when four more claims were staked, but in the summer of 1908 word finally got out that there was real gold to be had on Canyon Creek, and in the space of three months 49 new claims had been staked on that creek and on others in the vicinity. The winter of 1908–09 was very severe, however, and because the snow lay on the ground right into July, there was no more activity in the area until the summer of 1910. Over the next two years a few of the miners took out a small amount of gold after a great deal of arduous panning, but one by one the claims were forfeited, leaving only two in good standing by 1914. Two years later there was another brief flurry of staking but interest quickly flagged, and all claims were forfeited by the end of World War I. Of the prospectors who staked in the Canyon Creek area, only five were Sunshine Coast people: Charles and Frederick Thulin who had pre-empted at Halfmoon Bay, Thomas Lillie of Pender Harbour, and Peter J. Sanson and Joseph Silvey of Egmont. The rest were part of that vast company of wandering prospectors who join every rush for gold.

The next Sunshine Coast gold rush came in 1919 when 62 claims were staked on the Tzoonie River at the head of Narrows Inlet. Traces of silver and gold were the lure here, but the area is so precipitous that the prospectors could not interest investors in backing their exploration work. As a result, instead of doing their annual assessment work to hold onto their claims, they simply restaked the same claims with brand new names every year, to the frustration of the Ministry of Mines. By 1922 the only prospector still carrying out assessment work on the Tzoonie River was Peter J. Sanson of Egmont, and he appears to have forfeited his claims in the late 1920s.

Joseph "Paddy" Hatt of Egmont, trapper and gold miner. 1941.
COURTESY OF SECHELT COMMUNITY ARCHIVES.

Treat or Beaver Creek on Jervis Inlet was the site during the 1930s of a mysterious gold mine belonging to an old trapper named Joseph "Paddy" Hatt. Whenever the harvest was poor on Hatt's trapline in the mountains beyond Princess Louisa, he would disappear up Treat Creek and return to Pender Harbour with his old double-ended sailboat loaded with ore. Hatt never filed a claim on his mine, and since he was very secretive about its location, it became just another "lost gold mine" when he died.

Not all of the very ancient igneous and metamorphic rock that was raised from the seabed during the Cretaceous geological period to become mountaintops was obliterated by the relentless grinding of the last ice age, and it is this rock, sandwiched into the hollows and gullies between the Sunshine Coast's granite peaks, that contains nearly all the mineral deposits of any economic importance. Prospecting and finding the minerals in this rock has never been easy. The terrain is incredibly rugged, and in the early years of the 20th century, there were few roads in the mountains since the logging industry had not yet entered its truck-logging phase. To make prospecting even more difficult, the best mineral showings occur above 3,000 feet where the working season is seldom more than five months long, and in years of heavy snowfall as little as two months—not enough time to make the average mine economically feasible.

In spite of these drawbacks, prospectors began searching for gold, silver and copper here as early as the 1860s. The first serious effort to develop a mine was made in 1874 when Alexander Donaldson set off into the mountains east of Clowhom Lake at the head of Salmon Inlet. At the 3,100-foot level of a mountain that would later bear his name, he found an outcrop of copper and staked six claims. Within three years he had completed his assessment work and obtained Crown grants on the two most promising claims. Then to finance further exploration, Donaldson formed the Howe Sound Copper and Silver Mine Company and began selling shares. His prospectus boasted that the lode was a "true fissure vein." It continued:

> The profile of the lode can be examined to the depth of 200 feet from the surface as it crops out in the face of a cliff, having doubtless been laid bare by some convulsion of nature. The lead is thus clearly defined from the base of the precipice to the top, and may be still farther traced along the surface of the ground for at least a mile from where it first makes its appearance. The vein is wedge-shaped, being thickest at its base where the ore is also richest.[2]

To further encourage investors, Donaldson sank a 30-foot test tunnel. A private assay of the best specimens of the ore showed 60 percent copper and 91 ounces of silver to the ton; however, the average specimens tested in the Geological Survey lab were a little less promising, showing only 40 percent copper and 50 ounces of silver.

Government mining engineer R.B. Harvey, who inspected the mine in June 1877, was very enthusiastic about the find.

The ore is rich in character, made up of what are known as Peacock and

*Grey ore and oxide of copper. It carries also a large percentage of silver. It is
the richest ore of this character I have ever seen on this Coast or in England.
I firmly believe that the lode will, at a greater depth from the surface,
prove to be richer in silver than in copper . . . I believe in time the country
between Howe Sound and Jervis Inlet will be a great mining district.[3]*

Only one aspect of the new mine worried Harvey—there was no road
to take out the ore—and he recommended that work begin on this project
immediately. The mine was only two and a half miles from Salmon Inlet, but
the only way to get to it at that time was via a seven-mile horse trail from the
inlet up Sechelt Creek to the point where that creek is joined by Slippery Creek.
From there, the miners packed everything up Slippery Creek canyon and over a
bald granite peak to the mine site. But although Donaldson's company worked
the mine sporadically until 1883, no attempt was made to build a road. Instead,
the company carried out enough ore on pack animals for a small shipment to a
smelter at Swansea, Wales. The results were never made public.

It was only 15 years later that trappers who were setting up their lines on
Jane Creek on the east side of Howe Sound (just outside the Sunshine Coast
area), discovered another outcrop of copper. This was the big one, and by 1906
one of BC's longest working and most successful mines was in operation at
Britannia Beach. The same year the Britannia mine began shipping ore, two
Los Angeles speculators disguised as prospectors, Ellis and Willard Mallory,
announced that they had struck the continuation of the Britannia vein of
copper ore at Mill Creek on the west side of Howe Sound, close to the spot
where the Woodfibre mill stands today. They staked five claims that, they said,
held 3 million tons of bornite as well as molybdenite "in paying quantities."[4]
Excitement in the mining community was immediate because the site of the
Mallorys' claims lay on a direct line between the mine at Britannia Beach and
Donaldson's Howe Sound Copper and Silver Mine Company claims, both
proven copper bodies.

By May 1906 the Mallorys had "sold" the site to Edward Cowper-Thwaite,
who "represented a group of London capitalists with extensive mining properties in South Africa, the United States and Mexico."[5] The selling price was
reputed to be $250,000 with 10 percent down and the balance in 90 days.
Cowper-Thwaite announced that he was letting immediate contracts for
deepwater piers and ore bunkers, the installation of a tramway, and a five-drill
compressor plant. His new company, the Britannia West Copper Company,
would be hiring 150 miners and carpenters by the fall, and the mine would,
according to Cowper-Thwaite, be shipping within six months. Shares were
available at five dollars each, and Captain Cates of the steamer *Britannia* was

hired to take potential investors to look over the site. Engineers D.S. McGilvary and R.A. Shreve published glowing reports, with McGilvary claiming that "production and annual profit . . . will only be limited by the size and extent of their equipment."[6]

Britannia West's announcement coupled with the reality of the mine at Britannia Beach started a rush of prospecting in the area, and 30 mineral claims were staked in 1908 in the Britannia Beach and Howe Sound area. Within two years most had been forfeited. By this time Britannia West had been exposed as a scam, but not before hundreds of investors had been bilked of their money. Neither the Mallorys nor Cowper-Thwaite were ever prosecuted as they were long gone by the time their scheme was exposed.

There was no mining activity on Mount Donaldson after 1883, and a Ministry of Mines inspector who attempted to survey the site of Donaldson's mine in 1914 could find no one who had ever visited the claim to act as his guide. Mining interest had shifted to Jervis Inlet by then, to an area that forms the northern end of the line that begins at Britannia Beach and travels through Mill Creek and Mount Donaldson. All of the claims staked along this line showed concentrations of copper.

The Baramba Mining Company acquired six claims in 1912, a mile beyond the head of Hotham Sound and about 1,500 feet above sea level. Fired with enthusiasm over the quality of the minerals exposed in their first 80-foot-long open cut, the company built a camp and set up a blacksmith shop on the mountainside. During the next three years they ran 330 feet of tunnels in attempts to intersect the main ore body. In 1915, convinced that success was imminent, they built a floating wharf at the head of Hotham Sound in preparation for shipping ore, but they never found the rich mineral vein they were seeking. For the next eight years, the company's annual reports to the Ministry of Mines indicated that they were keeping up their annual assessment work, and in 1923 the company even incorporated with a capitalization of half a million, but it was essentially a mining company without a mine. The postscript to the story is contained in the Ministry of Mines Annual Report for 1929. The mining inspector, having climbed to the camp to investigate, found it long deserted. On the wall of the camp office was a calendar for the year 1916.

Although there was an economic slump in BC during the early years of World War I, prospecting during those years on the Sunshine Coast never lost its allure. Just north of the Baramba Mine, prospector Harry Jolley cut a switchback trail up the mountainside and staked six claims at the 1,900-foot level then leased them out to a mining company to continue exploration. By 1928 there were only a few holes in the ground to show that man had passed that way.

Ben Coates' copper mine was a 40-foot tunnel straight into the mountain-side at Jervis Inlet's Jack Bay. A former Texas Ranger who had the bad luck "to get his man at the wrong time,"[7] he had turned up in Egmont in 1914, built a cabin in the bay east of Egmont Point and started prospecting. Whenever he ran out of blasting powder, he went fishing or took a job in the woods to earn some money. He settled after a time in a shack on Blakely's Island in Pender Harbour, but he never gave up on his mine, even though no one recalled him ever shipping any ore. Ben Coates died at the age of 101 in 1942, still convinced that another blast or two would bring him to the ore body.

Thomas Lillie, a bachelor Scot who had spent 10 years prospecting the length of Jervis Inlet from a home base in Pender Harbour's Hardscratch district, staked the Mendella Group of claims in 1917, three miles beyond the mouth of Britain River. His property extended from the waterline to the 850-foot level where he carried out most of his exploration work. His nearest neighbour was the Norman Copper Company of Vancouver, which was oper-ating three miles below Britain River where they had driven two adits into the lower slopes of Mount Diadem. Neither the Mendella nor the Norman claims showed much commercial value and were forfeited two years later.

The next year Lillie and a partner, Theodore Groven, staked again, this time farther up Mount Diadem beyond the Norman claims. Prospects looked good for the two men but they had only begun exploration when the disastrous Jervis Inlet forest fire of 1919 forced them to flee for their lives. They made better progress the following year, but in November 1920 the bottom fell out of the copper market, and prices dropped so low that even the highly successful Britannia Mine on Howe Sound was forced to close. With future prospects bleak, Lillie and Groven were unable to raise financing to carry on their explorations that year. The mines ministry inspector, who had been turned back by fire when he attempted to survey the Lillie–Groven claim in 1919, came back in the early summer of 1922 but was unable to find his way up the mountain because of an impenetrable pall of smoke from fresh fires. By the time he returned in the autumn, both Lillie and Groven had fallen over a cliff near their claims and been seriously injured. Lillie returned to Pender Harbour to recuperate, but the next spring, walking home from Donley's store where he had gone for tobacco, he dropped dead of a heart attack. His share in the mine was sold to Philip White of Vancouver, but the claim was abandoned a couple of years later.

Groven, who lived with his wife in a small bay near Britain River, continued to stake claims in the area, optimistic that someday he would strike it rich. Then one day in 1938, the crew of the mission boat *Rendezvous* spotted a small white signal flag fluttering above the Grovens' shack. Mrs. Groven explained that her husband had rowed off early that morning to intercept the Union Steamships' boat to collect mail and groceries and had not returned. The *Rendezvous* found his boat washed ashore three miles down the inlet with Groven dead inside it.

By 1928 exploration was underway on only two groups of claims in this area: the Red Mountain claims operated by the Britain River Mining Company 4,000 feet above sea level on the east side of Mount Diadem and those held by Mount Diadem Mines Limited adjoining the Red Mountain claims to the northeast. The Red Mountain claims, so named because they were situated on bluffs stained bright red by iron oxides, were so high that no permanent camp was ever built. Instead, a tent camp was set up each summer and exploration halted in early fall. A mines inspector who came calling in early September 1927 arrived in drizzling rain to find dense fog at the mine elevation and the miners already packing up for another year. Both groups of claims looked promising, but this counted for little when the stock market crash came in 1929 with the Great Depression hard on its heels. Although all of this area would be prospected and staked repeatedly in the next 60 years, the low quality of the ore has always ruled out exploitation.

Initial prospects on the south side of the inlet were more encouraging. At Treat or Beaver Creek, about five miles south of Vancouver Bay, Henry Whitney Treat of Seattle had acquired seven claims around 1915. They were located high on the southern slope of the prominent peak known locally as Treasure Mountain because glacial erosion is so pronounced here that in a number of places the ore bodies were already exposed. During the summer of 1917 Treat brought in a crew to make three open cuts and a series of short adits that revealed ore with an average assay of 28 percent iron with about 1 percent copper. With this encouragement, he installed an aerial tramway from the mine workings to the beach where he built a wharf. But when Treat died suddenly in 1920, the mine was abandoned.

High above a creek that flows into Killam Bay near Egmont Point, a Vancouver prospector named E. Prendergast staked the Red Jacket claims in the 1930s. Unfortunately, they ranged from 3,200 to 4,000 feet above sea level, and before he could even begin exploration work, he had to build four miles of switchback trail over some of the most precipitous ground in the country. Then, having completed his trail, he abandoned his claims.

Mining activity on the Sunshine Coast has always existed in these cycles, with prospectors staking, exploring and forfeiting, then moving on to fresh mountainsides to do it all again. By the 1920s many of the new generation of prospectors were climbing the mountains that the generation before them had climbed, and staking the old forfeited properties in the hope that the economic climate was now right or that newer technologies would reveal ore bodies hidden from their forerunners or at least make the ore economic to mine. Thus, as the market for copper improved in the mid-1920s, prospectors returned to Mount Donaldson. Surveyor Noel Humphries of Sechelt was hired to re-establish the old pack trail up Sechelt Creek from Salmon Inlet and widen it so that heavy equipment could be brought in. At the top of the mountain, beside the old Howe Sound Copper and Silver Mine workings, he found a large anvil, blacksmith bellows, tools, boxes of dynamite and black powder. At nearby Crater Lake a pile of whipsawed lumber waited beside an unfinished cabin; the whipsaw lay nearby.

Two of Donaldson's old claims became part of a 400-acre site belonging to a new company, Pacific Copper Mines Limited, that was incorporated in 1928. Four million shares were offered to the public at 25 cents each. A mining camp was constructed near the old mine workings, 4,500 feet above sea level, but Pacific Copper's engineers failed to locate the high-grade ore that the Howe Sound Copper and Silver Mine Company had announced 50 years earlier. The company's directors then arranged for a "Radiore Survey," but this electrical prospecting procedure also proved disappointing. Pacific Copper retrieved its equipment from the mountaintop and began acquiring mining properties elsewhere. "The shareholders," commented the BC Mines Ministry's annual report for 1931, "have been given a good run for their money."

In 1952 handlogger Herman Solberg and his daughter Bergie decided to try their luck on the mountain. Bergie had been caretaking Universal Logging's camp at the foot of the trail leading up Sechelt Creek and had brought her collection of animals there, including a couple of horses. Herman Solberg sent his daughter up the mountain on horseback to the old mine, but like those before her, she came out empty-handed.

BACKYARD MINING

The mines belonging to the Klein brothers of Pender Harbour are probably the only thoroughly documented "backyard mines" on the Sunshine Coast. The story of Fred Klein's mine began with a Scot named Dave Gibb who came to the Harbour in the mid-1920s to live off remittance money reputed to be more than $500 a year—an enormous sum in those parts and those years. Gibb entertained himself with a pack of expensive cougar dogs with which he ranged the mountainside, and on one of his expeditions around 1929 he spotted an outcropping of chalcopyrites, the commonest of the copper ores. As Gibb was not interested in anything as arduous as mining, he guided Fred Klein to the spot and Fred staked it, much to the amusement of the Pender Harbour colony who were thoroughly aware of the going price for copper. But Klein's copper mine became the community's gold mine a few years later when Fred persuaded the government to give him a grant to build a trail up to it, and he was able to employ half the men in the Harbour to do the job. All they got was two dollars a day and they had to give one free day's work for every paid day, but since most of the men of the community were unemployed, no one complained.

In 1939 Sheep Creek Mining took an option on Klein's mine and drilled a 200-foot tunnel to get under the ore body. When they found nothing, they drilled a tunnel from the opposite direction. This time they ran into a little copper and the bitter truth: it was just a surface deposit, perhaps a thousand tons of really high-grade copper with no vast ore body beneath it. Sheep Creek left the property without taking out any ore. The company found little consolation in the fact that the sample they sent for assay turned out to have one of the highest grades ever found in this province.

The Kleins, however, had not finished with the mine. In the early 1950s, two of Fred's brothers, John and Pete, owned a company called Pender Harbour Explorations through which they managed their logging operations, and at this time they were eyeing a patch of timber on the slope of Mount Hallowell. Unfortunately, there was no road going in that direction and it occurred to them that the original trail to the mine could be improved to provide access. The two brothers therefore took a lease on Fred's mine, and since they already owned trucks and drilling equipment, they applied to the government for a $15,000 grant to build a road in order to reopen the mine. Their new road began just north of the Pender Harbour high school and ran for three miles straight up to the 3,200-foot level of the mountain.

Ironically, after the road was in, they were unable to log the patch of trees they coveted because the ground there was too steep for their equipment. Instead they became miners. Operating from an open cut, they separated the ore by hand into an ore bin. Dump trucks then hauled the rock down to Oyster Bay and unloaded it onto a platform, and from there scows were loaded for shipment to the smelter at Tacoma. Although only two scow-loads ever went out, the first carrying nearly 400 tons, the second somewhat less, both showed a substantial profit.

There remained one more attempt to exploit the mine after the brothers were through with it. In 1955 Sileurian Chieftain Mines took an option on it and shipped out several hundred tons of ore. But within a year they, too, were gone, having exhausted the accessible ore.

Fred was not the only Klein with a mine. In the late Depression years another brother, Bill Klein, with his son Norman also owned one. Located on the slope south of Sakinaw Lake, this mine produced about 70 tons of high-grade silver ore. Today, Bill Klein's Mine, as it was called locally, is only marked by "a bit of a hole in the ground."[8]

New interest in the Pender Harbour–Egmont area came in the early 1980s when Steve Hodgson of Roberts Creek staked the first of the Chalice Mines claims near Waugh Lake. According to the company, one of the showings was a quartz vein over six feet in width that held gold, silver and copper. By 1985 when Chalice was listed on the Vancouver Stock Exchange, the company's claims covered more than 16,000 acres around Waugh and North lakes, and they had already spent $300,000 on prospecting, geological mapping, and geochemical and geophysical surveys in preparation for drilling. However, by 1992 they had found the gold deposits were not continuous, and they abandoned their claims. Two years later Menika Mining Ltd. staked claims in the same area; company president Charles Boitard pointed out to reporters that a geological report in the mid-1980s had discovered 30 showings of gold mineralization on the Chalice claims. "I think they didn't know what they had," said Boitard.[9]

There are hundreds more old "mines" on the Sunshine Coast, holes in the ground that cannot be explained by documents held by the Ministry of Mines. They are in most cases the result of miners tunnelling without licences, generally screening their operations by pre-empting land that showed promise of minerals. In other cases, the ministry's records show mining claims staked where no one ever intended to mine; these were generally filed by homesteaders who wanted to live in areas that were closed to pre-emption but open to mining. Many of these were filed during the 1960s in Jervis Inlet.

By the 1990s mineral claims formed a patchwork over most of the Sunshine Coast map, with almost all the old properties staked once again. The entire northern end of the peninsula was under exploration by Menika Mining and the corridor down the middle was held by Tri-Sil Minerals. The Mount Diadem, Treat Creek and Tzoonie River areas were being reinvestigated, and high atop Mount Donaldson, a square of bald rock had been marked out once again. It would seem a pointless task to keep searching where others have found so little, but it is the very nature of prospecting that inspires a dogged belief in the existence of gold—and other valuables—in "them thar hills."

ENDNOTES

INTRODUCTION: A DREARY AND INHOSPITABLE COUNTRY

1. Vancouver, George. *A Voyage of Discovery,* page 597
2. Roberts, Harry. "The Naming of the Sunshine Coast." *Remembering Roberts Creek— 1889–1955,* page 45
3. Ibid.

PART TWO: PUTTING THE SUNSHINE COAST ON THE MAP

1. Vancouver, page 584
2. Vancouver, page 583
3. Puget, Peter, unpaged
4. Vancouver, page 584
5. Puget, unpaged
6. Vancouver, page 585
7. Puget, unpaged
8. Vancouver, page 586
9. Vancouver, page 587
10. Puget, unpaged
11. Ibid.
12. Vancouver, page 587
13. Puget, unpaged
14. Ibid.
15. Vancouver, page 588
16. Puget, unpaged
17. Vancouver, page 589
18. Vancouver, page 590
19. Vancouver, page 590
20. Downie, W. "Explorations in Jervis Inlet and Desolation Sound"
21. Dawson, L. S. *Memoirs of Hydrography,* page 135
22. Ibid.

PART THREE: THE NATIVE PEOPLES

1. Puget, unpaged
2. Ibid.
3. CBC interview with Clarence Joe, 1965
4. Interview with Dick Hammond by Rosella Leslie, July 13, 2006. Sechelt Community Archives
5. Durieu, Paul. Letter to the Editor. *Mainland Guardian,* June 16, 1875, page 3
6. Bunoz, E.M, page 197

7. Ibid.
8. Duff, Wilson. "The Impact of the White Man"
9. "The Alleged Indian Outrage at Jarvis Inlet." *Mainland Guardian,* December 24, 1874
10. "A Great Injustice." *Mainland Guardian,* June 9, 1875, page 3
11. Durieu, Paul. Letter to the Editor. *Mainland Guardian,* June 16, 1875, page 3
12. "The Sechelt Mission Excursion." *The Daily World,* Vancouver, June 4, 1890, page 4
13. Ibid.
14. Interview with Theresa Jeffries, April 1990
15. Ibid.
16. "Self-government—a spirit reborn." Commemorative Issue, *Sunshine Coast News,*
    October 6, 1986, page 1
17. Ibid.

PART FOUR: SETTLERS AND TOURISTS

1. Burnside, Stuart. "Hardy and Resourceful." *Coast News Weekender,* November 26, 1992.
2. Whitaker, Herbert. Prospectus
3. Interview with Dr. Alan Swan by Rosella Leslie, April 12, 2002. Sechelt Community
    Archives
4. Erle Stanley Gardner. *Log of a Landlubber,* page 142
5. Blanchet, M. Wylie. *The Curve of Time,* page 27
6. Interview with Alfred Taylor, January 19, 1991

PART FIVE: LOGS AND LOGGERS

1. Jackson, L.S. "A Logger's Tale." *Sunshine Coast News,* July 12, 1956
2. Ibid.
3. Interview with Baxter, undated. Sunshine Coast Museum and Archives
4. Orchard, C.D. "Interview with Dewey Anderson"
5. McElvie, B.S. Letter to Eustace Smith
6. Jackson, L.S. "A Logger's Tale." *Sunshine Coast News,* July 12, 1956
7. Interview with Sophia Loraine Brackett (nee Bell) by Rosella Leslie, April 24, 2002.
    Sechelt Community Archives
8. Interview with Arnold Gustavson by Betty Keller, November 28,1990
9. Ibid.
10. Interview with Ted and Eileen Girard by Rosella Leslie, November 28, 1991
11. Interview with John Bosch by Rosella Leslie, November 8, 1991
12. Interview with Bill Bestwick by Rosella Leslie, November 19, 2003
13. Carmichael, Herbert. "Pioneer Days in Pulp and Paper," page 201
14. Interview with Robert Noyes, October 26, 1990
15. Ibid.
16. "Hundreds of Years of Logging Ahead." *Sunshine Coast News,* January 4, 1951

17. Orchard, C.D. "Interview with Dewey Anderson"
18. Allison, A.P. Telegram to J.L. Green, BC–Iowa Shingle Company, Sechelt, October 12, 1921
19. Interview with John Bosch, November 8, 1991
20. Interview with Alan Douglas Wood by Rosella Leslie, March 28, 2002. Sechelt Community Archives
21. Interview with Dr. Alan Swan by Rosella Leslie, April 2002. Sechelt Community Archives.
22. Ibid.

PART SIX: DEEP WATER, SMALL BOATS AND BIG FISH

1. Vancouver, page 584
2. M. Wylie Blanchet. *The Curve of Time,* page 14
3. Matthews, James S. "Memorandum of conversation with William A. Grafton at City Hall, March 24, 1934." *Early Vancouver,* Vol. 3, 1934
4. Dawe, Helen. Conversation with C. Wyngaert, Helen Dawe Collection, Sechelt Archives, undated
5. Jackson, L.S. "A Logger's Tale". *Sunshine Coast News,* February 4, 1954
6. Sinclair, Bertrand. *Poor Man's Rock,* page 106
7. Interview with Ida Higgs, October 16, 1990
8. Telephone interview with Robert Anstead by Rosella Leslie, October 27, 2008
9. Beck, Phillipa. "Dawe Slams Jervis Water Export Proposal." *Sunshine Press,* July 10, 1990, page 2

PART SEVEN: QUARRIES, MINES AND ETERNAL OPTIMISM

1. Interview with Rudy Riepe, February 27, 1991
2. Dawson, George M. *Report of Progress, Geological Survey of Canada, 1876–77,* Vol. 3/2
3. Harvey, R. B. "Howe Sound Copper and Silver Mine." *Report of the Minister of Mines,* Victoria, BC, June 26, 1877
4. *Prospectus.* Britannia West Copper Company Ltd., July 6, 1906, page 2
5. "Britannia West Copper Company." *Vancouver Province,* May 19, 1906, page 1
6. *Prospectus.* Britannia West Copper Company Ltd., July 6, 1906, pages 30–31
7. McNutt, Gladys. "The Egmont Story: Part 4," August 1, 1955
8. Interview with Roy Phillips, June 20, 1991
9. *Sunshine Press,* September 19, 1993

SELECTED BIBLIOGRAPHY

"A Great Injustice." *Mainland Guardian,* June 9, 1875: 3

Anderson, Bern. *Surveyor of the Seas: The Life and Voyages of Captain George Vancouver.* University of Toronto Press, Toronto, 1960

Andrews, Ralph W. *Glory Days of Logging.* Superior Publishing, Seattle, 1956

Andrews, T.R. Memorandum, Department of Recreation and Conservation, December 6, 1974, File 144-3

Annesley, Pat. "No Fantasy Fishman." *Equity,* October 1987: 13

Annett, William. "Tom May: As the captain of BC salmon farming, he leads a business on an uncharted course." *Canadian Business,* August 1988: 41

Annual Report of the Ministry of Mines, Province of British Columbia, 1876–1948

Annual Report of the Department of Railways, Province of British Columbia. King's Printer, Victoria, 1919, 1920, 1922 and 1923

Annual Report of the Ministry of Energy, Mines and Petroleum Resources, Province of British Columbia, 1980–1989/90

"Aquaculture in British Columbia." Deacon Morgan McEwen Easson Limited Research Report, January 25, 1988

Aquaculture in B.C.: Getting Started. Ministry of Agriculture and Food, revised May 1986

"Aquarius Seafarms Ltd. (AQS)." Deacon Morgan McEwen Easson Limited Research Report, August 22, 1988

Avery, Donald H. *Canadian Immigration Policy and the Alien Question 1896–1919: The Anglo-Canadian Perspective.* PhD Thesis, University of British Columbia, 1973

"B.C. Oyster Industry." *The Globe and Mail,* July 18, 1979: A1

Bacon, W.R. *Geology of Lower Jervis Inlet, British Columbia,* British Columbia Department of Mines, Bulletin #39, 1956

Beaumont, Ronald C. "She Shashishalhem: The Sechelt Language." *Language, Stories and Sayings of the Sechelt Indian People of British Columbia.* Theytus Books, 1985

Beck, Phillipa. "1,513 Year Old Tree." *Leader,* August 9, 1991: 4

Benson, Bradley. "Aquaculturists Flock to Coast." *Sunshine Coast News,* October 21, 1985

Bergren, Myrtle. *Tough Timber: The Loggers of British Columbia—Their Story.* Elgin Publications, Vancouver, 1979.

Blanchet, M. Wylie. *The Curve of Time.* Gray's Publishing Ltd., Sidney, BC, 1980

Bloomfield, Patrick. "Fish Story with a Twist Hatches on the Pacific." *Financial Post,* July 1, 1988: 18

Boyd, Robert Thomas. Introduction of Infectious Disease Among the Indians of the Pacific Northwest, 1774–1875. Unpublished thesis, University of British Columbia, 1985

Brown, W.W. and J.B. Stewart. *Port Mellon, B.C.: Being An Account of Its First Fifty Years.* Vancouver, 1954

Bunoz, Bishop E.M., O.M.I. "Methods of Apostolate, Bishop Durieu's System." *Etudes Oblats,* Vol. 1, 1942: 193–209

Calhoun, Bruce. *Mac and the Princess; The Story of Princess Louisa Inlet.* Ricwalt Publishing, Seattle, 1976

Canada Shipping Act Commissioner's Court, re the S.S. *Belcarra.* Vancouver, August 19, 1911

"Canada's Oldest Tree on Sunshine Coast." Western Canada Wilderness Committee Educational Report co-published with Friends of Caren, Vancouver, undated

Carmichael, Herbert. "Pioneer Days in Pulp and Paper." *British Columbia Historical Quarterly,* Vol. 9/3: 201–212

Commercial Aquaculture in Canada, Department of Fisheries and Oceans, 1988

Commission on the Salmon Fishery Industry in British Columbia, Canadian Federal Royal Commission Reports, Ottawa, April 20, 1903

Cummings, J.M. and J.W. McCammon. *Clay and Shale Deposits of British Columbia.* British Columbia Department of Mines and Petroleum Resources, Bulletin #30, 1952

Cutter, Donald C. *Malaspina and Galiano: Spanish Voyages to the Northwest Coast: 1791 & 1792.* Douglas & McIntyre, Vancouver, 1991

Dawe, Helen. *Helen Dawe's Sechelt.* Harbour Publishing, Madeira Park, 1990

Dawson, L.S. *Memoirs of Hydrography including Brief Biographies of the Principal Officers Who Have Served in H.M. Naval Surveying Service Between the Years 1750 and 1885.* The Imperial Library, 1885

Deegan, Rick, and Anne Parkinson. *British Columbia Aquaculture Industry Update.* Aquaculture Information Bulletin No. 3-2, BC Ministry of Agriculture and Fisheries, February 1988

Directory of the Lumber Industry of the Pacific Coast. Timberman. Portland, Oregon, 1924 and 1927

"Dominion Timber Regulations." *Year Book of British Columbia and Manual of Provincial Information 1897–1901.* Queen's Printer, Victoria, 1902 and 1911

Douglas, Robb. *Skookum Tugs: British Columbia's Working Tugboats.* Photos by Robb Douglas; text by Peter Robson and Betty Keller. Harbour Publishing, Madeira Park, BC, 2002.

Downie, W. "Explorations in Jervis Inlet and Desolation Sound." Report to the Province of British Columbia, Department of Lands, December 12, 1859

Duff, Wilson. "The Impact of the White Man." *The Indian History of British Columbia,* Vol. 1, Provincial Museum of Natural History and Anthropology, 1964

Egan, Brian. "Bloom slams Agamemnon Channel." *The Fish Farm News,* Vol. 2/10 (October 1, 1989)

Egan, Brian. "Receiverships plague the industry." *The Fish Farm News,* Vol. 2/11 (November 1, 1989)

Egan, David, and Alan Kenney. "The British Columbia Salmon Farming Industry— An Industry in Transition." *World Aquaculture Magazine,* Vol. 21/2 (June 1990)

Elsey, C.R. *Oysters in British Columbia.* Bulletin No. 34, Biological Board of Canada, 1933: 5–34

Evans, Diane. "Chalice Mines Now Trading; High Hopes for Egmont Gold." *Sunshine Coast News,* March 25, 1985: 1

Farrow, Moira. "Salmon farm on Nelson Island thrives—guard duck and all." *The Vancouver Sun,* April 16, 1981

Farrow, Moira. "Oyster farming: It's a tough life." *The Vancouver Sun,* October 6, 1982

"Fish Farm Inventory Inaccurate." *The Vancouver Sun,* December 23, 1986: C1

Fish Farming: B.C.'s New Venture on the Coast. Province of B.C. Ministry of Agriculture and Fisheries, Aquaculture and Commercial Fisheries Branch, 1987

"Fish Hatchery Plan on Chapman Creek." *Sunshine Coast News,* April 23, 1984

"Fish Hatchery Rezoning." *Sunshine Coast News,* July 7, 1986

Fisher, Robin. *Contact and Conflict: Indian–European Relations in B.C., 1774–1890.* University of British Columbia Press, 1977

Fisheries Statistics of Canada, 1926–1936, King's Printer, Ottawa, 1926–1936

Fowler, Rodney A. "The Oblate System at the Sechelt Mission 1862–1899." Unpublished honours essay, Simon Fraser University, April 1987

Fralick, James E. *Feasibility of Salmon Farming as a Small Business in BC.* Thesis, University of British Columbia, 1978

Fralick, James E. Economic Aspects of Salmon Farming in British Columbia. B.C. Ministry of Environment, Marine Resources Branch, Paper No. 1, June 1980

Fraser, Dave. "Weldwood Camp Boosts Sunshine Coast Economy." *Sunshine Press,* May 22, 1990: 20

Fuller, Frank. "Gilbert Joe." *Labour History,* Vol. 2/3:16

Gallagher, Tim. "Going Belly-up on the Farm." *British Columbia Report,* January 8, 1990: 33

Graham, Donald. *Lights of the Inside Passage.* Harbour Publishing, Madeira Park, 1986.

Green, Mervyn T. *British Columbia Industrial Locomotives: An All-time Listing Including Museums and Short Lines.* Second Edition, self-published, Richmond, BC, January 1986

Hadley, Michael L. *God's Little Ships: A History of the Columbia Coast Mission.* Harbour Publishing, Madeira Park, 1995

Hargreaves, George. Survey Diary. Survey between Burrard Inlet and Pender Harbour, May to October 1874, mss, BCARS

"Hatchery on Again." *Sunshine Coast News,* May 28, 1984

Hill, Beth. *Upcoast Summers,* Horsdal & Schubart, Ganges, B.C., 1985

Hodgins, H.J. Sechelt Forest Survey and Preliminary Management Recommendations, BC Forest Service, Forest Surveys Division, 1933

Hopkins, Gordon. "From Tug to Passenger Boat and Back to Tug Again." Mss, undated, Vancouver Maritime Museum, Vancouver, BC

Horwood, Harold. "The Salmon and the Uncivil Servants." *Reader's Digest,* November 1976: 81–85

Howay, Frederic W. "Early Shipping on Burrard Inlet." *British Columbia Historical Quarterly,* Vol. 1 (1937): 8–16

Howay, Frederic W. and Ethelbert O.S. Scholefield. "Walter Hepburn," and "Frank Llewellyn Buckley". *British Columbia from the Earliest Times to the Present.* S.J. Clark and Son, Vancouver, 1914: 936–9

Howe Sound News. Howe Sound Pulp and Paper Limited, Port Mellon, BC, Vol. 1/3 (May 1990), Vol. 1/4 (September 1990) and Vol. 2/4 (February 1991)

Jackson, L.S. "A Logger's Tale." *Sunshine Coast News,* January 21, 1954–July 12, 1956

Jones, Gordon G. and Bruce L. Jones. *Advances in the Remote Setting of Oyster Larvae.* Ministry of Agriculture and Fisheries and The Aquaculture Association of B.C., Victoria, January 1988

Kendrick, John and Robin Inglis. *Enlightened Voyages: Malaspina and Galiano on the Northwest Coast, 1791-1792.* Vancouver Maritime Museum, Vancouver, 1991

Kincaid, Trevor. "The Oyster Industry of the Pacific Coast." *Pacific Fisherman 1916–1919 Yearbook,* Seattle, 1920

Knight, Rolf. *Indians at Work An Informal History of Native Indian Labour in British Columbia 1858–1930.* New Star Books, Vancouver, 1978

Lawrence, Joseph Collins. Markets and Capital: A History of the Lumber Industry of British Columbia 1778–1952. Thesis, University of British Columbia, 1957

Lazenby, A.L. "Catalogue of Original Timber Leases, 1870–1906." Mss, BC Archives, Victoria, 1982

"Leadbetter Seized Opportunities." *Columbia–Willamette Business Journal,* Hall of Fame Section October 22, 1990: 3

Lemert, E.M. "The Life and Death of an Indian State." *Human Organization,* Vol. 13/3 (1954)

"Licensing for Fish Farms Streamlined by New Agreement." *The Vancouver Sun,* September 7, 1988: C1

Lode-Gold Deposits in Southwestern British Columbia. British Columbia Department of Mines Bulletin #20, Part IV. Revised, November 1946

Macdonald, R.D. and J.W. Murray. Sedimentation and Manganese Concretions in a British Columbia Fiord (Jervis Inlet). Geological Survey of Canada, Department of Energy, Mines and Resources, Paper 73-23, 1973

McCammon, J.W. *Surficial Geology and Sand and Gravel Deposits of the Sunshine Coast, Powell River and Campbell River Areas.* Ministry of Mines and Petroleum Resources, Bulletin No. 65, Victoria, 1977

McElvie, B.A. Letter to Eustace Smith, January 22, 1952. The Orchard Forest History Collection, University of British Columbia Library, Special Collections Division.

McMynn, R.G., Commercial Fisheries Branch. Memo to Lloyd Brooks, Deputy Minister, Department of Recreation and Conservation, File 14-15

McNutt, Gladys. "The Egmont Story, Parts 1 to 13." *Sunshine Coast News,* May 26, 1955– November 17, 1955

"Mariculturist Addresses Power Squadron." *Sunshine Coast News,* March 19, 1984: 15

Mathews, W.H. *Calcareous Deposits of the Georgia Strait Area.* Department of Mines Bulletin No. 23, Victoria, 1947

Mayne, R.C. *Four Years in British Columbia and Vancouver Island.* London, 1862

"Mermaid Strikes Rock." *Colonist,* March 29, 1904: 8

Mitchell, Donald Hector. *Archaeology of the Gulf of Georgia Area, a Natural Region and its Culture Types.* PhD Thesis, Department of Anthropology, University of Oregon, 1968

Newcombe, C.F. Menzies' Journal of Vancouver's Voyage: April to October 1792. Archives of British Columbia, Memoir No. 5, King's Printer, Victoria, 1923

"Nodules of Manganese Oxide in Jervis Inlet." *The Vancouver Sun,* January 31, 1967: 1

"Lumber Costs Do Not Balance With Revenue." *The Vancouver Sun,* December 2, 1921: 13

"Ocean Construction Supplies Limited Building BC Since 1886." Supplement to the *Journal of Commerce,* June 9, 1986

Operating Salmon Farms on Sunshine Coast. Aquaculture Resource Centre, March 20, 1991

Orchard, C.D. "Interview with Lloyd C. Rodgers at Victoria on December 8, 1956." The Orchard Forest History Collection, University of British Columbia Library, Special Collections Division.

Orchard, C.D. "Interview with Copley, G.R." The Orchard Forest History Collection, University of British Columbia Library, Special Collections Division

Orchard, C.D. "Interview with C. Dewey Anderson, February 18, 1957." The Orchard Forest History Collection, University of British Columbia Library, Special Collections Division.

"Oyster Picking Permits." BC Shellfish Mariculture Newsletter. Ministry of Environment, Marine Resources Branch, Vol. 1/1 (January 1981)

"Pacific Aqua to take significant writedown." *The Globe and Mail,* January 20, 1987

"Pacific Aqua Foods." *The Globe and Mail,* August 25, 1987: B16

"Pacific Aqua to count fish in inventory." *The Globe and Mail,* December 23, 1986

"Pacific Aqua Foods Ltd." Deacon Morgan McEwen Easson Limited Research Report, January 25, 1988

Palmer, Vaughn. "Salmon the Harvest on Meneely Family Farm." *The Vancouver Sun,* May 21, 1974

Parton, Lorne. "Opponents Cite Disease, Prices." *The Province,* July 20, 1988

Pearse, Peter H. Report of the Royal Commission on Forest Resources, Timber Rights and Forest Policy in British Columbia. Vol. 2, Victoria, 1976

Peterson, Lester R. *The Gibson's Landing Story.* Peter Martin Books Canada, Ottawa, 1962

Pickard, G.L. "Physical Features of B.C. Inlets." Proceedings and Transactions of the Royal Society of Canada, Canadian Committee on Oceanography, Third Series, Vol. L. Meeting of June 1956. The Royal Society of Canada, Ottawa, 1956

Price, Al. "Winds Devastate Fish Farms." *Sunshine Press,* February 14, 1989

Puget, Peter. Log of the Voyage of the Discovery, 1791–1795. Mss, University of British Columbia, Special Collections Division.

Pynn, Larry. "Fish Farms Pose No Threat, Sunshine Coast Assured." *The Vancouver Sun,* October 19, 1985

Quayle, D.B. "From a B.C. Oyster Biologist's Notebook, 1932." The British Columbia Shellfish Mariculture Newsletter, Pacific Biological Station, Nanaimo, BC, Vol. 2 (1982)

Quayle, D.B. *Pacific Oyster Culture in British Columbia.* Canadian Bulletin of Fisheries and Aquatic Sciences No. 218, Department of Fisheries and Oceans, 1969

Register of Placer Mining Claims 1895–1910. Department of Mines and Resources, Mineral Titles Branch, Vancouver

Report and Recommendations. British Columbia Fisheries Commission, Ottawa, 1922

Roberts Creek Historical Committee. *Remembering Roberts Creek 1889–1955.* Harbour Publishing, Madeira Park, BC, 1978

Rogers, Fred. *Shipwrecks of British Columbia.* J.J.Douglas, North Vancouver, 1973

"Rough Waters Dampen Salmon Farm Fever." *Financial Post,* January 26, 1987

"Royal Pacific Sea Farms." Discovery Foundation BCRD Vol. 4/3 (February 1988): 20

Rushton, Gerald. *Whistle Up the Inlet: The Union Steamship Story.* J.J.Douglas Ltd, Vancouver, BC, 1974

"Scantech saga rolls on." *Sunshine Coast News,* November 25, 1985

"SCRD Proposes Halt to Inlet Fish Farms." *Sunshine Coast News,* March 24, 1986

Sechelt Inlets Coastal Strategy. Catherine Berris Associates Inc., Vancouver, BC., 1990

Sinclair, Bertrand W. *Poor Man's Rock.* Little Brown & Co., Cambridge, Mass., 1920

Southern, Karen. *The Nelson Island Story.* Hancock House, Vancouver, 1987

Stevenson, John S. *Molybdenum Deposits of British Columbia.* British Columbia Department of Mines, Bulletin No. 9, 1940

Sumida, Rigenda. The Japanese in British Columbia. Thesis, University of British Columbia, Economics Department, 1935

Summary Report of the Geological Survey Department of Canada. Sessional Paper #26, Ottawa, 1906

Sunshine Coast Regional Profile. Socio-Economic Profiles. BC Central Credit Union, Economic Department, Vancouver, Vol. 29 (1985)

"The Mill and the Environment." *Howe Sound News,* Howe Sound Pulp and Paper Limited, Port Mellon, April 1989

Thomas, R.C. Guidelines and Procedures for Licensing of Private and Commercial Fish Farms. Department of Recreation and Conservation, Fish and Wildlife Branch, File 33-00, January 5, 1972

Tillapaugh, D.L. and J.C. Edwards. A Permit and Licence Guide for the Prospective Aquaculturist. Ministry of Environment, Marine Resources Branch, Victoria, June 1980

Timber Applications, Department of Lands, 1905–1908. BCARS, Victoria, B.C.

Tobin, Brian A. The Pulp and Paper Industry of BC. Graduating essay, University of British Columbia, Department of Economics, 1930

Turner, Nancy J. *Food Plants of Coastal First Peoples.* Royal British Columbia Museum and UBC Press, Vancouver, 1995

Turner, Robert D. *Logging by Rail: The British Columbia Story.* Sono Nis Press, Victoria, 1990

Tysdal, Rod, MacMillan Bloedel Limited, Stillwater Division. Letter to Betty Keller. Unpublished, December 10, 1987

Unwin, Frank E. "Log Towing on the B.C. Coast and Puget Sound." *Canadian Merchant Service Guild Year Book, 1933–34.* Toronto, 1934

Valiela, D. The BC Oyster Industry: Policy Analysis for Coastal Resource Management. Westwater Research Centre, Technical Report No. 19, December 1979

Van der Burg, Jessie M. A History of the Union Steamship Company of British Columbia 1889–1943. Mss, Vancouver Maritime Museum, Vancouver, B.C.

Van den Wyngaert, Francis J. *The West Howe Sound Story: 1886–1976.* Pegasus Press, Vancouver, 1980

Vancouver, George. *A Voyage of Discovery,* 3 Volumes. Robinson & Edwards, London, 1798

Wagner, H.R. *Spanish Explorations in the Strait of Juan de Fuca.* Santa Ana, California, 1933

Watt, Alison. A History of the Sechelt People with Special Reference to the Provincial Park Sites on the Sunshine Coast. Mss, Interpretation Inventory Development Project, Ministry of Environment and Parks, 1981

Western Pulp Partnership, Squamish Pulp Operation. Western Forest Products, Woodfibre, BC, 1990

Whitaker, Herbert. Prospectus [for the proposed Sechelt Townsite Company]. Vancouver, *c.* 1901

Wolferstan, Bill. *Cruising Guide to British Columbia, Volume III: Sunshine Coast, Fraser Estuary and Vancouver to Jervis Inlet.* Whitecap Books, Vancouver, 1982

Worden, Caryl, and Evo Marcon. Economic Profile of the Sunshine Coast. Sunshine Coast Economic Development Commission, Sechelt, BC, 1991

Yamashira, George. A History of the Occupations of the Japanese in British Columbia. Mss, University of British Columbia Library, Special Collection Division, 1942

Yates, Leslie. "Fish Farm Working Despite Difficulties." *Peninsula Times,* August 27, 1975

Yates, Leslie. "Salmon Farm Battle Fought on Three Fronts." *Peninsula Times,* September 3, 1975

Year Book of British Columbia and Manual of Provincial Information, 1897–1901. King's Printer, Victoria, 1901 and 1911

INDEX

ACKNOWLEDGMENTS

We are especially indebted to Lola and Jim Westell who helped us probe the archives of the Elphinstone Museum for the first edition of this history, and to Billie Steele for opening her Sechelt Archives to us. And for this new updated edition we are extremely grateful for the help of Reana Mussato, Alison MacPherson and Gary Morisson of the Sunshine Coast Museum and Archives.

We would also like to thank the following people for their help with both the original edition and this new edition: Steve and Monica Acciaroli, Gwen Asseltine, Bradley Benson, John Bosch, Sophie Brackett, Inge Bremer, Robert Briggs, Earl Brown, Robert S. Cameron Sr., Gordon Cawley, Mike Clements, Ambrose M. Cronin III, Jackie Day, Dianne Evans, Ron Fearn, Beth Feldman, John Fields, Elaine Futterman, Ruby Gamble, Judy Gill, Eileen and Ted Girard, Tony Greenfield, Eileen Griffith, Arnold Gustavson, Robert Hackett, Dick Hammond, Syd Heal, Marilyn Heaps, Paul and Mavis Jones, Ida Donley Higgs, Steve Hodgson, Ed Husby, John Hutchison, Terry Jacks, P.S. "Pete" Jackson, Gladys Klein, Ed and Betty Laidlaw, Ron Leblanc, Eva Lyons, Bill McDermid, Sybil A. "Nan" MacFarlane, William McNaughton, Linda May, Michael "Bill" May, Elizabeth Leadbetter Meier, Pat Ness, Phil Nicholson, Ken Northrupp, Bob Noyes Jr., Walter Nygren, Reg Paine, Joe Paul, Roy J. Phillips, Donald V. Ramsay, Jack Ratzlaff, Lorne Reesor, Mr. and Mrs. Gordon Reeves, the late Richard N. Reeves, John Seabrook, Norma E. Selig, Karen Silta, John Slind, Bergliot Solberg, Steve Southin, Dr. Alan Swan, Eleanor Swan, Harold and Bea Swanson, Alfred Taylor, Ron Thicke, Robert Turner, Arthur M. Twigg, Jon van Arsdell, Ben Vaughan, Betty Virtue, John and Mary West, Florence Williams, Ray Williston, Wiljo Wiren, Cherry Sinclair Whitaker, Jean Whittaker, W.E. Whittall.

Tom Bell, Ministry of Environment, Lands and Parks; Dr. Neil Bourne, Pacific Biological Station; Darlene Bulpit, Sechelt Nation Resource Management Dept.; Malcolm Cattanach, BC Forest Service; Dr. John Clague, Geological Survey of Canada; Dr. Craig Clark, Pacific Biological Station; Peggy Connors, SCRD; Dave Crosby, SCRD; Rick Deegan, Ministry of Agriculture and Fisheries; Dr. Herb Dragert, Pacific Geoscience Centre; Graeme Ellis, Pacific Biological Station; Jim Fralick, Ministry of Agriculture, Fisheries and Food; Ron Ginetz, Department of Fisheries and Oceans; Paul Harper, BC Forest Service; Bill Harware, Ministry of Agriculture, Fisheries and Food; Theresa Jeffries, Sechelt Indian Government; Cathy Kenny and Sigfried Lehman, SCRD; Dr. Leitch, Geological Survey of Canada; Kerry Mahlman, School District 46;

George Miller, Pacific Biological Station; Bill Moore, SCRD Economic Development; Alana Phillips, BC Cetacean Sightings Network, Vancouver Aquarium; Dr. Dan Quayle, Pacific Biological Station; Lloyd A. Webb, Department of Fisheries and Oceans; Ian Whitbread, Ministry of Tourism, Recreation and Culture.

Bob Anstead, Sunshine Coast Salmon Enhancement Society; George Brandak, UBC Library, Special Collections Division; James Delgado, Vancouver Maritime Museum; Dora Glover, Sunshine Coast Aquaculture Association; Christopher Keller, Department of Botany, University of Washington; Len McCann, Vancouver Maritime Museum; Jeff Marliave, Vancouver Public Aquarium; Steve Marsh, Sechelt Aquaculture Resource Centre; David L. Stone, Underwater Archaeological Society of BC; Anne Yandle, UBC Library, Special Collections Division.

Wayne Cammel, Rivtow Ltd.; Pat Crawford, BC Hydro; Laura Dixon, Construction Aggregates Ltd.; Al Driscoll, BC Hydro; Mike Dusenbury, Jack Cewe Ltd.; Bill Elphinstone, B.A. Blacktop; Roger Engeset, Wood Bay Salmon Farms Ltd.; Loren Eve, Construction Aggregates Ltd.; Mike Gray, Harmony Seafoods; Len and Myra Kwiatkowski, Clowhom Lodge; Brian Lucas, Airspan Helicopters; Dan Paul, Weldwood of Canada; Joachim Pierre, Construction Aggregates Ltd.; Rudolph Riepe, Tri-Sil Minerals Inc.; Dieter Shindelhauer, Chalice Mines; Jack Sutherland, Lafarge Concrete Ltd.; Rod Tysdal, MacMillan Bloedel Ltd.

ABOUT THE AUTHORS

Betty Keller has lived in Vancouver, BC's Fraser Valley, the Okanagan and Kootenay areas, as well as in Nigeria. She taught in BC secondary schools, at Simon Fraser University and the University of British Columbia. A founding member of the SunCoast Writers Forge, she was the producer of the Sunshine Coast Festival of the Written Arts and the Sunshine Coast Writers-in-Residence Program for 12 years. Author and co-author of sixteen books of non-fiction and fiction, Betty has been the recipient of many awards, including The Canadian Biography Award (1980), The Lescarbot Award (1991), The Queen's Golden Jubilee Medal (2002), The Bill Duthie Booksellers' Choice Award (2003), and The Roderick Haig-Brown Regional Prize (2005). Please visit www.quintessentialwriters.com.

Rosella Leslie was born in Alberta, but has lived on the Sunshine Coast for almost thirty years. Her feature articles and short fiction have appeared in local and national magazines, and she is the author of several books, including *The Sunshine Coast: A Place To Be* (Heritage, 2001) and a novel, *The Goat Lady's Daughter* (NeWest Press, 2006). Her second novel, *The Drift Child*, will be published by NeWest in 2010. A past member of the board of directors of the Sunshine Coast Festival of the Written Arts and member of the SunCoast Writers Forge, she was a co-winner of the Roderick Haig-Brown Regional Prize for *A Stain Upon the Sea: West Coast Salmon Farming* (Harbour, 2005). For more information please see www.quintessential writers.com.